Input, Interaction,
and the Second Language Learner

Input, Interaction,
and the Second Language Learner

Susan M. Gass
Michigan State University

LEA LAWRENCE ERLBAUM ASSOCIATES, PUBLISHERS
1997 Mahwah, New Jersey

Lawrence Erlbaum Associates, Inc., Publishers
10 Industrial Avenue
Mahwah, NJ 07430

Cover design by Kathryn Houghtaling

Library of Congress Cataloging-in-Publication Data

Gass, Susan M.
Input, interaction, and the second language learner / Susan M.
Gass
p. cm.
Includes bibliographical references and index.
ISBN 0-8058-2208-9. — ISBN 0-8058-2209-7 (pbk.)
1. Second language acquisition. 2. Language and lan-
guages—Study and teaching. I. Title.
P118.2.G368 1997
418—dc21   96-47420
                                                CIP

Books published by Lawrence Erlbaum Associates are printed on
acid-free paper, and their bindings are chosen for strength and dura-
bility.

Printed in the United States of America
10 9 8 7 6 5 4 3 2

To G. Z-G. and H. H. G.
for a lifetime of input and interaction

Contents

Preface

The goal of this book is to provide a view of the relationship among input, interaction, and second language acquisition. As such, it should prove useful for those whose primary concern is with the acquisition of a second or foreign[1] language as well as for those who are primarily interested in these issues from a pedagogical perspective. I do not explicate or advocate a particular teaching methodology, but I attempt to lay out some of the underpinnings of what is involved in interaction—what it is and what purpose it serves. Some of these issues are addressed in chapter 7.

Researchers in second language acquisition are concerned with the knowledge that second language learners do and do not acquire and how that knowledge comes about. This book ties these issues together from three perspectives: an input–interaction framework, information processing, and learnability. The book has two primary audiences—those whose interest is in second language acquisition per se and those whose interest is in second language acquisition as a basis for understanding language classrooms.

---

[1]I intend the term *second* in *second language acquisition* to refer to both second and foreign language learning situations. In other words, the term is intended to cover nonprimary language acquisition. I use the terms *acquisition* and *learning* interchangeably with no theoretical implications intended.

Current second language instruction is based on the assumption that learners need to be actively involved in gaining input through interaction. It is frequently the case that this methodology is thrust on teachers without an understanding of what they are doing or why. Questions such as "what good does group work do?" are often not asked; rather, teachers assume that group work has a positive effect. This book is explicitly concerned with these issues.

There are many people who have been influential in the writing of this book. First are my colleagues and friends in the field of second language acquisition whose works I have read, consumed, and devoured for many years. Notably, the works of Michael Long and Teresa Pica have been of great influence. Their thinking has helped shape mine in so many ways. Litsa Varonis was my partner in crime for many years. We began a longstanding collaborative relationship in 1980 and have worked together as friends and colleagues for more than a decade. It goes without saying that many of the ideas in this book were born from the numerous conversations we have had over the years. If any of them are misguided, the fault is (mostly) mine. There are my students, too numerous to mention, who participated in classes and seminars that I have taught on the subject of input and interaction. I cannot name them all, but I am grateful to every last one of them for challenging and pushing me to explain what I mean. I will single out a few who stand out as having been exceptional in pushing me: Catherine Fleck, Margo Glew, Sabine Helling, B. Kumaravadivelu, Usha Lakshmanan, Nevin Leder, and India Plough, and Ildiko Svetics. I have been indeed fortunate to have had you in my seminars. I am particularly grateful to Sabine Helling, for reading and commenting on an earlier draft and for causing me to rethink portions of this book, and to Catherine Fleck, for reading an earlier draft of this book and for saving me from many embarrassing slips and errors.

It is common to thank one's family in a work of this sort, and I will continue this tradition. My family has always been supportive of my work, and this project has been no exception. Seth and Ethan have often found bits and pieces of manuscript lying by the computer and have not hesitated to tell me that such and such is poorly written or is just plain "garbage." Although I may have not always been ecstatic at hearing the feedback, I do appreciate it and feel blessed to have such astute children. Burgundy and Manchego have also contributed in their usual and unusual ways. During their puppy days, many pages of this manuscript were found "mysteriously" chewed up. It is fortunate that computers and backup disks exist; if not, this manuscript would not have survived the puppy stages of two Newfoundlands. Finally, my husband, Josh, has been my major supporter. Fortunately, he did not chew up any pages.

He has never wavered in his desire to see this book complete (it is just that he is so darn sick of hearing me say that I wanted it finished and would like to see a sense of normalcy return to our household—or maybe it is just that he wants me to help more with the laundry and cooking—"no, not the cooking, just the laundry," he says). Thanks, Josh, for being there (and for doing the laundry). And finally, Gertrude Zemon-Gass and H. Harvy Gass, to whom this book is dedicated.

I owe a debt of gratitude to the Department of English and the College of Arts and Letters at Michigan State University for some time off from teaching so that I could work on this project. It has been a long time in coming, but it is now done.

The staff at Lawrence Erlbaum Associates are always wonderful to work with. This project has certainly been no exception. Judith Amsel has been enthusiastic in seeing this project to completion. Many thanks, Judi, for being there as editor and friend.

Modeling Second Language Acquisition[1]

1.0. INTRODUCTION

The concept of *input*[2] is perhaps the single most important concept of second language acquisition. It is trivial to point out that no individual can learn a second language without input of some sort. In fact, no model of second language acquisition does not avail itself of input in trying to explain how learners create second language grammars.[3] Input has been characterized differently in different theories of second language acquisition, ranging from Krashen's model (Krashen, 1980, 1982, 1985), in which input (in the form of comprehensible input) assumes a major role, to studies within the Universal Grammar (UG) framework (e.g., White, 1989b), in which input assumes a lesser but more specific, central role. The goal of this book is to provide a view of the relation between input and interaction, on the one hand, and second language learning, on the other, and, in so doing, to understand both theoretically and empirically the nature and function of input.

The starting point is the uncontroversial premise that second language acquisition is a complex phenomenon that cannot be described in its entirety and in its complexity by any existing model today. What is essential in understanding how individuals go about acquiring second languages is to understand how various research areas and theories relate to one another.

Perhaps the most divisive issue in current language acquisition research (both first and second) is the extent to which acquisition is a function of innateness. Those who adhere to an innateness position maintain that a learner comes to the learning task with structural knowledge that allows him or her to construct a grammar of the language being learned on the basis of limited data. The opposing position holds that language acquisition and social interaction are in mutually dependent roles and that language acquisition cannot be understood devoid of the context in which it occurs.

Research within an innateness paradigm focuses on the nature of the innate structure (UG), with the claim that in order to understand formal constraints on language, one needs to isolate the linguistic system and investigate it apart from a consideration of external (e.g., social) influences. Although many researchers accept this position for child language acquisition, the question is less clear with regard to second language acquisition. Is innate knowledge about language available to adults learning a second language? (See White, 1996b, for a review.)

Those operating in a social interactionist perspective argue that language and social interaction cannot be separated without resulting in a distorted picture of the development of both linguistic and cognitive abilities. This is perhaps more relevant for first language acquisition than for second because, from this point of view, language and cognitive development are both embedded in context. That is, young children are learning about the world at the same time as they are learning language. If this is the case, one cannot hope to understand the development of grammatical knowledge unless one focuses on the way grammatical knowledge interacts with other aspects of the learning situation.

It may seem paradoxical to claim that both positions have merit. Yet, it is the premise of this book that one must consider not which of these positions is the correct one but how these positions interrelate and how both might contribute to a more complete understanding of the way second languages are learned. To that end, I describe a model (Gass, 1988a; Gass & Selinker, 1994) that may be useful in conceptualizing the various facets of acquisition. The model is an attempt to characterize what a learner does in moving from exposure to second language input to the production stage of output.[4]

1.1. A FRAMEWORK FOR SECOND LANGUAGE ACQUISITION

Research over the years has attempted to characterize the type of input that is available and necessary for acquisition (see chapter 3). These characterizations have focused on the extent to which input is modified, controlled, or limited by the input giver (usually a native speaker [NS], textbook, etc.). Even when input is potentially available to a learner, however, we must ask what happens to it (see Fig. 1.1). Five stages are proposed

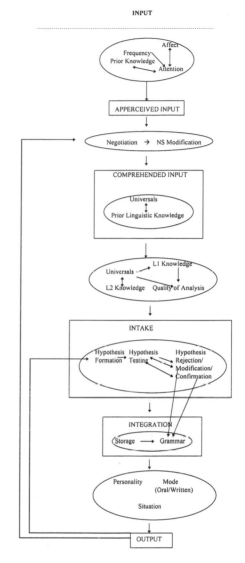

FIG. 1.1. A model of second language acquisition.

to account for the conversion of input to output: apperceived input, comprehended input, intake, integration, and output. I deal with each of these levels and elaborate on the factors that mediate between one level and another. This type of model finds support in the child language literature. For example, Slobin (1985), on the basis of cross-linguistic data, posited strategies necessary for the processing and representation of incoming data. These strategies include attention, storage, pattern matching, and general problem solving.

1.1.1. Apperception, or the Age of Enlightenment

It is important to note in any discussion of acquisition that inherent in the term acquisition is a degree of ambiguity. On one hand, acquisition is viewed as an endpoint. This would be the case when referring to something having been acquired (e.g., the past tense, the passive). Here, varying criteria have been used in second language acquisition research (e.g., percentage accurate, first occurrence). On the other hand, acquisition can be viewed as a process beginning with input apperception and culminating with integration of new linguistic information into an existing linguistic system, output then being the manifestation of newly integrated or acquired knowledge. The model described here (Fig. 1.1) represents a dynamic view of the process of acquisition.

A well-established fact about second language acquisition is that not everything that learners hear or read is utilized as they form second language grammars. That fact is indicated in Fig. 1.1 by the sievelike line at the top. Some language data filter through to the learner, and some do not. A concern in second language acquisition research has been with the limits on what filters through to the learner and what determines those limits.

The first stage of input utilization is the recognition that there is something to be learned, that is, that there is a gap between what the learner already knows and what there is to know. This is called *apperception. Apperception* is the process of understanding by which newly observed qualities of an object are initially related to past experiences. Thus, past experiences influence the selection of noticed material (see Robinson, 1995; Schmidt, 1990, 1993a). Apperception is an internal cognitive act in which a linguistic form is related to some bit of existing knowledge (or gap in knowledge). We can think of apperception as a priming device that prepares the input for further analysis. Thus, apperceived input is that bit of language that is noticed in some way by the learner because of some particular recognizable features. It is in this sense that I refer to this as the *age of enlightenment*: It is at this crucial juncture that the light of recognition goes on, and, the learner realizes that some gap needs to be filled. This can also be referred to as *selective cueing*.

1.1.2. Comprehended Input

Apperception relates to the potentiality of comprehension of the input; another level in the process of acquisition is comprehended input. In earlier treatments of input (notably that of Krashen, 1977, 1980; see chapter 3), a central concept was that of comprehensible input. There are two important differences between comprehensible input and comprehended input. First, the former implies that the speaker, rather than the hearer, controls the comprehensibility. With comprehended input, the focus is on the hearer (the learner) and the extent to which he or she understands. A second difference has to do with the nature of comprehension. In Krashen's sense of the word, *comprehension* is treated as a dichotomous variable; something is either understood or it is not. He was apparently using the common meaning of the word (in fact, the *American Heritage Dictionary* defined *comprehension* in part as "the act or fact of grasping the meaning . . ."). In this book, comprehension takes on a broader significance with the implication that there are different levels of comprehension that can take place. In this sense, *comprehension* represents a continuum of possibilities ranging from semantics to detailed structural analyses. In other words, one can comprehend something at the level of meaning; that is, one can have an understanding of the general message. On the other hand, deeper analyses may take place. Learners might understand the component parts of an utterance and thus gain an understanding of the syntactic or phonological pattern represented.

It may at first appear that the differences between the notion of comprehensible input and comprehended input are inconsequential. However, I maintain that this is not the case because both differences discussed here have significance for the level of intake. In the first case, the distinction between speaker and hearer control is crucial because the learner ultimately controls the intake. In the second case, the recognition of different levels of analysis is important in that the likelihood of input becoming intake is in part dependent on the level of analysis achieved.

1.1.3. Intake

Intake is the process of assimilating linguistic material; it refers to the mental activity that mediates input and grammars. I refer to this as *selective processing*. This, of course, suggests that intake is not merely a subset of input (see also chapter 6). It is in the intake component that psycholinguistic processing takes place. That is, it is where information is matched against prior knowledge and where, in general, processing takes place against the backdrop of the existing internalized grammatical rules. It is where generalizations are likely to occur, it is where memory traces are formed, and finally, it is the component from which fossilization stems.[5]

1.1.4. Integration

After the intake component has performed its task of processing the input and matching it against existing knowledge, there are at least two possible outcomes, both of which are a form of integration. One is the development per se of one's second language grammar, and the other is storage. The distinction is between integration and nonintegration of new linguistic information.

Gass and Selinker (1994) outlined four possibilities for the outcome of input. The first two take place in the intake component and result in integration, the third takes place in the integration component, and the fourth represents input that exits the system early in the process.

The first possibility is hypothesis confirmation or rejection (intake ⇒ integration). Input may be useful to assist in confirmation or rejection of a current hypothesis. That is, a learner may have created a particular hypothesis about some grammatical form. On being confronted with new input data, learners receive confirmation of the original hypothesis and strengthen that particular knowledge, or they receive information that causes them to reject the original hypothesis. In the first case, integration occurs. In the second case, the hypothesis is modified and awaits further confirmation from the input.

The second possibility is apparent nonuse (intake ⇒ integration) of the input. Apparent nonuse occurs when the information contained in the input is already incorporated into a learner's grammar. However, the fact that the information is already incorporated into a grammar does not necessarily exclude it from being utilized—although it may be used in a different way from what one normally thinks of. When the information contained in the input is already a part of one's knowledge base, the additional input might be used for rule strengthening or hypothesis re-confirmation. Part of becoming a fluent speaker of a second language involves the automatic retrieval of information from one's knowledge base. The knowledge base is developed through practice or repeated exposure to exemplars. Thus, information that may appear redundant may be serving an important purpose in terms of the access the learner has to that information.

The third possibility is storage (intake ⇒ delay or incubation period ⇒ [integration]). Input is put into storage, perhaps because some level of understanding has taken place, yet it is not clear how integration into a learner's grammar can or should take place. An example will help to make this clear. A Spanish-speaking ESL student had heard the word *so*, as in the sentence: *So, what did you do yesterday?* He could neither figure out what it meant nor how to use it, and, after hearing it again in an ESL class, asked a direct question about the meaning. From this, one can infer that he had stored this information and was waiting for it to be available for integration. In other words, the learner had created a hypothesis, but because there was insufficient evidence (i.e., input) to determine the validity of the hypothesis, the information was put into storage, awaiting enough information to confirm or disconfirm the hypothesis. It is reasonable to assume that the storage component is more likely for vocabulary and smaller chunks of language than for large syntactic strings. This may be due largely to the fact that it is more difficult to hold large bits of language in memory for a long period of time.

In the final instance, nonuse (comprehended input ⇒ [intake] ⇒ exit), learners make no use of the input. This may be because they have not succeeded in comprehending it at a useful level.

1.1.5. Output

The fifth stage is output. In one sense this is not truly a stage in the acquisition process but is more aptly characterized as an overt manifestation of that process. In another sense, output plays an active role in acquisition in that it serves as a means of hypothesis testing. In other words, once learners have created a particular hypothesis about a second language form and use that form in production (orally or in a written format), they may receive feedback and as a result modify the original hypothesis. This then constitutes a means for output (in the sense of produced output) to serve as feedback into the intake component (this is discussed further in chapter 6).

A second point to note is the role output plays in forcing a syntactic rather than solely a semantic analysis of language (Swain, 1985). When individuals are listening, they may gain a general understanding of the message without understanding the language-specific syntax of the target language. This is done by relying on other aspects of the conversational situation, such as real-world knowledge or past statements in the conversation. When speaking, however, elements of a sentence or an utterance, must be put in some order.[6] Swain (1985) referred to this as *comprehensible output. Comprehensible output* means pushing the learner "toward the delivery of a message that is not only conveyed, but that is conveyed precisely, coherently, and appropriately" (Swain, 1985, p. 249). Hence, in production some sort of (at least) rudimentary knowledge of syntax is necessary. This conceptualization of output necessitates a feedback loop to comprehended input.

1.2. ATTENTION, AWARENESS, CONSCIOUSNESS

Before turning to a more detailed look at the five components of this model and consideration of the way they interact and the factors that are important in mediating among them, I turn to issues of attention, awareness, and consciousness. Together they form the cornerstone of the entire process—they are integral to the level of apperception.

In the recent second language acquisition literature, much attention (a pun intended) has been paid to the concept of attention. Some of this literature relates to the classroom context and to the debate between focus on form and focus on meaning. The other area of emphasis is more directly related to issues of psycholinguistic processing. I turn to this area here.

Given that second language learners are surrounded by second language (L2) data, some mechanism must be available to help them wade through and sort out these data. One way in which the input becomes more manageable is by the learner focusing attention on a limited and hence controlled amount of data at a given point in time. By limiting the data to which one attends, learners can create a set of data that allows them to move from input to output in the way characterized in the preceding sections. What this assumes is that language processing is like other kinds of processing: Humans are constantly exposed to and often overwhelmed by various sorts of external stimuli and are able through attentional devices to tune in to some stimuli and to tune out others. James' (1890) very early definition characterized *attention* as "the taking possession by the mind, in clear and vivid form, of one out of what seems several simultaneously possible objects or trains of thought" (as cited in Posner, 1994, pp. 403–404).

Another concept that is frequently discussed in the literature is awareness. Definitions are somewhat scattered, but a common one according to Schachter, Rounds, Wright, Smith, and Magoto (1996) is that "an individual is able to detect and verbalize the pattern that he has learned" (p. 2).

1.2.1. Attention as Presupposition to Awareness

Early works devoted to the role of attention in second language acquisition were those of Schmidt (1990, 1993b, 1993c, 1994b). Schmidt's main point was that noticing something in the input is crucial to acquisition. That is, before something can serve as intake, it must be noticed. This is not unlike what was claimed in preceding sections with regard to apperception, which serves as a priming device or as a prerequisite to the intake component. Where the present model and Schmidt's part company is that for Schmidt "intake is that part of the input that the learner notices" (Schmidt, 1990, p. 139). Thus, once the learner notices something in the input, it automatically becomes intake: "If noticed, it becomes intake" (Schmidt, 1990, p. 139).

In considering the concept of noticing, Schmidt argued that all noticing is conscious: A learner in noticing something is conscious of the fact of noticing. In fact, he specifically stated that "subconscious learning" is oxymoronic (Schmidt, 1990, p. 139). The word *conscious* is clearly one that is fraught with difficulty. Schmidt (1990), in describing theories of consciousness, claimed that they all converge on the idea that consciousness can be identified with "online phenomenological awareness" (p. 138).

A further point to consider is that most theories of consciousness deal with two distinct types: unconscious and conscious. Unconscious processes "are not under voluntary control and are difficult to modify, but are fast, efficient, and accurate, and are responsible for skilled performance and most details of cognitive processing" (Schmidt, 1990, p. 138). This is similar to what is often referred to as *automatic processing* (see McLaughlin, 1987).

On the other hand, conscious processes are "the experiential manifestation of a limited capacity central processor" (Schmidt, 1990, p. 138). Similar to controlled processing, they are slow and often deliberate.

Schmidt (1994a), in discussing awareness, seems to have equated awareness and consciousness. He cited the *American Heritage Dictionary* definition of *aware* as "Conscious; cognizant; alert: *aware of the consequences*"; and *conscious* as "1.a. Having an awareness of one's own existence and environment. b. Capable of complex response to environment. c. Not asleep; awake. 2. Subjectively known: *conscious remorse*. 3. Intentional; deliberate: *a conscious insult*."[7] This view is shared by Crick and Koch (cited in Horgan, 1994), who argued that consciousness is synonymous with awareness and that the underlying mechanism of awareness is one that combines attention with short-term memory.[8]

In sum, in this view, noticing by definition involves awareness and consciousness. Further, Schmidt (1993b, 1993c) argued that noticing involves a subjective experience and an ability to articulate that experience. Although Schmidt (1993b) acknowledged that determining what a learner has or has not noticed is virtually impossible, at least in naturalistic learning situations, he claimed that one can show that something has not been noticed "by the failure of subjects to report their awareness of a stimulus if asked immediately following its presentation" (p. 25). Thus, noticing includes awareness, and awareness presupposes attention. Hence, attention is central to any concept of noticing.

A major impetus for Schmidt's view of noticing as involving consciousness and awareness as necessary conditions for acquisition comes from his diary studies from when he was in Brazil learning Portuguese. During his 5-month stay in Brazil he studied Portuguese formally (5 weeks), spent time interacting with NSs of Portuguese, and kept diary records. Additionally, he arranged to be tape-recorded at 1-month intervals. In trying to determine the relation between noticing and eventual output, his notes (i.e., diary, class notes) were compared with the tape recordings of his speech. These records were analyzed in a number of ways. For example, there was an attempt to see if the relation between frequency in the input and eventual output could be established. Although there was some relation, it was insufficient to account for what Schmidt actually produced. What did appear to be significant was the relationshp between what he noted in his diary (either by forms that he wrote down or by notes that he wrote about the forms) and the emergence of these forms in his speech. As Schmidt (1990, p. 140) noted, he was able to

"identify the apparent source of innovation as something very specific that someone had said to me that had caught my attention, such as the following example:

Journal entry, Week 21 . . . I'm suddenly hearing things I never heard before, including things mentioned in class. Way back in the beginning, when we learned questions words, we were told that there are alternate short and long forms like *o que* and *o que é que, quem* or *quem é que*. I have never heard the long forms, ever, and concluded that they were just another classroom fiction. But today, just before we left Cabo Frio, M said something to me that I didn't catch right away. It sounded like French *que'est-ce que c'est* [sic], only much abbreviated, approximately [kekse], which must be *(o) que (é) que (vo)cê* . . .

Journal entry, Week 22. I just said to N *o que é que você quer* but quickly: [kekseker]. Previously, I would have said just *o que*. N didn't blink, so I guess I got it right . . ."

Schmidt went on to report that these forms had been present in the input. In fact, 43% of the question words on the first tape were of this type. He had "heard them and processed them for meaning from the beginning, but did not notice the form for five months" (1990, p. 141). It was the overt noticing of the form that Schmidt claimed led to his use of the form. Again Schmidt equated noticing with conscious awareness and ability to articulate; if the forms were processed for meaning, they were noticed or apperceived earlier.

1.2.2. Dissociation of Attention and Awareness

A more appropriate model for attention, and one that does not rely so heavily on conscious awareness, is that presented by Tomlin and Villa (1994) based on work by cognitive psychologists. They describe attention as consisting of three phases: alertness, orientation, and detection.

Alertness refers to the overall "readiness to deal with incoming stimuli or data" (p. 190). Alertness is closely related to the rate at which information is selected for further processing. That is, the greater the alertness, the faster information will be processed, although the rate of accuracy may be adversely affected. In a second language context, there are many ways that one can see the effects of alertness. Clearly, in a classroom context, alertness (perhaps in the form of being "bright-eyed and bushy-tailed") may lead to a greater ability to take in the information being presented. All teachers are familiar with the Monday morning syndrome in which students seem not to be awake and in which the class seems to move along at a slower pace. Alertness can also be seen in the form of general motivation to learn. Highly motivated students and learners seem able to take in more information at a faster rate than do less motivated students.

Orientation, the second phase of awareness, is a facilitator of detection; it directs attentional resources to a particular bit of information while excluding other information. When attention is oriented to a particular bit of data, there will be either a positive or a negative effect, depending on whether the information that is focused on is expected or not (see also chapter 2, section 2.1.1.3). Tomlin and Villa gave the example of research concerning homographs. Consider the meanings of *trunk* (i.e., a proboscis of an elephant, a large traveling container, the main woody axis of a tree, and the back of a car—at least in American English). All things being equal, if a person is presented with this word, one or more of these meanings may be activated, possibly based on frequency of use or on one's profession, both of which are forms of orientation. This activation can also be manipulated through orientation (e.g., by presenting alongside the word a picture representing one of the meanings). When orientation occurs, secondary and tertiary meanings are inhibited, and the oriented meaning is facilitated. Considering this in a classroom context, one could argue that the presentation of information (be it lexical, semantic, phonological, or grammatical) to learners in fact orients them toward that material.

The third phase of attention is detection, or the "cognitive registration of sensory stimuli" (Tomlin & Villa, 1994, p. 192). It is "the process that selects, or engages, a particular and specific bit of information" (p. 192). It is most closely aligned with apperception and what Schmidt described as noticing, although it significantly differs from Schmidt's view in that awareness is not required. In all cases, it is a necessary prerequisite to further processing. Tomlin and Villa point out three main aspects of detection. First, information detected causes great interference with the processing of other information. Second, information detected (i.e., cognitive registration) exhausts more attentional resources than even orientation of attention. Finally, detected information is available for other cognitive processing. The relevance to second language acquisition is great because the cognitive registration of some example or bit of language is crucial to the next stage, that of intake and eventual integration into one's second language knowledge base.

The question remains: To what extent is awareness a necessary part of attention and of learning in general? *Awareness* "refers to a particular state of mind in which an individual has undergone a specific subjective experience of some cognitive content or external stimulus" (Tomlin & Villa, 1994, p. 193). Allport (1988) argued against a uniform entity of phenomenal awareness. According to Allport, three (theoretically independent) conditions must be met in determining whether or not an individual is aware of some experience. First, the individual must show some behavioral or cognitive change (i.e., direct response) as a result of the experience. Second, he or she must be able to report awareness of the experience (see also Cheesman & Merikle, 1985, for work on confident self-reporting), and third, the person must be able to describe the experience.

That alertness and orientation can be dissociated from awareness is probably uncontroversial. Although being alert may be a prerequisite for other parts of attention, there is no way of knowing what will be attended to, because alertness is only a way of being prepped for attending. Similarly, *orientation* refers to the fact that one's attentional resources are being directed toward an object or a bit of language, and so on. It, too, is prerequisite to detection and thus does not necessarily involve awareness in the sense defined by Allport. On the other hand, detection is the area in which awareness is most likely to occur. The question is, is awareness a necessary condition?

Tulving (1989, p. 8) proposed what he called the doctrine of concordance:

> It holds that there exists a close and general, even if not perfect, agreement between what people know, how they behave, and what they experience. Thus, conscious awareness is [assumed to be] required for, and therefore accompanies, the acquisition of knowledge, or its retrieval from the memory store; retrieved knowledge guides behaviour, and when this happens, people are aware of the relation between the knowledge and the behaviour; future behaviour is planned and ongoing behaviour is executed under the watchful eye of consciousness.

Although this view is still maintained by some, most researchers generally agree that one can distinguish between conscious and nonconscious processing (Farthing, 1992; Kihlstrom, 1987). *Conscious processing* is "processing that occurs with awareness of the contents being processed" (Farthing, 1992, p. 127). Farthing further pointed out that awareness of the contents may occur at any stage (i.e., beginning, middle, or end). *Unconscious processing*, on the other hand, is processing "that occurs without awareness of the contents being processed" (p. 127). This does not mean that conscious processing involves an introspective awareness of mental processes. It means only that people are aware of the contents or the outcomes of the processes. Farthing gave the example of lexical retrieval. When a word is read, one analyzes the visual pattern and matches it against word shapes in long-term memory until the correct association between the visual image and the meaning is made. One is not aware of the processes involved, only of the outcome—that there is or is not a match.

1.2.3. Attention, Awareness, and Learning

One way of conceptualizing the dissociation between awareness and performance (i.e., learning in the case of second language acquisition) is with recourse to explicit and implicit knowledge (Schacter, McAndrews, & Moscovitch, 1988). Explicit knowledge is knowledge that individuals use in the performance of a task while having conscious awareness that they possess that knowledge. Implicit knowledge represents the converse. It is knowledge used to perform a task without conscious knowledge of possessing that knowledge.

There is evidence in the cognitive psychology literature for subliminal perception (i.e., nonconscious recognition of stimuli that cannot be consciously recognized—for example, stimuli that are too brief for detection by the human eye; see, Cheesman & Merikle, 1986; Farthing, 1992; Marcel 1983a, 1983b; and Merikle & Cheesman, 1986; see Holender, 1986, for counterevidence). Even with subliminal perception, however, do we have subliminal learning, that is, learning without awareness?

To understand what might be involved in nonconscious perception of unattended stimuli, imagine yourself in line at a cafeteria. Imagine also that you are engaged in a serious conversation with the person in front of you and are thereby ignoring what is going on around you. Suddenly you hear your name mentioned, and you turn around. You have no recognition of what the other party's conversation was about. You were in no way attending to it. Farthing (1992) took this as evidence for nonconscious monitoring that automatically recognizes all incoming stimuli. It is therefore evidence for the fact that unattended stimuli can be perceived and hence for a separation of attention and perception.

There is further evidence from both cognitive psychology and from second language acquisition that learning can take place without awareness of what is being learned. Carr and Curran (1994) reported studies showing the dissociation between structural learning and attention or awareness. In other words, some of the mechanisms of structural learning are independent of consciousness. In work by Nissen and Bullemer (1987), subjects shadowed a sequence of lights by pushing buttons. There were four lights in a row with a button under each one. The lights flashed one at a time in a continuous series. Subjects had to press the button under the light that flashed as quickly as possible. Their reaction times were measured. The order of the lights was structured with a sequence that repeated itself every 10 flashes. Importantly, then, there was structure underlying the sequence of lighted bulbs even though the subjects did not know what the structure was or even that structure existed. Despite this, their reaction times showed that structural learning did take place. The speed and accuracy of subjects' ability to press buttons improved with repeated exposure to the patterns. Performance was compared to that of subjects for whom the lights appeared randomly (see also Bullemer & Nissen, 1990; Cohen, Ivry, & Keele, 1990; Curran & Keele, 1993; Nissen, Knopman, & Schacter, 1987; Perruchet & Amorim, 1992; Willingham, Nissen, & Bullemer, 1989).

In subsequent research, attempts were made to gain information about structural awareness and conscious utilization of structural information more explicitly. Subjects were asked whether or not they noticed a sequence and, if so, to describe the sequence. This assessed knowledge about structure. To determine the extent to which they were able to utilize that knowledge, researchers presented participants with a light and asked them to predict what the next light in the sequence would be. The results are interesting and varied. In responding to whether or not they noted a pattern, some participants said that they noticed no pattern, others said that they thought they noticed, but only supplied fragmentary descriptions, and others said that they noticed a pattern and were able to describe that pattern accurately. The results for the light prediction task were similar. Some participants performed at chance, others were above chance, and others were nearly perfect (see also Cohen et al., 1990; Nissen & Bullemer, 1987; Nissen et al., 1987; Willingham et al., 1989). What is particularly noteworthy is that there was little relation between performance on the reaction time part of the experiment and performance on the prediction task. There were subjects who said that they noticed no pattern (supported by the fact that they appeared not to notice any pattern when performing the prediction task) but who outperformed the control group. Similarly, although there were some increases in accuracy in the prediction task, these increases do not appear to be supported by evidence of structural learning in performance on the reaction time part of the experiment. In sum, a direct relation between improvement in performance on the initial reaction time experiment and awareness does not appear (Willingham et al., 1989, as reported by Carr & Curran, 1994).

Of course, one could argue that in the light experiment perhaps some attention was paid to the structure of the blinking lights. Here, we are in a situation requiring the burden of proof. Because one cannot easily prove that something did not take place (e.g., one cannot prove innocence in the killing of Nicole Simpson and Ronald Goldman, except perhaps through DNA testing, assuming no reasonable alibi and a possible proximity to the murder scene), the burden of proof, particularly in the face of strong evidence, appears to be on the shoulders of those who argue that indeed attention was focused on structure and that there was awareness.

One can point to research from second language acquisition that also suggests learning without attention or awareness. One example from second language acquisition research comes from data on relative clauses. Based on data from languages diverse both typologically and geographically, Keenan and Comrie (1977) proposed the accessibility hierarchy, a way of describing the relation among different relative clause types cross-linguistically. The underlying principle is that the types of relative clauses in any language can be described on the basis of the following hierarchy:

SU > DO > IO > OPREP > GEN > OCOMP[9]

There are two universal facts:[10] First, all languages have subject relative clauses, and second, predictions can be made such that if a language has a relative clause of type *X*, then it will also have any relative clause type higher on the hierarchy, or to the left of type *X*. Thus, if we know that a language (let us say English) has object of comparative relative clauses (e.g., *I saw the man that I am taller than*), we know that it also has all other relative clause types. If we take a language that has genitive relative clauses, such as Italian (*Vedo la donna il cui figlio ti ho parlato* ["I see the woman whose son I told you about"]), we can infer that all relative clause types except object of comparative are possible. From an inspection of the hierarchy, there is no way of predicting the lowest relative clause type. All that can be said is that when the lowest type is known, we are able to make claims about all other relative clause types that that language has.

Claims have been made that the hierarchy reflects not only universal facts of relative clauses but also ease of relativization. It is further assumed that if this is universally the case for native speakers, it should also be the case for second language speakers. That is, difficulty should not differentially affect languages that an individual uses. Evidence used to support this claim comes from Gass (1979a, 1979b), who presented data from learners of English with a wide range of native languages (e.g., Italian, Arabic, Portuguese, Farsi, French, Thai, Chinese, Korean, and Japanese). The data supported the view that production of relative clauses by second language learners could be predicted on the basis of the Accessibility Hierarchy. Subject relative clauses showed the greatest frequency and accuracy, followed by direct object relative clauses, and so forth. With the exception of the genitive,[11] the predictions of the Accessibility Hierarchy are borne out.

With specific regard to the potential separation of awareness and learning and with our knowledge of the implicational relation among relative clause types, we can ask if learning a relative clause type lower on the hierarchy would generalize to knowledge of other relative clause types. Based on studies by Gass (1982) and Eckman, Bell, and Nelson (1988), the answer appears to be *yes*. In Gass (1982), two groups of second language learners were given specific instruction on relative clauses. One group was instructed on subject and direct object relatives; a second group learned object of preposition relatives. After the period of instruction, both groups were tested on all relative clause types. The group that had received subject and direct object instruction performed well only on those two relative clause types but no others, whereas the second group performed well not only on their instructed relative clauses (i.e., object of prepositions) but also on the relative clauses higher on the accessibility hierarchy.

Eckman et al. had four groups of learners, a control group and three experimental groups, each of which received instruction on one relative clause type: subject, direct object, or object of preposition. Although there was improvement for the groups learning the three types of relative clauses, the greatest improvement occurred in the group that was given instruction on the lowest position of the hierarchy (i.e., the object of preposition group). The group with the next greatest improvement was the direct object group and then the subject group. The conclusions of both these studies were that learners show maximum generalization up the hierarchy. What is crucial for our purposes is that learning particular relative clause types occurred without any attention drawn to the specific structures in question; in fact, input was not even available to the learners of those particular structures. This goes against the strong version of the noticing hypothesis (Schmidt, 1990, 1993b, 1993c): "Attention to input is a necessary condition for any learning at all, and that what must be attended to is not input in general, but whatever features of the input play a role in the system to be learned" (Schmidt, 1993b, p. 35). If no input existed, how could attention to input be a necessary condition for all aspects of learning?[12]

Recent experimental work by Schachter et al. (1996) suggests that awareness in and of itself (in their work, awareness is operationalized by the presentation of explicit rules to learners) is not a determining factor in learning. Another part of their work considered the role of attention. Learners were placed into groups that differed on the extent to which participants were required to attend to a particular syntactic feature. There was evidence of attentional learning, and there was also evidence of learning in a nonattentional mode. Thus, Schmidt's strong hypothesis cannot be maintained.

The preceding arguments are not intended to suggest that attention and awareness are not important in the process of learning a second language. To the contrary, the arguments are intended to show that attention and awareness are not the only factors. Some of the factors involved in second language learning are internal to the learner, and others are external to the learner. Those that are internal to the learner are of two sorts, those that are available to introspection and those that are not. Examples of introspective types of internal factors are just those aspects of learning that a learner can be aware of, such as vocabulary or certain grammatical features. These can be manipulated (i.e., oriented) by others (e.g., teachers) so as to have a greater likelihood of having attention drawn to them and hence of being noticed. Others are not (readily) available for introspection and cannot be manipulated. These aspects of language do not require attention or awareness for learning. Examples of the latter may stem from language based on UG (see chapter 2).

1.3. MEDIATING FACTORS

1.3.1. From Input to Apperception

To this point, I have dealt with five levels in the process of moving from input to output, and I have dealt with the notions of attention and awareness as central factors in this process. I now turn to a discussion of some of the factors that are influential in moving from one stage to another. The first question to be asked concerns apperception. Why is some input apperceived, whereas other input is not? Why are some aspects of language noticed by a learner, whereas others are not? What are the mediating factors at this initial stage? Put differently, what factors serve as input filters?

One factor is time pressure, particularly at early stages of acquisition. At early stages of learning a second language, much of the input is difficult to separate into words or phrases or other units that may be manageable[13] by the learner. When the input comes from oral input, it is particularly difficult to hear anything that may be recognizable in any way. The problem is somewhat smaller when dealing with written input because the learners are not necessarily limited to one exposure to the input. Furthermore, they are guided by the division of units into words by means of visual breaks at the beginning and end of those words.

A second factor is frequency, possibly at both extremes. Something that is very frequent in the input is likely to be noticed. On the other hand, particularly at more advanced stages of learning at which expectations of language data are well established, something unusual because of its infrequency may stand out for a learner. For example, in a particular context that is familiar to the learner, a new word or phrase may appear. It then may be noticed by the learner and thus be available for eventual integration into the learner's system.

A third factor that influences apperception has been described as affect. Within this category are social distance, status, motivation, and attitude. This is exemplified by the work of Krashen (1977, 1980, 1982), who proposed that individuals have an affective filter. Another explanation was put forth by Schumann (1976), who argued that social distance can prevent a learner from obtaining input data. If learners feel psychologically or socially distant from the target language community, the language input will not be available. This may be the case because learners physically remove themselves from speakers of the target language.

A fourth factor that may determine whether language data are apperceived has to do with the broad category of associations and prior knowledge. In fact, apperception has been defined as the process of understanding by which newly observed qualities of an object are related to past experiences. Learning involves integration of new knowledge with prior knowledge. Importantly, one needs some sort of anchor with which to ground new knowledge. An example is in order. Recently, an American was traveling on a bus in Japan. She had studied Japanese for a brief period of time, but her knowledge was minimal. There was an announcement on the bus that apparently stated the names of upcoming stops. She heard a stream of speech that was generally incomprehensible, but a few bits of sound jumped out at her, which she later realized were *san cho-me* ("third district") and *yon cho-me* ("fourth district"). These phrases were recognizable to her because she had prior knowledge of numbers (*san*, "three," and *yon*, "four") and remembered seeing *cho* on Japanese addresses in the past. This recognition led her to hypothesize that she was hearing names of bus stops.

Hence, prior knowledge is one of the factors that determine whether or not the input is meaningful. Prior knowledge is to be interpreted broadly and can include knowledge of the native language, knowledge of other languages, existing knowledge of the second language, world knowledge, language universals, and so on. All play a role in a learner's success or lack of success in interpreting language data, in that they ultimately determine whether a learner understands and what level of understanding takes place.

Salience of form is yet another aspect that appears to be relevant in determining what is noticed. Bardovi-Harlig (1987) used salience of form to explain the acquisition of grammatical structures that could not be explained by means of markedness. Her concern was the acquisition order of sentences like 1 and 2 by L2 learners.

1. Who did Mary give the book to?
2. To whom did Mary give the book?

Theoretical considerations based on markedness predict the acquisition of the structure in Example 2 before the structure in Example 1.[14] However, the data show the reverse pattern; the structure in Example 1 is acquired before the structure in Example 2. She identified *salience* (which she defined as the availability of input) as the main factor contributing to the unexpected outcome. Because learners are exposed to a greater quantity of input for sentences such as Example 1 as opposed to Example 2, the acquisition patterns are what they are. The role of salience in second language acquisition research received additional support from Doughty's (1991) study of relativization. She compared three groups of subjects engaged in a computer-assisted language learning project. The groups differed in the format of presentation of the language material. In addition to a control group, there were two experimental groups: a meaning-oriented treatment group and a rule-oriented treatment group. As the names suggest, in the rule-oriented treatment group were explicit metalinguistic statements about relative clauses, whereas in the meaning-oriented treatment group there were no such explicit statements. If salience can come about through focusing a learner's attention on particular grammatical features, then the rule-oriented treatment group should do better on a posttest than the other two groups. This was not the case; the two experimental groups improved more or less equally. However, a closer examination of the experimental materials brings us back to the question of what makes something salient. There are many ways in which increased salience can be brought about. Among these are frequency of input (possibly at both ends—that is, highly frequent and highly infrequent items or structures) and form-focused instruction.

Returning to Doughty's (1991) study, we see that both saliency and redundancy (i.e., frequency) were built into the tasks of the meaning-oriented treatment group. In the experimental material, the meaning-oriented treatment group saw passages with certain features, namely head nouns and relative clause markers, highlighted on the screen. Additionally, typographical capitalization of the juxtaposed head noun and relative clause marker made these parts of the passage visually salient to the learner. Thus, if salience has an important role in second language acquisition, Doughty's results (given her particular methodology) would be predicted because both forms of pedagogical intervention focused on drawing learners' attention to relative clause formation.

Bayley (1994) also used salience as an explanation for language use. In his study of phonetic acquisition, he noted that the salience of the past tense form affects the extent to which an L2 learner uses a particular past tense marker.

Although all of this leads us to the conclusion that salience affects acquisition, it clearly begs the question of precisely what makes a form salient. Is it word stress, position in a sentence, relation to something already known, frequency? The answer to each of these (as well as to a much longer list) is undoubtedly "yes." Regardless of the specific factors involved in making linguistic form salient, salience can be said to help ensure that particular forms are noticed by the learner and hence lead to rule strengthening (see discussion in section 1.1.4). It helps the learner confirm patterns that may already be on the way to being established or it helps the learner create new patterns, links, or connections.

A final factor to mention is that of attention (see the extended discussion in section 1.2). In fact, many of the aforementioned factors determine, to some extent, what a learner does or does not attend to. The crucial question is whether a learner attends to the input at a given point in time. One can think of many reasons why the input is not attended to. Many of these are trivial and do not concern second language acquisition—(e.g., falling asleep in class); others are not trivial (e.g., an a priori realization that the input is not manageable). Attention is important because it allows a learner to notice a mismatch between what he or she knows about the L2 and what is produced by speakers of the second language. If one is going to make modifications in one's grammar, one must first recognize that changes need to be made. Thus, readjustment of one's grammar is triggered by the perceptibility of a mismatch. In fact, the necessity of recognizing that something needs to be learned may in part explain aspects of nonlearning, which often occurs between two closely related languages where differences in certain parts of the linguistic system are not readily discernible.

Attention may also affect whole areas of language, such as pragmatics. It is often the case that pragmatic behaviors (e.g., when and how to apologize, to compliment, to refuse; cf. Blum-Kulka & Olshtain, 1984; Olshtain & Blum-Kulka, 1985) are learned late, if ever. These are often areas that learners do not readily recognize as differing cross-linguistically or cross-culturally. Rather, deviations in the area of pragmatics are often seen as negative reflections of individuals or of groups of people. That these are not seen as part of the language that needs to be learned results in the obvious fact that they are not learned; native language pragmatic behavior persists even after numerous years of exposure despite, in many instances, fluency in all other linguistic areas. Two examples illustrate this.

1. From Halmari (1995)

Pizza deliverer:	Double or Nothin' Pizza?
Non-native speaker (NNS):	This is A.B., hi.
Pizza deliverer:	*What* was your name?
NNS:	(annoyed) A.B.
Pizza deliverer:	(annoyed) Why do I wanna know your name?

In this example, a Finnish woman who had been living in the United States for many years and who was fluent in English (except for a minor trace of a Finnish accent, she was virtually indistinguishable from a NS of English) continued to use names as a form of greeting, as is the norm in Finnish:

2. From Hakulinen (1993, pp. 155–156)
TELEPHONE RING

Sirkka:	Sirkka Kotolaineh
	(name surname)
Pertti:	Pe:rtti huomen-ta
	(name morning + PART)
Sirkka:	H:uomen-ta
	(morning + PART)

As seen in Example 1, the use of names in telephone conversations was a continuing mode of greeting despite significant input to suggest that this practice is not followed in American English.

In the following example, a Finnish man who had been conducting business in the United States for many years was still accustomed to using the Finnish business practice of including a long discussion unrelated to business prior to entering into the business part of the conversation.

3. From Halmari (1993, pp. 416–417)

1.	Native speaker (NS):	Okay. How are you doing today?
2.	NNS:	I'm real bad. I was so—w-we have been so angry with my wife because we have problems with the computer.
3.	NS:	(laughs) Hah-hah-hah-hah-ha!
4.	NNS:	You don't believe how how these people how they are—er, they are sending us to four different companies. I never buy an EB—IBM any more.
5.	NS:	Oh REALLY?
6.	NNS:	Yeah.
7.	NS:	You have a big problem with your IBM?
8.	NNS:	Ye:s.
9.	NS:	How funny.
10.	NNS:	Yeah and I think that it is the basically that the first guy who sold it to us he put the wrong serial number in the guarantee papers.
11.	NS:	O:h.
12.	NNS:	We have a warranty on it but the serial number is different. He has made a m-smesh to us and it's going to cost almost two thousand DOLLARS.
13.	NS:	Oh N:O!
14.	NNS:	So I'm pissed.
15.	NS:	I- I would be very pissed too hah -hah!
16.	NNS:	[Yeah.
17.	NS:	O:h what an awful thing that-s that's a lot of cars you have to sell.
18.	NNS:	Yeah. I have to ship a many many many cars.
19.	NS:	That's a lot of cars for a lousy computer.
20.	NNS:	Yes. (laughs)
21.	NS:	Same for me too.
22.	NNS:	Oh?
23.	NS	*So.* I'm returning your call regarding a *rate* that you want.

The native speaker only minimally engaged in the conversation (lines 3, 5, 9, 11, 13). He began the conversation with a perfunctory "How are you doing today?" to which he undoubtedly expected only a limited answer. In line 17, he started (unsuccessfully) to bridge to a business context. However, perhaps because the Finnish man expected to be engaged in a lengthy mutual nontopical discussion, he did not pick up on the segue into the business purpose of the call. Most likely, at the end of this encounter each thought the other odd. What is important in this context is that this subtle aspect of American English business behavior was lost on the Finnish man despite many years of interactive exposure.

These categories (i.e., time, frequency, affect, prior knowledge, salience, and attention) are not intended to be necessarily independent. For example, attention may be related to or influenced by affective variables. If learners have little desire to deal with the target language community, they may block out all the input, attending only to that which is necessary to conduct business or to get through the day. Similarly, affective variables may be influenced by prior knowledge. Whether learners are positively or negatively disposed toward the target language or target language community is presumably determined by prior linguistic knowledge (perhaps they do not like the sound of the language or find the language difficult to learn) or even by prior experience with the speakers of the target language. Thus, a significant role is assigned to prior knowledge or experience as activators of selective attention.

1.3.2. From Apperception to Comprehension

The preceding discussion has dealt with issues that may determine why input is noticed by the learner. There are also factors specific to conversational interactions that are relevant to how the input can be shaped so that it can be comprehended. That is, once the input is noticed, what is involved in helping it be comprehended? Here, I include the concept of negotiation of meaning and foreigner talk (see chapters 3 and 5). Negotiation and modification differ from the previously mentioned factors in that they involve production and feedback. They are not necessary conditions but rather serve to increase the possibility of a greater amount of input becoming available for further use. Yet another factor that aids comprehension is redundancy. Pica, Doughty, and Young (1986; Pica, Young, & Doughty, 1987) showed that redundancy, in terms of exact as well as semantic repetitions, aids in the comprehension process. Further support comes from Doughty (1991), who, in a study discussed earlier on the acquisition of relative clauses through a computer-aided design, found that the experimental group that received lexical and semantic rephrasings of the relative clause sentences performed best on a measure of comprehension. She further pointed to the specific area of semantic rephrasings as a key to input comprehension.

In dealing with comprehension, there are many aspects of language that second language learners must learn. These include not only the more common areas of syntax and phonology (including knowledge about segments, syllable structure, and prosody) but also less commonly mentioned areas such as discourse, pragmatics (see section 1.3.1), and vocabulary.

There are a number of means by which one can reach a particular analysis. For example, the most common way of getting at a syntactic analysis is by first having an understanding of the meaning. However, one can also imagine having an understanding of the syntax yet not being able to arrive at a meaning, for example, in the case of idioms or proverbs.

What is the difference between apperceived and comprehended input? Apperception is conceptualized as a priming device. It prepares the learner for the possibility of subsequent analysis. For example, in learning a language with contrastive consonant length, a learner might apperceive that consonant length is an important aspect of the language (this could be on the basis of first language [L1] or on the basis of experience with the L2). In comprehending, however, the task facing the learner is to analyze the input in order to determine the consonant length in some particular context and then to relate the particular consonant length to a specific meaning. To take a specific example, Italian uses consonant length for the purpose of differentiating the meanings of words: /cap:elli/ "hair" versus /capelli/ "hats." A learner of Italian has to recognize first that Italian differentiates between words on this basis (i.e., apperception), then recognize the difference between /cap:elli/ and /capelli/ (i.e., comprehension), and then match /cappelli/ with the concept "hair" and /capelli/ with the concept "hats" (another level of comprehension).

1.3.3. From Input to Intake

Intake can be conceptualized as apperceived input that has been further processed. One factor that determines whether or not a particular instance of comprehended input will result in intake is the level of analysis of the input that a learner achieves. For example, an analysis at the level of meaning is not as useful for intake as an analysis made at the level of morphology, lexicon, or syntax. Recall the American in Japan mentioned in section 1.3.1 who, while traveling on a bus, heard *san cho-me* and *yon cho-me*. She initially recognized *san* and *cho*. She had some vague knowledge of the word *cho* but received a deeper understanding of the phrase when later someone informed her that *me* means "eye" and that *cho-me* actually has something to do with smaller districts ("as far as the eye can see"). The proposal that different levels of analysis differentially affect intake is supported by Faerch and Kasper (1986), who, in the context of foreign language teaching, argued that one way to improve formal correctness is to provide learners with tasks designed to promote recognition of formal features rather than overall comprehension of meaning, and by Call (1985), who argued for the importance of syntax and structural awareness in listening comprehension. A second factor is the time factor. Pressures of conversational interaction may preclude sufficient analysis for the purposes of intake. In this case the input (although comprehended) may have no further role in acquisition or may be put into temporary storage. For example, recently an English-speaking learner of Japanese was at lunch with a Japanese man who had just learned that she had studied Japanese. He said to her, *"Nihonni ikimasuka?"* ("Are you going to Japan?") She did not understand much of anything but figured out from the word *Nihon* ("Japan") that he was asking her something about Japanese. In fact, she thought that he had said *Nihongo* ("Japanese"). She kept this phrase in mind until a few minutes later; when she had time to mull it over, she was able to figure out precisely what he had asked her. Thus, although the input was initially virtually incomprehensible (although it was apperceived), it served as input into the next level at a later point in time.

What will determine whether the second language is comprehended or not? Prior linguistic knowledge is an important factor (see Gass & Selinker, 1994). Prior linguistic knowledge includes native language knowledge, existing second language knowledge, language universals, and knowledge of other languages. These same factors are important in the determination of apperception as well. This is not surprising, because linguistic knowledge is in some ways cumulative. One needs a place to attach new information to and some basis for the analysis (i.e., comprehension) of new information. Comprehension cannot take place in a vacuum. Prior knowledge forms the basis for comprehension (in either a narrow or broad sense).

What mediates between what has been comprehended and what is eventually important for intake? I have already mentioned that the quality of analysis (i.e., comprehended input) is an important factor. Clearly, knowledge of L1 and L2 are significant factors. Additionally, whether or not a particular feature is part of UG (i.e., representing something innate) will bear upon eventual intake; whether or not a particular feature is part of a universal typological feature will also bear upon eventual intake. Those factors are not to be understood as necessarily independent. Features that are part of universal knowledge or are present in the native language (or other languages known) are most likely to be candidates for deeper analysis and hence for intake.

Hypothesis formation takes place with the addition of new information. A beginning learner (let us assume a native speaker of Spanish) hears the English sentence "It's pretty," forming the hypothesis that English sentences can be of the form Verb + Adjective. This conclusion is arrived at by attending to the form, apperceiving it in terms of a Spanish sentence, *"Es bonito,"* and understanding the sentence in terms of both its meaning and its syntactic structure. The error in the analysis occurs because *it's* is heard as being similar to *es*, and a similar syntactic structure is assumed.

Thus, the knowledge of L1 facilitates the learner's conclusion. Prior knowledge led to apperception, actual syntactic and semantic comprehension, and intake because the analysis matched up with something already known, that is, *"es bonito."*

The hypothesis of Verb + Adjective is tested against a reasonable assumption, that of native–target language similarity. The hypothesis is confirmed. At a later point in time, the learner might see the printed version of *it's* and question the single word analysis she had originally given to this form. This would cause her to modify this hypothesis and possibly further test it against new data. If the hypothesis is modified in such a way as to eliminate the first hypothesis, that first hypothesis is no longer relevant for grammar formation.

It is important to consider why comprehended input and intake need to be separated: Not all input that is comprehended becomes intake. For example, input may be comprehended only for the immediate purpose of a conversational interaction, or it may be used for purposes of learning. Faerch and Kasper (1980) proposed something similar when they differentiated between intake as communication and intake as learning. The first is language intake only for the purpose of immediate meaning in the course of a conversational interaction, and the second is intake incorporated into a learner's grammar. Intake in the approach being discussed in this chapter only includes the second of these possibilities because intake refers to the process of attempted integration of linguistic information. Thus, input that is only used in a conversation and for the sake of that conversation is not regarded as intake.

1.3.4. Moving to Integration

Integration is not necessarily a one-time affair. Rather, there are different levels of analysis and reanalysis from storage into the grammar and within the grammar itself as part of integration. Importantly, the integration component does not function as an independent unit. This is particularly significant because the model being discussed (and second language acquisition in general) is dynamic and interactive, with knowledge itself being cumulative and interactive.

Language information that is processed and deemed appropriate for language development and is not put into storage becomes part of a learner's knowledge system or grammar. A significant amount of research has been done in this area, indeed the bulk of the work in second language acquisition over the past few decades. This includes most of the work on linguistic and psycholinguistic aspects of acquisition.

What are some factors that mediate between comprehended input, intake, and integration? Some are similar to those factors that are also available at the level of apperception. For example, the organizational structure of the native language may shape the way the learner's grammar is structured. Existing knowledge of the second language will also shape the way integration takes place. Universal principles of language may also play a role in L2 grammar formation. Given a particular element in the input, there are universal factors that interact with it, resulting in a generalization of the initial input to other related domains.

A factor that provides the impetus or motivation for changes in one's knowledge base is the recognition of a mismatch between what is present in the input and the learner's grammar. For learners to modify their speech, they must first recognize that there is something in need of modification—a perceived mismatch between native speaker speech and their own learner-grammars.

Evidence for integrated knowledge can be seen in one of two ways. First, there can be changes in the rule system that surface in the output. This is what is typically thought of when one considers developmental changes. Second, there may be changes in the underlying system although no output change. Changes in underlying systems with no surface manifestation are typically subsumed under the category of reanalysis. In a second language context, we can also think of reanalysis in two ways. A reanalysis of the underlying system may affect the potential for output. For example, a learner may have learned the lexical item *orange juice* as a single lexical item, *orangejuice*, and only at a later point in time will he or she reanalyze it as *orange + juice*. This reanalysis sets the stage for the potential forms *apple juice, grapefruit juice*, and so on. Thus, reanalysis allows for the potential creation of novel forms. On a syntactic level, prefabricated patterns may be analyzed with, initially, little output change. Hakuta (1974) cited the speech of Uguisu, a 5-year-old Japanese child learning English. In the first month of data collection the following were typical utterances:

4. Do you know?
5. Do you want this one?

In later periods it became obvious that *do you* was a (possibly monomorphemic) question marker. When reanalysis finally took place and *do you* was analyzed into its component parts with the result a productive rule of question formation, there was no output difference. Sentences 6 and 7 are taken from the fifth and sixth month of data collection, respectively.

6. How do you break it?
7. Do you put it?

Thus, even though reanalysis did not result in output differences in this part of her grammar, the underlying systems must be different, as evidenced by output in other forms in her grammar.[15]

1.3.5. Culminating in Output

Learners' output is often equated with their grammar. For example, it is frequently inferred that changes in the output represent changes in a learner's grammar. However, the two should not be equated. That the output is not identical to one's grammar is suggested by a number of factors. Among these is the recognition of individual differences in what learners are willing to say. Personality factors such as confidence in one's ability to produce correct target language sentences may influence whether or not a learner produces target language material. Additionally, learners produce different linguistic forms that have varying amounts of accuracy depending on the task performed. For example, what learners can produce in writing is not what they can produce in speaking; what they can understand from a printed page is not equivalent to what they can understand from an oral stimulus. Also, different grammatical information may be used in different genres. Undoubtedly, this has to do with the ability to use different channels to express linguistic information. It is also a matter of limitation of access that one has to one's knowledge base.

Confidence in one's ability is one determining factor in output, but we must also consider how strongly represented the knowledge is. There may be different degrees of strength of knowledge representation (perhaps related to the automaticity of language processing) that will in part determine output and how output will take place. An example is provided by Swain (1985, p. 248), quoting from an eighth-grade immersion student who said, "I can hear in my head how I should sound when I talk, but it never comes out that way." Thus, there appear to be limitations on the translation of second language knowledge into output.

In sum, the output component represents more than the product of language knowledge; it is an active part of the entire learning process (cf. Swain & Lapkin, in press). This is further discussed in chapter 6.

1.4. CONCLUSION

This chapter has presented a conceptualization of the ways in which the pieces of acquisition fit together, integrating aspects of language acquisition that are discussed in greater detail in the chapters of this book. The model in Fig. 1.1 is intended to reflect the dynamic and interactive nature of acquisition. It also shows the multiple roles that language transfer and universals have. Their roles can only be understood in relation to a specific part of the process. For example, language transfer, as part of prior knowledge, can have a filtering role, as in going from input to apperceived input, and a processing role, as at the level of intake.

Furthermore, such aspects as personality and affect, factors that are under the learner's control to the greatest extent, are important at the initial stages of apperception. Their role is less significant at the levels of intake and integration, areas affected primarily by linguistic (e.g., universals of either a formal or functional type) or psycholinguistic factors devoid of cultural and social context. Finally, personality and affect once again emerge as important factors at the level of output. In other words, those factors that are under a learner's control to the greatest extent have the greatest effect only at the peripheries.

Psycholinguistic processing and linguistic phenomena in the middle are more influenced by mental constraints that are less accessible to direct manipulation. One would thus expect a correlation between affective variables and what is apperceived on the one hand and what is produced on the other, and a lack of correlation between affective variables and aspects of, for example, UG.

In sum, there is a major role for apperceived input, determined to a large extent by selective attention. Selective attention aids in grammar development. In other words, an initial step in grammar change is the learner's noticing (at some level) a mismatch between the input and his or her own organization of the target language.

The remainder of this book takes as its premise the fact that acquisition is dynamic and interactive. I consider input and interaction in their many facets in attempting to understand their role in the complex process of acquisition.

NOTES

1. Much of this chapter is based on an article titled "Integrating Research Areas: A Framework for Second Language Studies," originally published as Gass (1988a).
2. The term *input* is in some sense a misnomer, particularly if one is used to conceptualizing it in terms of computers. *Input* in the L2 literature refers to the language to which a learner is exposed either orally or visually (i.e., signed languages or printed matter) and is to be distinguished from *intake* (see Corder, 1967, and the discussion in chapter 6), which is the language that is available to and utilized in some way by the learner. In this sense, then, the term *ambient speech*, terminology from the child language literature, is a more appropriate one because it implies nothing about the result of the input. However, for the sake of consistency with the existing second language literature, I continue to use the term *input* throughout this book.
3. The concept of *grammar* should be interpreted broadly, including the phonology, morphology, syntax, semantics, and pragmatics of the language.
4. As *acquisition* is an ambiguous term, so is *output*. It can refer to the process of production or to the product (i.e., speech or writing). So output as product is the result of the process of outputting.
5. Fossilization results when new (correct) input fails to have an impact on the learner's grammar.

6. This is not to suggest that understanding does not involve levels of representation, because there is clearly some structural or hierarchical order imposed on a string of sounds. What is intended is that the order may be imposed by real-world knowledge or by first language knowledge and may not bear any relation to the second language. For example, to understand a string of elements in which there is an animate noun, an inanimate noun, and a verb (denoting an action), a learner might impose a VSO order (assuming native speakers of a VSO language) even when the order of elements produced was SOV.

7. In this book I do not deal with *consciousness* as intent.

8. In the field of cognitive psychology, the concept of consciousness is highly debated. Can it be studied or not? Allport (1988) pointed out that for many the idea of studying "the phenomenon of consciousness" is a reality. On the other hand, others see consciousness as a cover term; for them (see McLaughlin, 1990a), consciousness cannot be conceived as a unitary phenomenon. Allport claimed that it is the "theoretical bogey of psychological theory [bad psychological theory], the *homunculus*—the little man in the head" (p. 160). Miller (1987) stated that "Consciousness is a word worn smooth by a million tongues" (cited in Velmans, 1991, p. 651). The incorporation into theories of second language acquisition of terms from other fields that are themselves filled with controversy is a potentially dangerous and unproductive enterprise.

Marcel and Bisiach (1988, p. 1) provided the following anecdotes to illustrate the acceptance and nonacceptance of consciousness.

> When someone returns after an absence, their home coming is not always straight forward nor their acceptance always universal. Three stories illustrate different aspects of this.
>
> In 16th-century France, a young peasant called Martin Guerre, not long married, quite suddenly left home. Some years later a man came to the village claiming to be Martin. The wife, tentative at first, accepted him and came to love him, as did many of the villagers. However, family disputes led to a judicial examination of whether the pretender was in fact who he claimed to be. Despite the fact that the man was appreciated by many for his various qualities, the official issue of his identity, for administrative and financial purposes, could not be ignored.
>
> In the biblical story of the prodigal son, different issues are at stake. For the father, the pleasure at the return of the prodigal to the fold outweighed the satisfaction derived from the constancy of the son who had stayed. Naturally, the dutiful son resented the welcome given to his prodigal brother and the lack of appreciation of his own less glamorous deeds.
>
> Our third story concerns the arrival in Mexico of Cortes. It was taken by many Aztecs to be the return of Quetzalcoatl. But it is said that some dared to voice the suspicion that Quetzalcoatl could not return since he had never even existed, was just a myth. The very idea of a serpent with feathers showed what an incoherent myth it was. However, yet others, especially some thoughtful Spaniards (anticipating Pirandello?), suggested that if something is believed to be the case, well, in some sense it *is* the case. Reprinted by permission of Oxford University Press.

As Marcel and Bisiach go on to point out, each of these stories in some sense reflect the reception given to the study of consciousness, including "those who either like or dislike the character, irrespective of his name, while others are concerned that the name and the appropriate identity should fit" (1988, p. 2), those who welcome the returnee back with full knowledge of the flaws, yet aware of the potential usefulness, and those who are either duped by the newcomer or, if not fooled, either reject the new individual or accept him as the best possible solution.

9. The abbreviations are to be interpreted as follows:

SU = Subject Relative Clause
> *Example:* I saw the woman **who** wants to be President of the United States.

DO = Direct Object Relative Clause
> *Example:* I saw the woman **whom** the man wanted to see.

IO = Indirect Object Relative Clause
> *Example:* I saw the woman **to whom** you gave the book.

OPREP = Object of Preposition Relative Clause
> *Example:* I saw the man **about whom** the other men were gossiping.

GEN = Genitive Relative Clause
> *Example:* I saw the woman **whose** brother borrowed my bicycle.

OCOMP = Object of Comparative Relative Clause
> *Example:* I saw the woman **whom** she is taller than.

10. This is an oversimplification of the facts. The interested reader is referred to Keenan and Comrie (1977) and Comrie and Keenan (1979).

11. One explanation for the unpredicted ordering of the genitive (it turned out to be more reflective of positions higher on the hierarchy) was that the phrase with the genitive marker (e.g., The man *whose brother* was at the restaurant) was perceived not as a genitive but as a unit in some other relation to the verb (in this case, as the subject of the verb *was*). On closer inspection of the sentences, it was noted that the genitive phrases were either subjects or direct objects within their own clauses, hence causing them to be interpreted as subject relative clauses or direct object relative clauses and explaining their more accurate use.

12. Schmidt (1995) in fact acknowledged that with parameters (see chapter 2, this volume) one could show that nonattentional learning and learning without awareness can take place.

> If it could be shown that one aspect of a parameter language serves as the trigger for automatic adjustment of all other aspects of the parameter, this would constitute powerful evidence for implicit learning, because the proposed principles controlling generalization not just to different lexicalizations of a single structure but to completely different structures are so abstract that learners certainly never become consciously aware of them.

The relative clause studies just discussed provide evidence in this direction.

13. In many cases learners find themselves engaged in conversation with a native speaker and know beforehand that little will be understood. In such instances they may do nothing more than provide minimal feedback to the native speaker so as not to appear rude, while tuning out the conversation completely.

14. Bardovi-Harlig based her arguments on work by Van Riemsdijk (1978). He noted that cross-linguistic evidence suggests that "preposition stranding" sentences are rare, limited to a few Indo-European languages. From a markedness perspective, preposition stranding comes when the *wh*-element has been extracted from the prepositional phrase. He argued that generally prepositional phrases do not allow extraction and that a prepositional phrase is a bounding node. Sentences with preposition stranding have entire constituents moved.

15. By *change*, I intend something more than expansion of forms. I mean a fundamental reorganization of some part of the grammar as opposed to addition or accumulation of new forms.

The Question of Evidence

2.0. PREAMBLE

This chapter deals with the nature of evidence available to learners. The focus is on the kinds of evidence that a learner needs in order to construct and revise grammatical knowledge successfully. The chapter also includes a review of some of the pertinent child language literature relating to negative evidence.

2.1. INTRODUCTION

Throughout the recent literature, two more or less distinct positions regarding the necessary evidence requirements for learning can be discerned. In general terms, we can summarize these as the nature and nurture positions.[1] The first refers to the possibility that learners (whether child L1 learners or adult second language learners) come to the learning situation with innate knowledge about language; the second position claims that language development is inspired and conditioned by the environment, that is, the interactions in which learners engage.

Much of the debate centers on certain kinds of knowledge and how learners (children or adults) can possibly attain that knowledge without being explicitly taught or without being exposed to it in some direct way. To understand this position, I present some of the basic tenets of UG and elaborate on certain aspects of linguistic knowledge that proficient speakers of a language have.[2]

What is UG? It is "the system of principles, conditions, and rules that are elements or properties of all human languages" (Chomsky, 1975, p. 29). As such, it "is taken to be a characterization of the child's prelinguistic state" (Chomsky, 1981, p. 7). The theory behind UG is that language consists of a set of abstract principles and parameters that form the core grammars of all natural languages. Principles constrain the kinds of linguistic phenomena that can occur at different levels of grammars. These constraints are assumed to be universal and hence valid for all languages. This does not mean that all languages avail themselves of all principles. Rather, there is a set of universal principles from which languages draw. For example, some languages require *wh*-movement in questions, whereas others do not. English is the former type; Korean the latter. For languages without movement, clearly no constraints on movement are needed. On the other hand, for languages with movement, there are constraints on which movement can exist.[3] The principle of subjacency is proposed as a universal principle constraining movement. It is relevant in English but not in Korean.

Parameters are principles that vary. That is, principles may operate in one way in some languages and in another way in other languages. In other words, there are different parameter settings. What is important and interesting from the perspective of second language acquisition is that parameters are composed of clusterings of properties. They specify the grammatical properties that are linked together in languages. A commonly cited example is the difference between Italian and English, the first being a [+prodrop] language (also known as a null subject language) and the latter a [−prodrop] language. In Italian (and languages like Italian, e.g., Spanish), verbs can appear without overt subjects, as in the following example:

1. *Compra   dei   libri   ogni   giorno.*
   buys (3rd sg.) some books each day
   "S/he buys books every day."

In Italian, the subject does not always appear before the verb, as can be seen in the following example:

2. *Mangia Giovanna una mela   ogni   giorno.*
   Eats   Giovanna an   apple each day
   "Giovanna eats an apple every day."

English, on the other hand, has obligatory subjects and does not allow subject–verb inversion. These two properties cluster together in languages; no language allows deletion of subjects but does not allow subject–verb inversion.[4]

The question to be asked concerns how children learn a complex set of abstractions when the input alone does not contain evidence of these abstractions. If the input does not provide the information necessary for the extraction of abstractions, there must be something in addition to the input that children use in grammar formation. Universal Grammar is hypothesized to be an innate language faculty that limits the kinds of languages that can be created. It thus serves as a constraint on the kinds of grammars that can be created and in a sense limits the hypothesis space that learners (i.e., children and possibly adults learning a second language) use in creating linguistic knowledge. Although there is still considerable disagreement as to the nature of UG, there is widespread agreement among linguists that children are born with some sort of innately specified knowledge. As discussed in chapter 1, the arguments in this book assume that acquisition is dynamic and must take into account not only details of linguistic knowledge and how that knowledge comes to be but also how language develops as a function of interactions in which learners engage. The question then is how innate knowledge interacts with the environment and input in the creation of linguistic knowledge.

The question could be raised, as indeed it was during the days in which behaviorist theories of language acquisition were in vogue, concerning correction. Why posit an innate language faculty if correction is a vital part of language acquisition? In other words, when errors occur, they are just corrected right out of the system. An important claim is made and elaborated: Children do not receive large doses of correction.

Before considering the empirical evidence for and against the role of correction, or more generally, negative evidence in child language, I turn to an examination of the kinds of complexities and abstractions that appear not to be available from the input and consider what it means to say that the input is insufficient. Consider the following examples from English, all based on the possibility of contracting *want to* to *wanna*:

3. George and Graham want to go to Cy's truck stop.
4. George and Graham wanna go to Cy's truck stop.
5. Visa, it's everywhere you want to be. (American TV slogan)
6. Visa, it's everywhere you wanna be.
7. Sue wants to go, but Dennis and Carol don't want to.
8. Sue wants to go, but Dennis and Carol don't wanna.
9. Do Carol and Pat want to go to the party tonight?
10. Do Carol and Pat wanna go to the party tonight?
11. Who do Kathi and Gabi want to see?
12. Who do Kathi and Gabi wanna see?
13. Who do you want to spread the rumor about?
14. Who do you wanna spread the rumor about?

Although these sentences are all possible in English, there are numerous instances in which no contraction of *want to* to *wanna* is possible. Consider the following:

15. Who do Joan and Dan want to spread the rumor?
16. *Who do Joan and Dan wanna spread the rumor?

Or consider the following pair of sentences, the first of which is ambiguous (i.e., "I want to succeed Teddy" and "I want Teddy to succeed"), whereas the second is not (i.e., only the first reading is possible):

17. Teddy is the man I want to succeed.
18. Teddy is the man I wanna succeed.

Because there is nothing in the input to inform a learner of the possibilities and impossibilities of contraction, something else must provide that information; clearly this information is part of what adult speakers know about English. It is at this point that UG is invoked, specifically the concept of traces, part of a UG principle (i.e., empty category principle) needed to account for a range of syntactic phenomena. In *wh*-questions, movement is involved in which the *wh*-word is moved from its underlying position to the front of the sentence. When this occurs, a trace (t) is left in the original position. The existence of this trace has important consequences for later syntactic operations. Consider the sentence pair given in 15 and 16 previously and here repeated:

15. Who do Joan and Dan want to spread the rumor?
16. *Who do Joan and Dan wanna spread the rumor?

The existence of the trace can be seen in 15′.

15′. Who$_i$ do Joan and Dan want t_i to spread the rumor?

This contrasts with the sentence pair in 13 and 14:

13. Who do you want to spread the rumor about?
14. Who do you wanna spread the rumor about?

where the trace can be seen in 13′.

13′. Who$_i$ do you want to spread the rumor about t_i?

The trace in 13′ comes at the end of the sentence, leaving *want* and *to* adjacent, whereas the trace in 15′ comes between *want* and *to*, effectively blocking contraction.

The ambiguity problem presented in sentences 17 and 18 can be understood in a similar way.

17. Teddy is the man (who) I want to succeed.

18. Teddy is the man (who) I wanna succeed.

The trace in 17 can be seen as follows:

17′a. Teddy is the man (who$_i$) I want to succeed t$_i$.
17′b. Teddy is the man (who$_i$) I want t$_i$ to succeed.

Sentence 18 can only have the interpretation of (a) because that is the only option in which contraction is allowed; contraction in (b) is disallowed by the position of the trace, which separates *want* and *to*.

Another example that illustrates the impossibility of coming to the appropriate generalization based on input alone is seen in the case of adverb placement. In English only the first three of the following possibilities exist:

19. Confidentially, Graham told the story about Gabi's disease.
20. Graham confidentially told the story about Gabi's disease.
21. Graham told the story confidentially about Gabi's disease.
22. *Graham told confidentially the story about Gabi's disease.

English has restrictions on where adverbs can be placed in a sentence. In principle (although sometimes competing sources make this impossible in practice), material cannot intervene between the verb and object, disallowing sentences such as 22. Assume a child is exposed to the input data (or comparable input data) in 19–21. Given that children are generally known to generalize from data, what prevents them from believing that English adverb placement is generally free? In fact, children do not make this generalization, and errors comparable to 22 do not occur. Were they to occur, in the absence of correction, there would be no way to retreat from this overgeneralized position and to end up with a grammar that allows 19 and 21 but not 22. To solve this learnability problem, it has been hypothesized that children initially adhere to the subset principle and adopt the narrowest grammar consistent with the input data. In this way, in the absence of corrective feedback, children only adopt the correct English grammar. Similarly, a child learning a language that does allow subject–verb–adverb–object orderings (SVAO; e.g., French) will also select a narrow grammar but from the input will learn that French allows SVAO.

Indeed, this knowledge is not discernible from the input alone. Abstract knowledge concerning underlying structures is necessary.

2.1.1. Specific Kinds of Evidence

The basic issue underlying a discussion of what is known variously as the learnability problem, poverty of the stimulus, or Plato's problem is, "How do we come to have such rich and specific knowledge, or such intricate systems of belief and understanding, when the evidence available to us is so meager?" (Chomsky, 1987, cited in Cook, 1988, p. 55). From a theoretical perspective learners can avail themselves of at least three kinds of evidence in the process of learning: positive evidence, negative evidence, and indirect negative evidence.

    2.1.1.1. Positive Evidence. *Positive evidence* refers to the input and comprises the set of well-formed[5] sentences to which learners are exposed. These utterances are available from either the spoken language (or visual language in the case of sign language) or the written language. This is the most direct means that learners have available from which they can form linguistic hypotheses. As discussed in section 2.1, positive evidence is insufficient for the development of a complete grammar: It is insufficiently rich in specificity, it underdetermines the final grammar, and it is often degenerate (see White, 1989b, for an explication of these issues). Lack of specificity can be seen by the fact that knowledge of language is in many instances an abstraction, whereas the data themselves do not immediately reveal abstractions.[6] That the data underdetermine the final form of grammars is related to the notion of abstractions as well. Recall the discussion of *want to* and *wanna.* The final form of the grammar (i.e., understanding when a contraction can and cannot be used) cannot be gleaned from the data themselves. Finally, data are often degenerate, representing patterns that appear to be ungrammatical. Chomsky (1965, p. 200) cited by Foster-Cohen (1993, p. 136) claimed that

> It seems clear that many children acquire first or second languages quite successfully even though no special care is taken to teach them and no special attention is given to their progress. It also seems apparent that much of the actual speech observed consists of fragments and deviant expressions of a variety of sorts.

As an example, consider that subjects in English are obligatory, but in certain instances subjects are deleted in casual speech:

    23. Wanna go?
    24. Seen any good movies lately?

Faulty conclusions can also be gleaned from grammatical utterances. In English, pronouns and nouns can be deleted in sentences with conjoined verbs, as in the following:

    25. The dog barked and ran down the street.

Upon first hearing a sentence such as this, it is possible to infer (incorrectly) that subject use is optional in English.

2.1.1.2. Negative Evidence. *Negative evidence* refers to the type of information that is provided to learners concerning the incorrectness of an utterance. This might be in the form of explicit or implicit information. The following are examples of explicit negative evidence and implicit negative evidence, respectively.

26. I seed the man.
    No, we say, "I saw the man."
27. I seed the man.
    What?

In the first example, the learner is receiving direct information about the ungrammaticality of what was said, whereas in the second example, ungrammaticality must be inferred. In 27 it is, of course, possible that the learner will not understand that this is intended as a correction and may think that the speaker really did not hear what was said. In section 2.2 the arguments concerning the existence of negative evidence are discussed in greater detail.

As a summary of the two evidence types discussed thus far, Long (in press) provided a very useful taxonomy that is reproduced in Fig. 2.1. Evidence can be positive or negative. If positive, it can be either authentic or modified. If modified, it can be simplified or elaborated. Negative evidence can also be of two types: preemptive (i.e., occurring before an actual error, as in a classroom context) or reactive. If reactive, it can be explicit

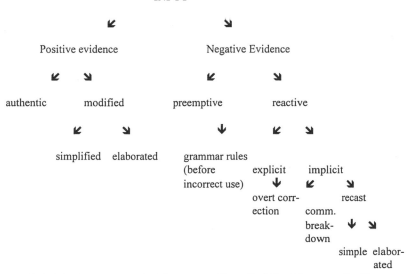

FIG. 2.1. A taxonomy of evidence types. From *Task-Based Language Teaching*, by M. Long, in press, Oxford, England, Blackwell Publishers. Reprinted with permission.

or implicit (see chapter 5). Explicit evidence is an overt correction. Implicit evidence can result in a communication breakdown or in a recast. Recasts, in turn, can be simple (e.g., repetition) or elaborated (e.g., a change to a generally grammatical form).

2.1.1.3. Indirect Negative Evidence. Indirect negative evidence is perhaps the most interesting of the types of evidence available to learners but unfortunately is the least studied, perhaps because no theoretical argument rests crucially on it. Chomsky (1981) stated:

> evidence to fix parameters may in principle be of three types: (1) positive evidence (SVO order, fixing a parameter of core grammar, irregular verbs, adding a marked periphery); (2) direct negative evidence (corrections by the speech community); (3) indirect negative evidence—a not unreasonable acquisition system can be devised with the operative principle that if certain structures or rules fail to be exemplified in relative simple expressions, where they would be expected to be found, then a (possibly marked) option is selected excluding them in the grammar, so that a kind of "negative evidence" can be available even without corrections, adverse reactions, etc. There is good reason to believe that direct negative evidence is not necessary for language acquisition, but indirect negative evidence may be relevant. (pp. 8–9)

Plough (1994) claimed that the term *indirect negative evidence* is a misnomer because it is not a form of indirect correction, or any sort of correction. Rather, it is an "indirect means of letting the learner know that a feature is not possible because it is never present in the *expected* environment" (p. 30). It may be easier to understand this concept in second language acquisition than in first because a crucial part of the notion rests on the concept of expected environment. Where do those expectations come from? Essentially, there are two choices: from the innately specified principles and parameters of UG or from the first language (or other languages known). Imagine an English speaker learning Italian. This learner hears sentences without subjects, as in the following:

28. *Vado   al   cinema stasera.*
    go (1 sg.) to the movies this evening
    "I'm going to the movies this evening."

29. *Mangiamo a casa   domani.*
    eat (3 pl.) at home tomorrow
    "We're eating at home tomorrow."

30. *Va   a Parigi sabato.*
    go (3 sg.) to Paris Saturday
    "He's going to Paris on Saturday."

Because there is a domain of expectations of obligatory subjects based on this learner's knowledge of English, this learner is likely to notice the absence in Italian. Examples can also be provided from the animal world. For certain types of primates, babies must learn the difference between predatory birds and nonpredatory birds. Seeing the former, the entire community screeches loudly when the birds approach. However, in the case of nonpredatory birds, the absence of screeches (in the context that screeches are to be expected) provides information that allows the babies to distinguish between predatory and nonpredatory birds.

A nonlinguistic example might further clarify this concept. Two applied linguists were recently in Poland where they spent a week before traveling by train to Prague. When they arrived in Prague, they noticed that the signs in the train station were written in Czech, English, and Russian. At that moment, they realized the absence of Russian on signs in Poland, a country that had been under Russian control until about the same time as the Czech Republic. As with linguistic indirect negative evidence, the absence of Russian in Poland was sufficient to make the linguists infer something about the Polish feelings concerning Russian domination. It was the presence of the Russian in Prague that created a domain of expectation for them, allowing them to notice the absence in Poland.

Given the possibility that negative evidence cannot be relied on in language acquisition (particularly child language acquisition), some other learning mechanism must be invoked. Lasnik (1989) and others (e.g., Archibald, 1993; Saleemi, 1990, 1992; Valian, 1990) argued that indirect negative evidence may be able to fill in for the absence of negative evidence (see Plough, 1994, for an in-depth review of this research). For the present purposes, it will suffice to give an example from Lasnik (1989). Consider the case of null subjects and in particular the case of children learning English. Languages of the world are of two sorts: Either they allow deletion of subjects or subjects are mandatory. Spanish and Italian are of the former type; English and French are of the latter type. If a child were mistakenly to assume that English is a [+ null subject] language (i.e., allowing the absence of subject pronouns), the data from English would not contradict this hypothesis because sentences with subjects are not incompatible with [+ null subject] languages. It is important to consider the concept of markedness,[7] which for the purposes of this discussion refers to the basic setting of a parameter cross-linguistically. In other words, in the absence of positive evidence, which setting is the most basic? Let's return to our child with the faulty [+ null subject] hypothesis. According to the original definition of indirect negative evidence, the child, not hearing [+ null subject] sentences, will use this information (i.e., will notice the absence of null subjects) and will reset the parameter to the correct English [− null subject]. For children learning Italian, the positive evidence will be used to reaffirm the correctness of the original setting of a [+ null subject] language. For children learning English, the absence of null subjects is used to come up with the correct grammar. Lasnik (1989) argued that the unmarked setting is [− null subject]; for English the first setting is the correct one and will not be disconfirmed by the evidence. Italian-speaking children will reset to [+ null subject] by noticing the absence of subjects in many sentences (e.g., *Vado al cinema*). Regardless of which of the two settings is taken as basic or as the initial setting, indirect negative evidence is used to disconfirm faulty hypotheses.

2.2. AVAILABILITY OF EVIDENCE

Earlier views of language acquisition were based on a behaviorist view of language. Central to this view was the role of correction. Children were imagined to learn language through a process of imitation and analogizing (cf. Bloomfield, 1933; Gass & Selinker, 1994; and chapter 3 for a synthesis). It was well accepted that imitation was often faulty and some theoretical mechanism was needed to correct faulty forms. That mechanism was correction—either in the form of direct correction, such as informing a child that a form was incorrect, or in the form of noncomprehension (e.g., "I don't understand you") or not receiving a desired object (e.g., a child asks for a toy and does not receive it) or a desired outcome (e.g., a child wants to go outside and the adult does not respond appropriately).

Section 2.1.1.2 briefly covered the concept of negative evidence, as it applies to child language acquisition. Negative evidence is a crucial concept because it forms the basis of the innateness argument: The need for innateness stems from the lack of correction. Central to this argument is the fact that direct intervention in which incorrect utterances are corrected is not present in the learning environment. Furthermore, when such correction is available, it may be sufficient to inform a child that a particular utterance is incorrect, but it often does not tell the child what needs to be done to correct the utterance and hence to revise a current hypothesis. The following examples illustrate that even when children receive correction and are informed about appropriate modifications, their grammars are often impervious to suggestions about change.

31. From Cazden (1972, p. 92); no age given
    Child:　My teacher holded the baby rabbits and we patted them.
    Adult:　Did you say your teacher held the baby rabbits?
    Child:　Yes.
    Adult:　What did you say she did?
    Child:　She holded the baby rabbits and we patted them.
    Adult:　Did you say she held them tightly?
    Child:　No, she holded them loosely.

32. From McNeill (1966, p. 69); no age given
    Child: Nobody don't like me.
    Mother: No, say "nobody likes me."
    Child: Nobody don't like me.
               (eight repetitions of this dialogue)
    Mother: No, now listen carefully; say "nobody likes me."
    Child: Oh! Nobody don't likes me.

33. Child, age = 3;2
    Child: I don't see no trees.
    Mother: I don't see any trees. Not no trees, any trees.
    Child: No any trees. No any trees.
    Mother: I don't see any trees.

Each of these examples shows some attempt to provide feedback to the child concerning the incorrectness of a hypothesis. In the first example, the attempt is made through correct modeling of the irregular past tense, yet the child continued to use the regular past tense form. In the second and third examples, the mother attempted to model and even to instruct the child overtly as to the correct form. In both instances, these attempts failed, and the child continues to use the incorrect form.

Given the absence of useable or used negative evidence, some additional means must be made available to a learner in order to learn the type of abstractions outlined in section 2.1 and to disallow overgeneralized grammars from which one cannot retreat on the basis of positive evidence alone. UG has been posited to satisfy these conditions. In other words, because positive evidence alone cannot limit the range of possible sentences and because negative evidence is not frequently and consistently forthcoming, innate principles must constrain a priori the possibilities of grammar formation.

For second language learning similar arguments have been made: Because of a lack of negative evidence, one needs to assume that adults have access to the same innate universal constraints or properties as children. However, there is a crucial difference: It is not clear that the assumption of lack of negative evidence in second language acquisition is warranted (Birdsong, 1989; Gass, 1988b; Schachter, 1988). If we consider that negative evidence is present primarily in conversational interactions, then we must investigate the nature and structure of conversations to understand the potential role of negative evidence in the acquisition of a second language. This is the subject of chapter 5.

The extent to which negative evidence can engage UG is in dispute. Schwartz (1993) argued that only positive evidence contributes to the formation and restructuring of second language grammars. This does not mean that there is not a role for negative evidence in her view. She posited two sorts of linguistic knowledge for second language speakers: competence, in the more or less traditional (linguistic) sense of the word, and learned linguistic knowledge (LLK). The former manifests itself in performance, the latter in what Schwartz called learned linguistic behavior (LLB). This is not unlike Krashen's distinction (see chapter 3) between acquisition, knowledge acquired largely unconsciously, and learning, knowledge acquired consciously (e.g., in a classroom context). That individuals learning both a first and a second language operate with two sets of rules (i.e., one set that generates what we produce and another set that we use when trying to approach standardized norms, as in the well-known phrase Winston Churchill used when referring to the rule that disallows prepositions at the end of sentences: "That is a rule up with which I will not put") is not particularly controversial. However, what is more controversial is that these two knowledge sources are separate and that negative evidence or correction can affect one but not the other. This argument is addressed by a reanalysis of White's (1991) data by Schwartz and Gubala-Ryzak (1992), who argued that the grammars of the learners in White's study are inconsistent with those found in natural languages. Given the unnaturalness of the grammar, one must conclude, according to Schwartz and Gubala-Ryzak, that these grammars cannot be generated by UG and hence are not reflections of interlanguage competence, which by definition in Schwartz and Gubala-Ryzak's framework is UG-generated. In other words, because learners end up with an impossible grammar, negative evidence (i.e., correction) and explicit instruction could not have tapped UG (or interlanguage competence). White (1992), although accepting some of Schwartz and Gubala-Ryzak's arguments, presented data based on Trahey and White (1993) showing that even positive evidence is not sufficient to trigger parameter resetting in the case of adverb placement. This runs counter to Schwartz and Gubala-Ryzak's claims that the appropriate positive evidence was not available and that the lack of appropriate positive evidence resulted in a lack of parameter resetting. In this argument is a major assumption, one that is clearly not yet settled (cf. Schachter, 1988, 1990, and Bley-Vroman, 1989), having to do with the availability of UG in second language acquisition.

   An in-depth discussion of this issue goes beyond the scope of this book, yet it is clear that it figures crucially in this debate. If, on the other hand, one does not distinguish between UG-based knowledge and other linguistic knowledge, then there is little question that negative evidence is crucial in revising interlanguage knowledge.

2.3. THE COMPETITION MODEL

The previous discussion was framed in the context of a linguistic approach to second language acquisition. There are other ways of conceptualizing the way learning takes place and the function of input in acquisition, ways that do not rely on innateness. For example, within connectionist approaches to language, it is important that patterns of associations among units are weighted but not fixed. Rather, new patterns may emerge, old patterns may disappear, and the strength of interconnections may be modified (see the discussion in chapter 1 on rule strengthening). Depending on the type of model, modification of association strength may make use of feedback or may make use of additional input against which to match current interconnections (Rumelhart & McClelland, 1986; Rumelhart, Smolensky, McClelland, & Hinton, 1986). This approach differs significantly from a purely linguistic (i.e., nativist) position in that what is stored in a learner's head is not a rule generalization; rather, what is stored are the various connection strengths. These connections, which differ in strength from one another, are activated depending on the input. On the basis of learner output alone, it is, of course, difficult to distinguish one conceptualization from the other because what will be seen in both is rule-governed behavior (although in the case of a connectionist approach, rules per se are not stored).

The remainder of this section includes a discussion of the competition model (see Bates & MacWhinney, 1982, 1989). This focus is the most developed with regard to second language acquisition. It differs from the view discussed in the previous sections in that the competition model is rooted in the belief that "the forms of natural languages are created, governed, constrained, acquired and used in the service of *communicative functions* [emphasis added]" (Bates & MacWhinney, 1989, p. 3). In other words, whereas a UG approach to acquisition is clear in its separation of the form of language from its function, the competition model has the two intertwined. The competition model's main concern is with language use; in fact, it was developed in large part to account for language processing. In contrast, a UG approach considers an idealized speaker-hearer's knowledge of language (i.e., competence) regardless of the context in which language is used and regardless of the mechanisms involved in putting language knowledge to use.

To understand the competition model, it is necessary to have some familiarity with cross-linguistic differences. The focus is on relations among elements in a sentence. An underlying assumption is that all languages have a means of determining relations among elements in a sentence. However, the way in which this determination is made across languages differs in many cases from language to language.

In the framework of the competition model, acquisition is driven by cues, among which are those that relate to correlations between form and function. The model itself is proposed to have a two-level structure, a functional level and a formal level. In the former, meaning is expressed; in the latter are surface forms. In the model's simplest form, direct mappings between these levels take place in language use.[8]

Language processing involves competition among various cues, each of which contributes to a different resolution in sentence interpretation. Although the range of cues is universal (that is, the limits on the kinds of cues one uses are universally imposed), there are language-specific instantiation of cues and language-specific strength assigned to cues. Consider two languages with different word order possibilities, English and Italian. English word order is rigidly of the form subject–verb–object (SVO), as in the following English sentence

34. The dogs eat the bone.

Native speakers of English use many cues to determine that *the dogs* is the subject of the sentence and that *the bone* is the object. Primary among the information (cues) that English speakers use is word order: In active declarative sentences, the first noun or noun phrase is typically the subject of the sentence. A second cue available is knowledge of the meaning of lexical items and real-world pragmatic knowledge (e.g., dogs eat bones rather than the reverse [bones eat dogs]). Third, English speakers use animacy criteria (i.e., whether the noun is animate or inanimate) to establish grammatical relations (i.e., in general, animate things do things to inanimate things). Finally, morphology (in this case, subject–verb agreement) contributes to interpretation because the plurality of *the dogs* requires a plural verb (*eat*) In sum, all elements converge in coming up with the interpretation of *the dogs* as the subject and *the bone* as the object.

In most cases, this information will lead a speaker or hearer to the correct interpretation. What about those instances in which not all cues converge? In these instances, the various cues are in competition. Assume a sentence such as

35. The bone eats the dogs.

English speakers are likely to run into some difficulty; there is competition as to which element will fill the subject slot. Considering the cues, we find that the answer is not straightforward. Using word order as a cue, *the bone* should be the subject; using meaning and animacy as cues, *the dogs* is the most likely subject; using morphology as a cue, it is *the bone*, which contains the only singular noun in the sentence. Thus, in this unusual sentence there is a breakdown in our normal use of cues; as a result, there is competition as to which member will fill the subject slot. Different languages resolve the conflict in different ways. English uses word order and agreement as primary determinants; thus, despite the oddity of the sentence, English speakers are likely to give an interpretation in which *the bone* is the subject.

Other languages, such as Italian, resolve the problem of interpretation in a different way. Italian has great flexibility in word order, as seen in the following examples (in some instances there is no overt subject):

36. Giovanni vuole una mela.   SVO
    Giovanni wants an   apple

37. Vuole   una mela.   VO
    Wants (3rd sg.) an   apple

38. Una mela Giovanni vuole.   OSV
    an   apple Giovanni wants

39. Vuole Giovanni una mela.   VSO
    wants Giovanni an   apple

40. Vuole una mela Giovanni, non è vero?   VOS
    Wants an   apple Giovanni, no?

41. La mela   la vuole Giovanni.   OVS
    The apple it wants Giovanni

42. Giovanni la   mela la vuole.   SOV
    Giovanni the apple it wants

There are a number of word order possibilities[9] in Italian. It is clear that Italian speakers cannot reliably use word order as a dominant cue in understanding relations among sentence elements. Morphological agreement, semantics, and pragmatics assume greater importance. In other languages, other factors may dominate or combine to dominate.

Indeed, cues are an important aspect of the competition model. There are two critical concepts, cue validity and cue strength. Cue validity is based on three factors (all of which can be expressed in mathematical terms; see Bates & MacWhinney, 1989); availability, reliability, and conflict validity. *Availability* refers to the extent that the cue is available. For example, if one were considering the cue of word order, the cue of preverbal position would be readily available in English but not in languages like Spanish or Italian where different word orders are allowed and where subjects are often omitted. *Reliability* refers to whether a particular cue leads one to an appropriate conclusion. To cite another contrast between English and Italian, preverbal position is highly reliable in English because the subject is nearly always in that position. It is not reliable in Italian because there are numerous instances when the object precedes the verb and others when the subject does so. *Conflict validity* refers to those situations in which there is conflict among cues. A ratio is formed based on the number of times a particular conflicting cue wins out divided by the number of times it is in conflict.

Cue strength refers to the weight given to the connection between two units. For example, the preverbal cue is weighted high for subjecthood in English but not for Italian.

2.3.1. The Significance of Input

Given that no innate mechanism is associated with this position (in first or second language acquisition), it is clear that input serves a major role, because the language learner uses input to establish the form–function relations, cue validity, and cue strength.

Bohannon, MacWhinney, and Snow (1990) pointed to the relation between positive evidence and negative evidence, the former being a form of negative evidence. As an example, assume a learner has internalized the form *breaked*. Upon hearing *broke*, the learner is simultaneously provided with positive and negative evidence. The former comes from actually hearing *broke*, and the latter comes from knowing that two forms with the same function cannot exist side by side. It is a balance of a sort. Evidence for one tips the balance in favor of that one and against the other. In order to explain this, Bohannon et al. invoked the uniqueness principle, that "there is only one truly correct way to express a particular intention or function. Given this, when the learner encounters two ways of saying the same thing, it is clear that one of them is wrong" (p. 223). They further argued that the uniqueness principle is one of "the most basic aspects of the human information-processing system" (p. 223). To bring this discussion back to the issue of competition, they referred to work of MacWhinney (1987, 1989a, 1989b), who argued that "the uniqueness principle is nothing other than the fundamental principle of mental competition" (Bohannon et al., 1990, p. 223).

To illustrate further, I consider forms that might be in competition, for example, an irregular past tense form, such as *singed* versus *sang* versus *sung*. If learners bring to the learning task something akin to the uniqueness principle, in which the parsimonious hypotheses about language are ones in which there is a one-to-one relation between form and function, then each instance of *sang* (i.e., positive evidence, or, in terms of the competition model, strengthening) is equivalent to negative evidence or cue weakening for the overgeneralized forms.[10]

2.4. CONCLUSION

This chapter presents the nature of evidence and the rationale for positing innate knowledge. Although many of the issues raised in this chapter originated in the context of first language acquisition, they are also similar if not identical to those raised in an L2 context. In particular, if second language learners are to achieve nativelike competence in a second language (a big if), they need to come up with the same sort of knowledge about the abstract structure of the target language as native speakers do, and this information is not available from the input. The situation is, of course, more complex because (adult) L2 learners have access to a full-blown language when they approach the learning of a nonprimary language. Does one then need to posit UG in the same way as one does for L1 learning? Can competition among forms and cues account for second language learning in the same way as some have claimed for first language acquisition? These and related issues have been topics of debate in the L2 literature for some time (see in particular survey texts of Cook, 1994; Ellis, 1994; Gass & Selinker, 1994; Larsen-Freeman & Long, 1991; Sharwood Smith, 1994; White, 1989b).

NOTES

1. See Pinker (1994, pp. 277–278) for a discussion of the irrelevance of this dichotomy. He took the position that the nature–nurture argument is a false dichotomy. He made the point that if wild children "had run out of the woods speaking Phrygian or ProtoWorld, who could they have talked to?" (p. 277). In other words, nature provides part of the answer, and nurture provides another.
2. The bulk of this chapter deals with UG accounts of second language acquisition. There are three primary reasons for this emphasis: It is the most well-developed linguistic theory, the role for input is clear, and it is the most deeply and broadly researched approach to (second) language acquisition. However, many argue (e.g., Bley-Vroman, 1989; Eckman, 1996; Schachter, 1988; Wolfe-Quintero, 1996) that there is no specific mechanism designed for language learning (i.e., the general nativism position). Rather, there are general "principles of learning that are not particular to language learning, but may be employed in other types of learning" (Eckman, 1996, p. 398). Both general nativism and innatist positions agree on the fact that something innate is involved in language learning; it is the nature of the innate system that is in question—is it only for the task of language learning or is it available for more general learning tasks? Although non-UG-based theories are considered at the end of this chapter, it is difficult to engage in a specific discussion of input with regard to general nativism, other than remarks such as

   > there is no serious theory of language acquisition that does not acknowledge that the human brain comes equipped with some means for organizing the language experiences that are presented to humans in the course of their development (Braine, 1994). There is a symbiotic, non-arbitrary relationship between the innate cognitive capacity for language learning and the input available in the environment, neither of which can be ignored (Wolfe-Quintero, 1996, p. 338).

   Wolfe-Quintero did point out, however, that input may have different kinds of roles ("as a trigger versus a shaper of language representations," p. 338).
3. The constraint predicts the ungrammaticality of the following English sentence:

   Who do you believe the claim that O.J. saw?

(coming from "You believe the claim that O.J. saw who?") because movement can only be across a single bounding node.

4. There are other grammatical structures that may or may not be part of this parameter (e.g., that–trace—see White, 1985; linking of auxiliaries and main verbs—see Hilles, 1986, and Hyams, 1986), but there is not agreement as to whether or not these properties are part of the prodrop parameter.

5. The question of the extent to which the input comprises well-formed sentences is discussed in chapter 3.

6. If primary data revealed abstractions, linguists would not need to spend so many years attempting to determine the abstractions.

7. Markedness can be defined differently in different frameworks. Furthermore, even within a single framework, there is by no means unanimity as to what is marked and what is unmarked.

8. This does not necessarily imply a one-to-one relation between form and function, nor does it imply a unidirectional relation. What it does imply is that form–function relations are established and processed together.

9. Many of these sentences are accompanied by intonational differences, and in some cases, notably those in which the object immediately precedes the verb, an object clitic pronoun is used.

10. It appears to be the case that second language learners generally know when they are right but not always when they are wrong. This can be understood in a model that allows for input to be the source of rule or cue strengthening. When certain forms are heard over and over again, they are as a result strengthened, resulting in confident knowledge on the part of the learner. On the other hand, when forms are not heard but created by learners, perhaps on the basis of overgeneralization or of native language patterns, there is little in the input to reinforce these patterns. Hence, their representation is weak and more susceptible to change or eradication, especially when some alternative form is present in the input.

The Nature and Function of Input

3.0. INTRODUCTION

This chapter begins (perhaps somewhat arbitrarily) by considering earlier conceptualizations of second language learning (i.e., pre-1970s) based on a behaviorist view in which the major driving force of language learning was the language to which learners were exposed (i.e., the input). Because it was held that learning a language involved imitation as the primary mechanism, the language that surrounded learners was of crucial importance as the source for imitation. To understand the role of imitation and hence the role of input, consider the following description from Bloomfield (1933) on how children learn their first language.

1. Under various stimuli the child utters and repeats vocal sounds. This seems to be an inherited trait. Suppose he makes a noise which we may represent as *da*, although, of course, the actual movements and the resultant sounds differ from any that are used in conventional English speech. The sound vibrations strike the child's ear-drums while he keeps repeating the movements. This results in a habit: whenever a similar sound strikes his ear, he is likely to make these same mouth-movements, repeating the sound *da*. This babbling trains him to reproduce vocal sounds which strike his ear.

2. Some person, say the mother, utters in the child's presence a sound which resembles one of the child's babbling syllables. For instance, she says *doll*. When these sounds strike the child's ear, his habit (1) comes into play and he utters his nearest babbling syllable, *da*. We say that he is beginning to "imitate." Grown-ups seem to have observed this everywhere, for every language seems to contain certain nursery-words which resemble a child's babbling—words like *mama, dada*: doubtless these got their vogue because children easily learn to repeat them.

3. The mother, of course, uses her words when the appropriate stimulus is present. She says *doll* when she is actually showing or giving the infant his doll. The sight and handling of the doll and the hearing and saying of the word *doll* (that is, *da*) occur repeatedly together, until the child forms a new habit: the sight and feel of the doll suffice to make him say *da*. He has now the use of a word. To the adults it may not sound like any of their words, but this is due merely to its imperfection. It is not likely that children ever invent a word.

4. The habit of saying *da* at sight of the doll gives rise to further habits. Suppose, for instance, that day after day the child is given his doll (and says *da, da, da*) immediately after his bath. He has now a habit of saying *da, da* after his bath; that is, if one day the mother forgets to give him the doll, he may nevertheless cry *da, da* after his bath. "He is asking for his doll," says the mother, and she is right, since doubtless an adult's "asking for" or "wanting" things is only a more complicated type of the same situation. The child has now embarked upon *abstract* or *displaced* speech: he names a thing even when that thing is not present.

5. The child's speech is perfected by its results. If he says *da, da* imperfectly,—that is, at great variance from the adults' conventional form *doll,*—then his elders are not stimulated to give him the doll. Instead of getting the added stimulus of seeing and handling the doll, the child is now subject to other distracting stimuli, or perhaps, in the unaccustomed situation of having no doll after his bath, he goes into a tantrum which disorders his recent impressions. In short, his more perfect attempts at speech are likely to be fortified by repetition, and his failures to be wiped out in confusion. This process never stops. At a much later stage, if he says *Daddy bringed it,* he merely gets a disappointing answer such as *No! You must say "Daddy brought it"*; but if he says *Daddy brought it,* he is likely to hear the form over again: *Yes, Daddy brought it,* and to get a favorable practical response. (Bloomfield, 1933, pp. 29–31. Excerpt from *Language* by Leonard Bloomfield copyright 1933 by Holt, Rinehart and Winston, Inc., and renewed 1961 by Leonard Bloomfield, reprinted by permission of the publisher.)

Indeed, there is no notion of anything innate in the child's quest to learn a new language; everything derived from the input and the interactions in which children were engaged (see Gass & Selinker, 1994, for a fuller description of this view of acquisition as it relates to second language learning). With Chomsky's review of Skinner in 1959, a new wave of theoretical insights regarding language and language acquisition was ushered in. Behaviorist theories fell into disfavor, and, as a consequence, so did interest in input, which was inextricably linked to behaviorism. Focus shifted to the internal mechanisms that a (child or adult) learner brings to the language-learning situation, with research emphasizing innateness and the nature of the innate system (for L2 studies, this was seen most notably in the works of Dulay & Burt, 1973, 1974a, 1974b, 1975; and Bailey,

Madden, & Krashen, 1974). Learners were viewed as creating language systems; therefore, the input they received was of minor importance. The significance of the study of input was minimized because it was believed that if much of learning depended on innate structures, then learners only needed to discover which of a limited number of possibilities are represented in their language. As discussed in chapter 2, input was believed to play only a minor role in this discovery; only a few instances of exposure were sufficient to trigger the appropriate language forms.

This chapter focuses on descriptions and functions of input, beginning with a brief description of findings from the child language literature because this literature informs much of the research in second language. This is followed by descriptions of input in second language acquisition. Chapter 4 deals with input within various theoretical perspectives of second language acquisition.[1]

3.1. MODIFIED LANGUAGE IN FIRST LANGUAGE ACQUISITION

No one would deny that the language addressed to nonproficient speakers of a language (be they children learning a first language or adults learning a second) differs from the language used when addressing adult native speakers of a language. What is less clear, however, is what that language is like and what function the modified language serves in acquisition.

As discussed in the previous chapter, the theoretical question underlying much of language acquisition research is the extent to which an innate mechanism drives acquisition as opposed to acquisition being conditioned and shaped by the linguistic environment and linguistic interactions in which a learner is involved. Much of the research on input in child language learning is in response to the Chomskyan (1965) notion that the language addressed to children was "restricted in scope, considering the time limitations that are in effect, and fairly degenerate in quality" (p. 31). On the one hand, this idea served as justification for the need of something other than input; on the other hand, it spawned a number of studies that suggested that caretaker speech is by and large well formed and in many instances semantically or syntactically simpler than speech addressed to adults.

Language addressed to young children was in earlier times known as baby talk. Reports of the register were frequently made by anthropological linguists, who were not detailed in their description. In general, this type of language is characterized by differences in intonation and pitch as well as syntax and semantics. However, to claim any effect for this type of modification in terms of acquisition, one would have to document these modifications universally. It is here that difficulties arise for those who argue for the necessity of these modifications (I return to this issue in section 3.1.2).

3.1.1. Responses to Children's Utterances

In the study of child language acquisition in general, and with regard to input in particular, an issue of central importance is the extent to which responses to children's utterances following utterances that are syntactically well formed differ from responses to those that are not. The significance of this issue relates to the discussion in chapter 2. To what extent is knowledge innate, and to what extent is it environmentally controlled? If there is a difference between responses to well-formed versus ill-formed sentences, then it could be claimed that the different response types are sufficient for the child to engage in self-correction; if, on the other hand, there are no differences, then children must have some other means of determining the grammaticality versus ungrammaticality of their utterances.

One of the earliest studies to examine this issue was that of Brown and Hanlon (1970). Based on their data, they claimed that the approval or disapproval of a child's utterance was not dependent on syntactic well-formedness but rather on the semantic truthfulness of the child's speech. Consider the following example:

> *Approval of syntactic ill-formedness*
> Adam: Draw a boot paper.
> Mother: That's right. Draw a boot on the paper.
>
> *Disapproval of syntactic well-formedness*
> Adam: And Walt Disney comes on Tuesday
> Mother: No, he does not.

Their data showed "explicit approval or disapproval of either syntax or morphology [to be] extremely rare . . . and so seems not to be the force propelling the child from immature to mature forms" (p. 202).

In the years following the publication of this landmark paper, other studies were conducted that appeared to contradict the Brown and Hanlon results or that at least appeared to call them into question. In particular, Hirsh-Pasek, Treiman, and Schneiderman (1984) found subtle differences in that parents were more likely to repeat ill-formed utterances than well-formed ones. In a similar vein, Demetras, Post, and Snow (1986) noted that there was more often a break in the conversational flow for clarification when sentences were ill formed as opposed to being error free.

In another study, Bohannon and Stanowicz (1988) examined responses to children's syntactic, semantic, and phonological errors. In terms of both responses and clarification questions, adults responded differentially. The authors made the interesting point that repetitions may have greater significance as feedback in that they provide two pieces of information: There is a problem with the utterance, and here is an alternative. Feedback in the form of denial only provides information of the first sort. Additionally, adults were twice as likely to provide a correction when the preceding utterance had a single error than when utterances had multiple errors. This may, of course, have to do with the relative ease of interpretation of utterances. That is, the more errors, the less likely that an interlocutor can determine the meaning. Without an understanding of the intended meaning, corrections are difficult, if not impossible.

3.1.2. Input in Non-Western Cultures

Research on input modifications in other cultures suggests that the kinds of modifications common in Western middle-class families are far from the norm[2] (see Lieven, 1994, for a review). In many cultures, researchers reported little or no direct talk to infants because, in the view of individuals in that culture, infants are clearly unable to respond to speech. However, we know that all children of normal intelligence and normal hearing learn to talk, and we know that individuals exposed only to noninteractive, nonmodified language do not learn a language. This latter point is documented by a number of studies. Sachs and Johnson (1972) reported on a hearing child of deaf parents; his source of oral language was television, which was not sufficient to allow him to learn oral language. Another frequently cited case, although from the domain of second language learning, stems from the research of Snow, Arlman-Rupp, Hassing, Jobse, Joosten, and Vorster (1976) who also reported on the inadequacy of television input for the acquisition of German by native-speaking Dutch children.

Although it may be that there are (many) societies that view an infant's role in an interactive setting differently than middle- or upper-middle-class Western families do, it is also true that none of these societies isolate the children from interactive language. Children are present while interaction is taking place, and there is often a different way of treating children linguistically than is the norm in that society. In fact, in "lap and back" societies, children, by virtue of being physically close to a caregiver, may be in the presence of input more frequently than "crib and cradle" babies, such as those in Western societies. For example, Schieffelin (1985) reported that the Kaluli of New Guinea do not begin talking directly to children until the children are clearly of an age where they can be conversant human beings.[3] This is generally the case when the child is able to utter two specific words: *mother* (nɔ) and *breast* (bo). These two words signal a stage in which the children are "shown how to speak [*to widan*]" (p. 531). One of the ways that the Kaluli treat children of language-learning age differently is through the use of a fixed expression, ɛlɛma, which means, "say like that."[4] This is said as a signal for a child to repeat an utterance. The next example illustrates how this works.

Mɛli 26 months
Mama (her cousin) 40 months
Mother

Mama ➜ Mɛli:	ge bokisi -ya diɛfɛnɔ
	you box LOC put 1ˢᵗ FUT
	'I will put you in the box.'

Mama ➜ Mɛli:
ge bokisi -ya diɛfɛnɔ
you box   LOC put 1ˢᵗ FUT
'I will put you in the box.'

Mɛli ➜ Mama:
ne   bokisi -ya   diɛfɛnɔ
I/me box   LOC put 1ˢᵗ FUT
?'I will put in the box.'

Mother ➜ Mɛli ⇨ Mama*: gi   bokisi -yɔ   hɛ?!
your box   NEUTRAL what about
ɛlɛma
say: IMP
'What about your box?!' say like that.

Mɛli ➜ Mama:
gi   bokisi -yɔ   hɛ?!
your box   NEUTRAL what about
'What about your box?!'

Mama (pointing to box) ➜ Mɛli: giyɔlɔ hɛ?!
yours what about
'What about yours?!'

Mother ➜ Mɛli ⇨ Mama: niyɔ dalab   ɛlɛma
mine have:3ʳᵈ PRES say: IMP
'I have mine. Say like that.'

Mɛli ➜ Mama:
niyɔ dalab
mine have 3ʳᵈ PRES
'I have mine.'

Mother ➜ Mɛli ⇨ Mama: niyɔ halo   ɛlɛma
mine up there say: IMP
'Mine is up there. Say like that.'

Mɛli ➜ Mama:
niyɔ niyɔ hadɔ-wɔ hɛ? Mama!
mine mine raw Q huh?
giyɔ hadɔ-wɔ
yours raw Q
'Mine, mine is raw? Huh? Mama! Is yours raw?'

*➜ indicates addressee; ⇨ indicates intended addressee.

Although it is clearly the case that the input is not modified in ways that people in many Western societies are familiar with, we need to ask about the function of the modifications seen in all societies. It is perhaps the case that the modifications of the more familiar sort as well as those seen in other cultures serve the function of isolating bits of the input to make it more manageable to work with. For example, television learning without an aid in associating meaning and structure is not sufficient for language learning. Some assistance needs to be given to children in order for them to begin to crack the code of the language being learned. Regardless of whether it is syntactic modification or whether it is of the repetition variety, assistance provides the child with a means for associating meaning and structure. The terms generally used to describe language addressed to nonproficient speakers (e.g., baby talk, foreigner talk, caretaker speech, etc.) are inadequate because they have been used to refer to changes to the structure itself. Rather, a more adequate and comprehensive term such as modification more aptly captures the notion that all cultures change something about the structure with the resulting effect of aiding the child through the maze of language, although the precise nature of the change varies considerably from culture to culture and is often a reflection of cultural beliefs about how language is learned.

3.1.3. Functions of Input

The preceding sections provide a cursory glance at the input modifications made to young child language learners. This is hardly a controversial point. What is less clear is the extent to which the modifications made are at all useful in learning a language (whether first or second). Although the first question may be interesting descriptively and certainly serves as an essential basis for the second issue, the second question is the one that can help unlock the puzzle of acquisition. Unfortunately, the jury is still out.

Although some studies appear to shed light on the issue, it is not always clear how to interpret the results. For example, in the Bohannon and Stanowicz (1988) study discussed in section 3.1.1, the data revealed that 60% to 70% of the children's utterances were produced without any comment from the adult. This appears to be problematic: Without regularity, how can a child come to rely on the feedback reliably? Furthermore, as Gordon (1990) pointed out, only 70% of the negative responses from adults to children actually followed incorrect utterances by children. Turning this around, 30% of the negative responses of adults (i.e., responses that could be taken to suggest that something was wrong with the initial utterance) followed utterances that were correct. If a child is attempting to use subtle corrections in the way that Bohannon and Stanowicz are suggesting, 30% of the time children will take a correct utterance to be incorrect and should theoretically modify their linguistic systems. However, if we take corrections not to be an initiator of an immediate change but rather as a catalyst that allows a learner to begin to search the input for more exemplars so as to confirm or disconfirm a current hypothesis, then the so-called inconsistency noted by Gordon is not problematic. In other words, a learner may be alerted to a potential problem and as a result will look for examples in the surrounding speech that allow confirmation or disconfirmation of the problem.

What is the expected lag time between the correction and the child's utterance modification? In order to claim a direct positive role for input, one would want to minimally show that what is frequent in the input emerges in a child's speech or that when new items or grammatical forms appear in the input, they soon emerge in children's speech. Unfortunately, most studies have been unsuccessful in determining correlations of this sort. There is some evidence, however, that input is fine-tuned to a child's level.[5] In these cases, however, one must be cautious as to what is driving what. Is the adult following the child's lead, or is the child following the adult's lead and actually learning from that lead? Furrow, Nelson, and Benedict (1979) and later Furrow and Nelson (1986) made the argument that input is adjusted to the child's level. Furthermore, the adjusted input, in making the language more comprehensible, serves a pedagogical purpose; it teaches children syntax.

Gleitman, Newport, and Gleitman (1984) observed that most of the input effects on the linguistic growth of child language are found in a young age group (i.e., 18–21 months). Furthermore, their findings suggest that the complexity of the input speech determines the child's linguistic growth. They claimed that this finding goes against what had normally been assumed: Input modifications, known in the child language literature as *motherese*, are valuable because they fine-tune the input, making it simpler and easier to understand. If complexity is the greatest predictor, then great simplification would appear to hinder rather than further language development.

> It is relatively easy to show that the language is learnable if the input includes complex sentences; it is awesomely harder to show learnability if the input is restricted to the simplest sentences. This position should not really come as a surprise. To learn a system whose structures are wide-ranging and various, it is common-sensical to suppose that data which mirror this range are most helpful. Data drawn from only part of the range might distort the conjectures the learner will make about the whole range. (Gleitman et al., 1984, p. 69)

In addition to the issue of complexity, Gleitman et al. discussed the role of salience (see chapter 1 for a related discussion). They noted that in their study (as well as in two previous studies investigating correlational relationships; Newport, Gleitman, & Gleitman, 1977, and Furrow, Nelson & Benedict, 1979) there was no significant relation between maternal input and child output with regard to declarative sentences. The explanation for the lack of correlation is difficult to explain, "on conjectures that the learner requires the simple declaratives, early in learning, as the rock on which to build the syntactic system (cf. Pinker & Lebeaux, 1982)" (Gleitman et al., 1984, p. 70). In contrast, in all the studies that they reported, there was a strong correlational effect in subject–aux inversion in yes–no questions. To return to the issue of salience, it is the learner who is selecting what is and what is not salient. Although the learner has to perceive salience, actual salience can be affected by such things as stress and loudness.[6] In the case of yes–no questions, Gleitman et al. claimed that the initial position, stressed and uncontracted, allows the child to readily perceive the structure.

Again, however, results are not always as straightforward as one would like. Hoff-Ginsberg (1985) found a correlation between auxiliary development and *wh*-questions. Given that in *wh*-questions the auxiliary is not in sentence-intial position, Gleitman et al.'s (1984) interpretation may not be correct. One possible explanation for the positive role of questions in the development of basic declarative structure is the role that questions play in speech with young children. In play, children are often inundated with questions[7] (e.g., "What is this?" "What are you doing?"). Children quickly learn that questions are the first part of a two-part sequence, the second part being an answer. In other words, they engage a child in ways that declarations do not. It may be that this engagement is what makes the entire structure salient.

Farrar (1990, 1992) considered the function of modeling for child language learners. Rather than looking at correlations between input (adult) and output (child), he considered the type of correction and the effect of the modeling. He considered the following responses to children's utterances:[8]

1. Recasts with correction
   Child: The dog running.
   Mother: The dog is running.

2. Noncorrective recast (expansion)
   Child: The blue ball.
   Mother: Yea, the ball is bouncing.

3. Topic continuation that models a target
   Child: I'm hot.
   Mother: Would you like some water?

4. Topic change that models a target
   Child: The plane crashed.
   Mother: Let's look at the dog book.

Through data from children 23 months of age, Farrar found that the use of grammatical morphemes was facilitated by corrective feedback; children were more likely to repeat grammatical morphemes after corrective feedback than they were to repeat the morphemes in instances of positive evidence only (as in Examples 2, 3, and 4).

In considering the function of the input, one must also consider learner differences. For example, Nelson (1977) argued that child learners can be classified as *referential* or *expressive* (see also Peters, 1977, who discussed Gestalt–Analytic differentiation, and Halliday, 1975, who discussed mathetic and pragmatic classification). Referential children focus on the use of language as it allows them to talk about things; expressive children focus on the social function of language. The former tend to learn early the names for things and people, whereas the latter are more likely to learn early verbs, adjectives, and social phrases (e.g., *all gone, thank you*). Referential children tend to be more analytic in their approach, whereas expressive children approach language more holistically.

There are at least two ways of thinking about the referential–expressive distinction, both related to the nature of the input. First, as Nelson (1977) proposed, the environment itself conditions the ways in which children conceive the function of language. Do adults use language primarily for its social function, or is a significant amount of time devoted to object naming? A second possibility is one proposed by Lieven, Pine, and Barnes (1992). They suggested that features of the language itself lend to the kinds of extractions that children make. This may in turn be related to the notion of attention. Tomasello (1988) argued that the way an adult attempts to direct a child's attention determines the extent to which that child will approach language, that is, either referentially or expressively.

Doing fine-grained analyses of actual input and output is an arduous task, to say the least; yet if we are to understand the effects of input on children's language, these studies are crucial. There is clearly a need to understand these effects not only from the perspective of frequency (which implies a simplistic input–output scheme) but also in terms of the developing language. In other words, we must consider changes over time. What needs to be addressed in the general study of language acqusition (be it first or second) is not only the direct relation between speech directed at learners and the learning process but also what enables these relations to exist.

3.2. SECOND LANGUAGES

In the second language context, modifications to non-native speakers, or *non-native directed speech*, seem more uniform because most studies report speech within a Western context. Many readers are familiar with the British television series "Fawlty Towers," in which Mr. Fawlty, the owner of a small hotel, speaks to an often noncomprehending Manuel, a hotel worker from Barcelona. Mr. Fawlty's speech is sometimes perfectly grammatical, "Would you take these cases to Room 7, please?" ["Hotel Inspector" episode], sometimes somewhat modified, "It's not fire; it's only bell" ["The Germans" episode], and sometimes phonetically modified ["The Germans" episode]:

5. Basil Fawlty: Go and get me a hammer.
   Manuel: ¿Cómo?
   Basil Fawlty: a xammer, a xammer.

Mr. Fawlty also uses pictures and gestures. When Manuel responds to the command, "Would you take these cases to room 7, please?" with "¿Qué?" Mr. Fawlty shows three drawings in rapid succession, one of a suitcase, one of an upward pointing arrow (↑), and one with the numeral 7.

3.2.1. Input and Simplification

One of the first scholars to focus on this specialized language variety was Ferguson (1971, 1975), whose major interest was an understanding of the nature of simplified varieties in general, as a window on the nature of the human capacity for language. His scope of inquiry was the presence or absence of the copula (i.e., an overt connecting link between a subject and complement, such as the verb *to be* in English, as in, "I **am** at my computer."). He noted that

> many, perhaps all, speech communities have registers of a special kind for use with people who are regarded for one reason or another as unable to readily undertand the normal speech of the community (e.g., babies, foreigners, deaf people). These forms of speech are generally felt by their users to be simplified versions of the language, hence easier to understand, and they are often regarded as imitation of the way the person addressed uses the language himself. (Ferguson, 1971, p. 143)

Thus, Ferguson proposed a source (i.e., imitation of a non-native speaker) and a function (i.e., to make the language easier to understand), although clearly neither of these was part of the thrust of his paper.

Meisel (1977) continued research on the notion of simplicity, suggesting that, indeed, the language used by native speakers when addressing non-native learners of a variety of languages (e.g., English, German, French, Finnish) is strikingly similar, all using common ways of simplifying language. Meisel took the simplification notion one step further and looked at learners' language from the point of view of the cause of simplification. Do learners' languages appear to be simplified versions of the target language because they are imitating the native speakers' foreigner talk, or, as Meisel suggested, are all learners using common simplification strategies as they attempt to communicate in a second language? Clearly, the latter possibility is more likely, as the literature published in the past 20 years has shown and as was discussed earlier in this chapter. Learners are actively engaged in a process of creating a second language, not in faulty imitation. The commonalities between foreigner talk and learner speech are in general due less to circular imitation than to the common use of linguistic resources humans make in both their first and second languages. Pine (1994) furthered the comparison between young language-learning children and nonproficient second language speakers, adding a comparison with speech directed to dogs (Hirsh-Pasek & Treiman, 1982), speech directed to infants (Snow, 1977), and child-directed speech by other children (Barton & Tomasello, 1994). In each of these instances is one common element: The interlocutors are not linguistically competent.

In considering the source of modified input, Meisel (1980) pointed out the difficulty in including imitation as a viable explanation, for the question becomes one of who is doing what to whom. This is illustrated by the following words from Bloomfield (1933), a staunch believer in imitation. "A jargon or a lingua franca is nobody's native language but only a compromise between a foreign speaker's version of a language and a native speaker's version of the foreign speaker's version, and so on, in which each party imperfectly reproduces the other's reproduction" (p. 473). Further, "speakers of a lower language [in contact situations] may make so little progress in learning the dominant speech, that the masters, in communicating with them resort to 'baby-talk.' This 'baby-talk' is the masters' imitation of the subject's speech" (p. 472). Although Bloomfield recognized that imitation cannot be the only answer, he noted that "There is reason to believe that it is by no means an exact imitation, and that some of its features are based not upon the subjects' mistakes but upon grammatical relations that exist within the upper language itself" (p. 472).

He also, perhaps somewhat contradictorily, furthered the circular imitation theory: "The basis is the foreigner's desperate attempt at English. Then comes the English-speaker's contemptuous imitation of this, which he tries in the hope of making himself understood" (p. 473). The results of A imitating B and B imitating A are utterances like the following that have been observed in contact situations:

You not like soup? He plenty kai-kai. ("Don't you like the soup? It's very good.")

Or

What man you give him stick? ("To whom did you give the stick?")

However, if imitation were going on in this circular fashion, how would progress ever be made?

3.2.2. The Nature of Non-Native Directed Speech

The study of input in second language acquisition had its beginnings in the late 1960s and early 1970s, with a major impetus coming from two works. The first was Corder's (1967) article in which he defined *input* as "what goes in not what is *available* for going in" (p. 9). In other words, in this definition, input is more akin to what he called intake (see chapters 1 and 6). A second important article was by Wagner-Gough and Hatch (1975), in which the authors argued that learners learn syntax from the input and interaction with NSs. At the time, this was a radical way of looking at the role of syntactic learning because the then-current orthodox position, particularly among those involved in classroom teaching, was that conversational interactions were used to practice forms, not learn them. The following examples from Wagner-Gough and Hatch illustrate the potential role of input in this young child's (a native speaker of Farsi) learning of an L2 (English). He takes forms that he has heard from the input (in this case the progressive) and uses it for a variety of functions.

a. Immediate intention
    I my coming. I my go my mother
    = I'm going to come to you. I'm going to ask my mother.
b. Distant future
    I don't know Fred a my going, no go. I don't know coming, go.
    = I don't know if Fred is going or not. I don't know if he's coming or going.
c. Past
    I'm find it. Bobbie found one to me.
    = I found it. Bobbie found it for me.
d. Process-State
    Msty, Msty go in there. Hey Judy, Msty going in there.
    = Msty is going in there. Hey Judy, Msty is going in there.
e. Imperative
    Okay, sit down over here! Sitting down like that!
    = Sit down over here! Sit down like that!

Since those early years of second language acquisition research, many studies have been conducted and numerous observations have been made of the speech used by NSs (teachers and nonteachers) when addressing NNSs. A first question that needs to be asked is whether native speakers in fact modify their speech when addressing NNSs? The vast majority of studies suggest that there is modification, but before looking in greater detail at the type of modification, it is also necessary to point out that so-called foreigner talk is not always present and not always stable.

3.2.2.1. Evidence for Little or No Modification.

Arthur, Weiner, Culver, Lee, and Thomas (1980) looked at evidence of modification in telephone conversations between airline agents and NSs on the one hand and airline agents and NNSs, on the other. The results were not uniform with regard to features that are typical of foreigner talk, such as length of response, complexity of response, and vocabulary size. Speech rate and redundancy did not differ significantly between the groups, although the differences were in the expected direction (i.e., faster speech rate for NSs and greater redundancy for NNSs).

Smith, Scholnick, Crutcher, Simeone, and Smith (1991) designed a study to investigate the issue of speech rate explicitly. Eighteen native speakers were paired with either a NS or a NNS. What was unique about this study was that it was done in a matched guise format. That is, the NS/NNS was the same person—a German–English bilingual–bicultural student. Furthermore, she was a professional actress. She adapted her behavior in three ways: speaking in standard English, speaking in accented English, and speaking in broken English. In the accented English condition, she showed mild difficulty with lexical choice and syntax, and she occasionally asked her partner to repeat or explain a difficult term or sentence. In the broken English condition, she showed much difficulty with both comprehension and production. She often asked for clarification or pretended to misinterpret things, and she produced sentences that were awkward in both structure and word choice. In addition, she used a heavy accent.

As with the Arthur et al. (1980) study, the results were mixed. There were clearly indications of typical accommodating behavior: Utterances were shorter to non-native speakers, questions were reworded, information was repeated, feedback and encouragement were provided. However, there were also examples of what the authors called *counter-accommodating* behavior. There was little evidence of slower speech rate to non-NSs, and, to the contrary, there were instances in which the speech rate was faster, as in the following example provided by the authors, although not officially part of their database.

6. Setting: Restaurant, attempting to order a hamburger
   NS = waitress
   NNS = Scandinavian tourist
   NS: And what kind of dressing do you want on your salad?
   NNS: Dressing?
   NS: What kind of dressing do you want on your salad? (spoken
           more rapidly)

NNS: (pause, nonverbal expression of confusion)
NS: Salad dressing . . . Y'know, like Thousand Island . . . or
       French
NNS: French?
NS: OK. And how would you like your hamburger?
NNS: How?

This excerpt shows classic foreigner discourse (see also chapter 5) in that
there is repetition as well as a choice question, in which the waitress offers
alternatives. There is also evidence of counter-accommodating behavior
when the waitress increases rather than decreases her speech rate. This is
also seen in the following example from their data.

7. NS: OK. So um, what is your major?
   NNS: Um? I in music.
   NS: Music. And is that um what your professional goals will re-
          volve around? (began slow and sped up)
   NNS: vas? Wha . . . ?
   NS: Is ah that what your professional goals will revolve around?
          (spoken even more rapidly)
   NNS: I uh uhm.
   NS: Oh, you don't understand?
   NNS: No . . .
   NS: OK. Well, let's skip that question.

In the following example, the NS apppears to be talking only to himself,
perhaps due to the frustration level reached by attempting to converse
with someone not a linguistic equal.

8. NS: OK, let's go on to another question. Uh—I don't think you're
          going to explain to me what the most serious problem in
          the world is today, so . . . (laugh) Oh, OK, here's the one
          after your goals. Uh, what do you see yourself doing ten years
          from now? (spoken rapidly)
   NNS: Sorry? I uh.
   NS: Ten years. (sigh) Ummmm (muttered under breath). Oh,
          this is fruitless.

In general, what was found was an inappropriate speech rate, complex
and confusing syntax and lexical items, and inappropriate repair strategies.
However, not all the data exhibited accommodating and counter-accommodating examples. That is, the talk of proficient to nonproficient speakers
is not simple nor straightforward. There is considerable give-and-take as
each interlocutor attempts to make language understandable or at times

even to extricate him- or herself completely from the conversation, as at the end of example 7.

A similar example of accommodation and counter-accommodation comes from work by Varonis and Gass (1985a), who reported a conversation between a native speaker of Spanish and a native speaker of English. This conversation was originally reported in the context of a discussion of miscommunication but is used here to highlight the way in which the NS accommodated a clear lack of proficiency and a clear lack of understanding *and* in which non-native directed speech did not accommodate the NNS's linguistic ability and linguistic needs. The NNS had been given a class assignment to call to find out the price of a television set. What he did not realize was that when he looked up a number in the yellow pages, rather than looking under television sales, he had looked under television repairs. The NS is thus speaking from the perspective of a repair shop while the NNS is speaking as if talking to a sales shop.

9. NNS: Hello
   NS: Hello could you tell me about the price and size of Sylvania color TV?
   NNS: Pardon?
   NS: Could you tell me about price and size of Sylvania TV color?
   PAUSE
   NS: What did you want? A service call?
   NNS: Uh 17 inch huh?
   NS: What did you want a service call? Or how much to repair a TV?
   NNS: Yeah TV color.
   NS: 17 inch.
   NNS: OK.
   SILENCE
   NS: Is it a portable?
   NNS: Uh huh
   NS: What width is it? What is the brand name of the TV?
   NNS: Ah Sony please
→ NS: We don't work on Sony's.
   NNS: Or Sylvania
   NS: Sylvania?
   NNS: Uh huh
   NS: Oh, Sylvania OK. That's American made.
   NNS: OK.
   NS: All right. Portables have to be brought in.
   NNS: Hm hm.
→ NS: And there's no way I can tell you how much it'll cost until *he* looks at it.

NNS: Hm hm.

➔ NS: And it's a $12.50 deposit.

NNS: OK.

➔ NS: And if he can fix it that applies to labor and if he can't he keeps the $12.50 for his time and effort.

NNS: Hm hm.

➔ NS: How old of a TV is it? Do you know off hand?

NNS: 19 inch.

NS: How old of a TV is it? Is it a very old one or only a couple years old?

NNS: Oh, so so.

NS: The only thing you can do is bring it in and let him look at it and go from there.

NNS: New television please

NS: Oh you want to know
                    SILENCE

NS: how much a new television is?

NNS: Yeah I want buy one television.

NS: Do we want to buy one?

NNS: Yeah

NS: Is it a Sylvania?

NNS: Sylvania TV color

NS: Well, you know even, even if we buy 'em, we don't give much more than $25 for 'em. By the time we fix 'em up and sell 'em, we can't get more than

NNS: Hm hm.

NS: $100 out of 'em time we put our time and parts in it (delivered in rapid speech)

NNS: Is it 17 inch?

NS: Well, I don't (long pause) the only thing I can tell you to do is you'd have to come have to come to the shop. I'm on the extension at home. The shop's closed
                    SILENCE

NNS: 19 inch? you don't have?

NS: Do we have a 19 inch?

NNS: Yeah.

NS: No, I've got a 17 inch new RCA.

NNS: OK. Thank you. Bye.

NS: Bye.

Initial evidence for accommodation can be seen in the native speaker's willingness to participate in this dialogue, which could have easily been terminated at the beginning when the NS responds that her shop does not work on Sonys (turn 15). Yet she persisted in an attempt to work with the caller to determine what the call was about. On the other hand, there is clear counter-accommodation. This, of course, presupposes that the NS was aware that there was a miscommunication in progress. One can only surmise that in fact this was the case, but this presupposition is bolstered by the fact that there were a number of long pauses in which the non-native speaker was clearly trying to adjust her thinking when the apparent topic of conversation turned out not to be correct. Despite the obvious fact of nonunderstanding, the NS did little linguistically to help her partner. She spoke rapidly, she used contractions (see for example turns 23, 25, 27), and she used idiomatic language (e.g., *off-hand* in turn 29). Hence, we see a native speaker, undoubtedly aware of the difficulty of a conversation, simultaneously engaged in accommodation (of an interpersonal nature) and engaged in counter-accommodation (of a linguistic nature).

One explanation for the store owner's behavior may be that she was reciting something that she has recited many times before (in particular, starting with "And there's no way . . ." to ". . . time and effort"), and she makes no adjustments in that recitation. That this was a canned speech coupled with her inexperience with a speaker of this level of proficiency may have resulted in a lack of modification.

3.2.2.2. Variability in Non-Native Directed Speech.
With regard to variability, it is important to note that all speakers, regardless of their interlocutor, accommodate and adjust their speech according to the needs of the conversation and of their conversational partners (cf. Giles & Smith, 1979). With NNSs, the situation is not so much different as it is exaggerated in the sense that the accommodation is less subtle and more frequent, and, importantly, the form of the speech to NNS may change during the course of a conversation. The change in input may be a result of a reassessment of an interlocutor's proficiency and hence a reassessment of an interlocutor's ability to understand.[9]

To illustrate the chameleon nature of non-native directed speech, consider the following data from Gass and Varonis (1985a). These data come from a telephone survey on food and nutrition in which NNSs randomly selected names from the local telephone directory and asked a series of preset questions. After two questions, the NNSs said, "Pardon me?" indicating to the native speaker respondent that there were difficulties in comprehension.

10. NNS: There has been a lot of talk lately about additives and preservatives in food. In what ways has this changed your eating habits?

   NS: Uh, I avoid them, I d-, I don't buy prepackaged foods uh, as much . . . . Uh, I don't buy . . . say . . . potato chips that

have a lot of flavoring on them. . . . And, uh, I eat better. I
think.

NNS: Pardon me?

NS: Ummm, pardon me? I, I eat better, I think. I, I don't buy
so much food that's prepackaged.

In this example, the NS makes the speech more transparent after the
"pardon me?" by changing "prepackaged foods" to "food that's prepackaged."

11. NNS: How have increasing food costs changed your eating habits?
    NS: Well, it doesn't, hasn't really.
    NNS: Pardon me?
    NS: It hasn't really changed them.

12. NNS: How have increasing food costs changed your eating habits?
    NS: Uh well that would I don't think they've changed 'em much
    right now, but the pressure's on.
    NNS: Pardon me?
    NS: I don't think they've changed our eating habits much as of
    now. . . .

In these examples the native speaker also makes the speech more transparent after an indication of nonunderstanding by taking the clipsized
verb form "hasn't really" and adding missing information: "hasn't really
changed them" (Example 11), and by taking a contracted pronominal
"'em" and giving the full noun phrase "our eating habits." In general,
considerable variation occurred from the beginning of the conversation,
in which the NNS appeared somewhat fluent (aided by the fact that she
was reading and had rehearsed a preestablished scripted set of questions),
to the end, after two indications of nonunderstanding.

The preceding description has dealt with ongoing changes in speech
resulting from a native speaker's changing perception of the extent to
which a non-native speaker understands. There are, of course, other
sources of variation. First, there are individual differences based on a
person's style of communication. The degree of variation may be due to
one's experience in talking to non-native speakers or in one's sensitivity
to and awareness of the interlocutor and the extent to which he or she
appears to understand. Second, and not unrelated to the first, is the actual
proficiency level of one's interlocutor.

Gaies (1979) presented data from eight teacher trainers and their speech
to each other as well as to ESL students at four proficiency levels. Table
3.1 presents a portion of his data to each of these five groups. In all cases,
there is a progression from lesser to greater syntactic complexity as a

TABLE 3.1
Comparison of the Syntactic Complexity of Teacher Trainer's
Baseline Data and Oral Classroom Language by Level

Level	Words per T-unit	Ratio of Clauses to T-units	Words per Clause
Beginner	4.30	1.02	4.20
Upper Beginner	5.75	1.14	5.04
Intermediate	6.45	1.24	5.18
Advanced	8.26	1.38	5.98
Baseline	10.97	1.60	6.84

Note. T-units are defined as "one main clause plus any subordinate clause or nonclausal structure that is attached to or embedded in it" (Hunt, 1970, p. 4). From *Studies in First and Second Language Acquisition* (p. 190), by F. Eckman and A. Hastings (Eds.), 1979, Rowley, MA: Newbury House. Copyright 1979 by Newbury House. Reprinted with permission of editors.

function of proficiency level. In fact, the proficiency level is a statistically significant predictor of the syntactic complexity of these teachers' speech.

In a similar example, we see the skillful linguistic ability of an experienced kindergarten teacher as she addresses children with different proficiency levels. Kleifgen (1985) presented data from a teacher with a class of students mixed in terms of language ability. There were native-speaking English children and non-native English-speaking children whose proficiency levels were mixed.

Below are examples from the speech of this teacher to various groups of students.

13. a. To a NS kindergarten class
        These are babysitters taking care of babies. Draw a line from Q to q.
        From S to s and then trace.
    b. To a single NS
        Now, Johnny, you have to make a great big pointed hat.
    c. To an intermediate-level native speaker of Urdu.
        Now her hat is big. Pointed.
    d. To a low intermediate level native speaker of Arabic
        See hat? Hat is big. Big and tall.
    e. To a beginning level native speaker of Japanese.
        Big, big, big hat.
    f. To a beginning level native speaker of Korean.
        Baby sitter.   baby.

This teacher is skillful in modifying her speech according to the proficiency level of her students. In looking at Kleifgen's study, one finds another interetsing phenomenon. For those students who showed improvement, the teacher's talk also changed over time; for those students who did not improve, the dynamic and changing nature of the teacher's talk was not apparent.

We have thus seen that so-called foreigner talk is not monolithic; rather, it changes according to individual and contextual factors. It appears to be in part due to prior experience and in part due to a common human desire to maintain conversations in which both parties participate.

3.2.3. Descriptions of Non-Native Directed Speech

Certainly non-native directed speech is variable. I now turn to some of the salient features of that talk before turning to a discussion of the function that this modified speech might have for the process of learning.

Although there are some stereotypical examples of ungrammatical input, most input to NNSs is grammatical. So what then makes it different? There are a number of dimensions, some of which are more obvious than others (I deal with interactional differences in chapter 5). Differences can be found at nearly all levels of language. Perhaps the most obvious are phonological differences.

3.2.3.1. Phonology. On the level of the speech signal, we often find speech that is loud, slow, and carefully articulated. For example, contractions are not often found in speech directed to low proficiency learners, and vowels that, in English are often reduced are less likely to be reduced. Additionally, there are more pauses and more fillers, such as *er, um,* and so on.

3.2.3.2. Vocabulary. Vocabulary to non-native speakers tends to be simple. For example, in describing an object that is blue, one would expect the generic term *blue* to be used rather than one of the more precise terms to describe various shades of blue (e.g., *navy blue, turquoise*). Idioms are used less frequently than in conversations with fluent speakers; the phrase "off-hand" used in Excerpt 9 (line 29) is exceptionally surprising because it is used with a nonproficient speaker.

3.2.3.3. Morphology/Syntax. In general, one finds simple syntax with low proficiency speakers (see section 3.2.2.2). One also finds explicit morphosyntactic information contained in speech directed to nonproficient speakers. For example, Larsen-Freeman and Long (1991) reported that in studies of foreigner talk in Japanese, Hindi–Urdu, and English, there are more examples of canonical word order than there are in native-directed speech (Long, Gambhiar, Gambhiar, & Nishimura, 1982). Onaha (1987) reported less ellipsis in foreigner versus talk to native speakers; markers in Japanese (such as those that mark semantic and grammatical relations) are frequently omitted in naturally occurring discourse among NSs but are more likely to be included in speech with NNSs. Other markers in Japanese, such as interrogative pronouns and honorifics, tend to be avoided in speech addressed to NNSs (Hiraike-Okawara, & Sakamoto, 1990).

3.2.3.4. Discourse. The structure of discourse in non-native directed speech is the subject of chapter 5. Suffice it to say at this point that conversations involving nonproficient non-native speakers are often peppered with nonunderstandings and attempts to resolve those nonunderstandings. These attempts are mutually constructed discourse structures that include clarification requests, comprehension checks, or-choice questions, and many others.

3.2.4. The Grammaticality of Foreigner Talk

When one thinks of the way native speakers of a language address non-native speakers, the stereotype that comes to mind is something reminiscent of the old "Me Tarzan, you Jane." However, a closer examination of the literature and examples of actual speech reveals little in the way of ungrammatical input. Nonetheless, there are examples of ungrammatical speech both in and out of the classroom. The following was observed in an ESL classroom. A teacher was trying to help a class understand the meaning of the word *suitcase.* Another student volunteered an answer and said, "It is bag for carry," to which the teacher responded, "Yes, right, bag for carry." Presumably, the student (and possibly other members of the class) received the correct message concerning the meaning of *suitcase*—that it is a bag used for carrying items, but they also received the incorrect message concerning the correctness of the syntax.

In 14 are examples of foreigner talk features (see Hatch, 1983).

14. a. Slow rate = clearer articulation
         Examples
              Final stops are released
              Fewer reduced vowels
              Fewer contractions
              Longer pauses
     b. Vocabulary
         Examples
              High frequency vocabulary (less slang, fewer idioms)
              Fewer pronoun forms
              Definitions
                   Overtly marked (e.g., This means X)

        Semantic feature information (e.g., a cathedral usual means a church that's a very high ceiling)

        Contextaul information (e.g., if you go for a job in a factory, they talk about a wage scale)

    Gestures and pictures

c. Syntax

    Examples

        Short and simple sentences

        Movement of topics to front of sentence

        Repetition and restatement

        New information at the end of the sentence

        Native speaker grammatically modified learners' incorrect utterances

        Native speaker fills in the blank for learners' incomplete utterances

d. Discourse

    Examples

        Native speaker gives reply in a question

        Native speaker uses tag questions

        Native speaker offers correction

Ungrammatical input is found in two situations: speech to someone of lower status or perceived lower status and speech to low-proficiency learners. With regard to the first situation, reports of ungrammatical input have been made largely in work situations (Clyne, 1977; foremen addressing workers) and in Germany in the research done on *Gastarbeiter* (guest workers; Clahsen, Meisel, & Pienemann, 1983; Klein & Dittmar, 1979). However, the "put-down" foreigner talk is not limited to that environment. Hawkins (1985) presented data based on a situation in which a non-native–native dyad plays a guessing game. In Example 15, the non-native speaker has an object that has been selected from a grab bag. The native speaker is trying to guess what the object is and says.

15. NS: Okay, little guy! Yeah, yours! Okay! Yours is it for eat?
     NNS: Eat. No.

The native speaker's ungrammatical "yours is it for eat?" is prefaced by a phrasc that indicates who is who in the relationship: "little guy" (clearly, if he were talking to a professor, he would undoubtedly not have used this term).

The following examples show how frequent ungrammatical input may be in speech to low-proficiency speakers. The non-native data come from two sets of interviews, each between a native speaker and a non-native speaker (the non-native speakers in each set are native speakers of Spanish). In one case the non-native speaker is a 5-year-old child (Cheo); in the other, it is an adult (Alberto). Portions of the data were originally reported by Cazden, Cancino, Rosansky, and Schumann (1975) and Schumann (1978) and were reanalyzed by Gass and Lakshmanan (1991).

A = Alberto, adult

16. NS: Ahm, is a boy.
    A: Is a boy.
    NS: Yeah, is that a good sentence or bad sentence?
    A: Good.
    NS: Good, O.K., ahm, ahm, is a dog.
    A: Is a dog? Good.
    NS: Good. Ahm, this apple.

17. A: Is part (/uh/) the week.
    NS: Good. Very good. Is this a weekend?
    A: No.
    NS: No.
    A: Is part of week.
    NS: Um hum, oh, is this a week day?
    A: No, is weekend.
    NS: Very good, good.

18. A: She is dead.
    NS: Good.
    A: De, dead.
    NS: Dead, yeah.
    A: Yeah, is dead.
    NS: Good explanation, good sentence.
    A: Yeah.

19. A: Uh, uh no good explain.
    NS: No good explain.

20. A: Oh sure. Drink too much.
    NS: Drink too much. What were you drinking?

21. A: Oh any person. No, no, no live more.
    NS: No live more?
    A: Yeah, no live, es, she, I need go and let in this funeral home.

22. A: Yeah, is charm.
    NS: Is charming or.
    A: Yeah, is charming.
    NS: Charming.

23. A: Yesterday my country change, ah, President.
    NS: Oh yeah? Now, is the new one a good one?
    A: Um?
    NS: Is a good President? Do you like him? No?
    A: No.
    NS: No.
    A: Is opposite of my ideas.

24. A: My country?
    NS: No, here, no.
    A: Here?
    NS: Is good?
    A: Yeah, this is good.

25. NS: Come at five o'clock.
    A: I not come, no? Is no is good?
    NS: Is; whatever you say is good. I'm interested to see what you say.

C = Cheo, child

26. C: Y/Is a boy. Y house.
    NS: Very good.

27. C: Es a house.
    NS: Very, very good.

28. C: Pu- water.
    NS.   What?
    C: Put-t, put it water.
    NS: Put water.
    NS: Good. Um, why is he doing that?

29. NS: You want to sit on the floor?
    C: Hum?
    NS: You want to sit on the floor? Sit up here?

30. NS: Does she speak English?
    C: No.
    NS: Nothing?
    C: No.
    NS: She doesn't talk? Always quiet? No talk?

31. C: Come to a little boyses.
    NS: Hum.
    C: [making noises of being satisfied: um, um]
    NS: Is a, a pencil.
    C: Pencil.

Clearly, speakers frequently used ungrammatical utterances to both Alberto and Cheo. What about the function of the ungrammatical input? In thinking about the significance of these data, it is important to note that pronoun use in Spanish is optional, depending in some measure on the discourse context. Thus, the following sentences are both acceptable:

32. Voy   a Barcelona.
    go (I) to Barcelona

33. Yo voy a Barcelona.
    I   go to Barcelona

In terms of learning, what this means is that both learners may be operating under the assumption that English is like Spanish in that pronoun use is optional. Assuming the correctness of this assumption, they receive confirmation of hypotheses from the input. In fact, when one looks at the frequency of the learners' use of zero pronouns and the frequency with which the interlocutor uses zero pronouns, there is a striking similarity. In both cases, data were collected over an extended period of time—in the case of Alberto, data were collected every 2 weeks over a 10-month period, and in the case of Cheo, they were collected every month over an 8½-month period. Figures 3.1 through 3.4 show comparisons of subjectless utterances

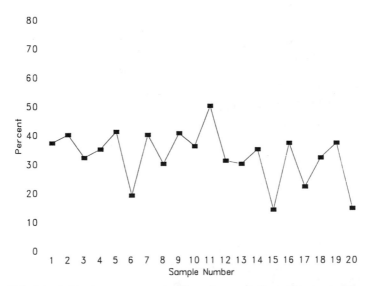

FIG. 3.1. Subjectless utterances in Alberto's speech. From "Accounting for interlanguage subject pronouns," by S. Gass and U. Lakshmanan, 1991, *Second Language Research, 7,* p. 190. Copyright 1991 by *Second Language Research.* Reprinted with permission.

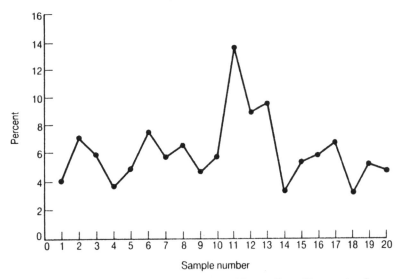

FIG. 3.2. Subjectless utterances in input to Alberto. From "Accounting for interlanguage subject pronouns," by S. Gass and U. Lakshmanan, 1991, *Second Language Research*, 7, p. 191. Copyright 1991 by *Second Language Research*. Reprinted with permission.

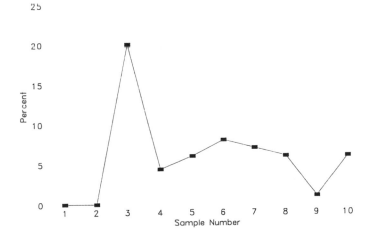

FIG. 3.3. Subjectless utterances in Cheo's speech. From "Accounting for interlanguage subject pronouns," by S. Gass and U. Lakshmanan, 1991, *Second Language Research*, 7, p. 195. Copyright 1991 by *Second Language Research*. Reprinted with permission.

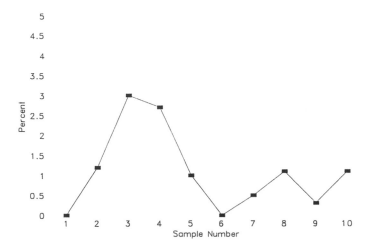

FIG. 3.4. Subjectless utterances in input to Cheo. From "Accounting for interlanguage subject pronouns," by S. Gass and U. Lakshmanan, 1991, *Second Language Research, 7,* p. 196. Copyright 1991 by *Second Language Research.* Reprinted with permission.

in the speech of each individual and speech to that individual (Alberto, Figs. 3.1 and 3.2; Cheo, Figs. 3.3 and 3.4). In each instance a greater use of subjectless utterances in the NS's speech corresponds approximately to a similar large number of subjectless utterances in the learner's speech.

This is not to say that there is a necessary cause-and-effect relationship; one could in fact argue that the NS is imitating the NNS. This discussion then is reduced to a chicken-or-egg argument. The point is that the non-native speaker, regardless of the NS's motivation, receives confirmation of a sort, telling him or her that subjectless utterances are acceptable. The confirmation comes in the form of repetition as well as in the form of NS-initiated utterances.

3.2.5. The Functions of Modified Input

The preceding section touched on the issue of the function of modified speech. In this section I continue that notion by exploring two types of modification, simplified speech and elaborated speech. It is important to note that in modified input, the input is often both simplified and elaborated. In other words, it is not always the case that input addressed to nonproficient speakers of a language is simplified in the sense of exhibiting some of the characteristics displayed in Example 14. Modification may also come in the form of greater elaboration.

In general, it is clear that some sort of comprehension is necessary. As was proposed in chapter 1, although comprehended input is a prerequisite to learning, comprehension does not guarantee learning. There are numerous instances where comprehension does take place but the time demands of a conversation do not allow retention of information. Furthermore, as suggested in chapter 1, it is necessary to consider different levels of comprehension. Comprehension of meaning may be less important than syntactic comprehension for eventual integration of linguistic information.

Regarding the notion of simplification, in those instances with reduced information (e.g., reduced syntactic information), one could argue that the fact that there is less information to process makes it more likely that learners will comprehend what is there. This is particularly the case if one recognizes that one of the first things that a learner needs to do to understand a stream of speech is minimally segment it into some meaningful units (e.g., phrases, words, sentences).

Simplification in terms of slower speech, greater pauses, or more pronounced intonation may allow more time for a learner to use the available information appropriately; that is, it allows more processing time (see Kelch, 1985). Phonetic modifications may also draw a learner's attention to salient parts of the discourse. However, simplification may also remove much of the redundancy present in language, making it more difficult to understand as opposed to facilitating comprehension, as is commonly believed. Reducing vocabulary to simple, common vocabulary items often makes a reader or listener work harder to figure out which of many possible meanings is being used. For example, the word *get* has many meanings. In a given context, does it mean *obtain*? Does it mean *receive*? Using a more explicit vocabulary item reduces the cognitive load on learners. They do not have to determine which of many possible senses is the correct one.

Much input is simplified in the sense that it is made more comprehensible, but often this is done through greater linguistic elaboration rather than through linguistic simplification. In fact, it may be that elaboration provides more information than is normally available. Issidorides (1988; 1991, as cited in Issidorides & Hulstijn, 1992, p. 148) found that the "presence of semantically redundant function words in utterances with normal suprasegmental cues does not hinder comprehension, and hence that their omission, as in FT, does not necessarily facilitate comprehension." Although this is a negative result, one can speculate that the positive counterpart, that is, that semantic redundancy increases comprehension, is plausible (see also section 1.4.2).

In section 3.2.2.2 the following examples were presented and are repeated here as 34 and 35:

34. NNS: How have increasing food costs changed your eating habits?
    NS: Well, it doesn't, hasn't really.

NNS: Pardon me?
NS: It hasn't really changed them.

35. NNS: How have increasing food costs changed your eating habits?
    NS: Uh well that would I don't think they've change 'em much
          right now, but the pressure's on.
    NNS: Pardon me?
    NS: I don't think they've changed our eating habits much as of
          now. . . .

In both, upon hearing an indication of nonunderstanding (*pardon me?*),
the native speaker elaborates on what was perceived to be a nonunderstood
response. The modification provides fuller information, in turn providing
a greater opportunity for comprehension to take place.

Parker and Chaudron (1987) reviewed a number of studies of input
simplification and input elaboration, concluding that there is a positive
effect on comprehension of elaborated modification. In a comparison of
modified input versus interactionally modified input, Gass and Varonis
(1994) found that both contributed to immediate comprehension but that
only interactionally modified input led to subsequently better linguistic
production.

Yano, Long, and Ross (1994) recognized the importance of understanding how linguistic simplification may lead to better comprehension
while reducing the amount of information available for learning. They
presented learners with three types of texts: unmodified, simplified, and
elaborated. The simplified texts consisted of reducing sentence length,
embedding, and multisyllabic words; the elaborated texts included para-
phrased information and definitions of low-frequency words. Their results
showed greater comprehension for simplified and elaborated versions as
opposed to the unmodified texts, although there was no significant difference between the simplified and elaborated texts. An interesting finding
relates to the type of comprehension that was being tested. For example,
when students were required to make inferences from the text, the elaborated text seemed to be the most beneficial.

In sum, it is frequently the case that the language addressed to NNSs
is modified. Unfortunately, because most data come from Western cultures,
or at least from industrialized cultures, there is no evidence from second
language learning situations in cultures such as the Kaluli. Nonetheless,
from the data obtained, not only have we seen the universality of modification, but we have also seen that the modifications appear to serve the
function of aiding comprehensibility. Although comprehensibility is a necessary condition, it is clearly not a sufficient condition for learning. Furthermore, it is not yet clear how different levels of comprehension feed
into acquisition, nor is it clear what precise factors make oral or written

language comprehensible. How the language is shaped and co-constructed by non-natives and their conversational partners to effect comprehension is discussed in chapter 5.

3.2.6. Triggers of Foreigner Talk

What is it that triggers foreigner talk? A corollary is, why do some individuals in some situations not modify their speech even in situations with an obvious language difficulty? There are a number of possibilities: stereotypes, actual language difficulty, prior experience, among others. It was noted previously that the native speaker in the example concerning the TV repair shop did not show much evidence of speech modification. The question is why not.

There seem to be two possible reasons for nonmodification; one is intentional, one unintentional. It has been argued (e.g., Meisel, 1977) that nonmodification is a way of talking down to an interlocutor. Incomprehensible speech puts one person at a distinct advantage and in a superior position. An unintentional possibility relates in all likelihood to lack of experience. There may be a certain amount of experience that one must have to be able to adequately judge the extent to which an interlocutor understands and to be able to make appropriate and somewhat fine-tuned adjustments to effect comprehension. Consider the following hypothetical conversation:

36. NS: Hey, dude, whad up?
    NNS: What?

Is it immediately obvious to all individuals what needs to be modified and how to do it? Or does it take some experience (and perhaps some educational experience) to understand that the initial greeting is highly colloquial and hence probably not within the linguistic range of a NNS?

Modification, on the other hand, comes from a willingness and desire to ensure a smooth, flowing conversation. It requires a recognition that some change is necessary and an understanding of what an appropriate change might be.

3.3. THE MONITOR MODEL

It is an understatement to point out that the most far-reaching model of learning in the second language literature is Krashen's monitor model, first described in the 1970s (e.g., 1977). Within the second language literature, the model itself initially had a great impact and spawned a number of empirical studies. The effect then fanned out to language teachers but became less influential in the second language literature as severe theoretical concerns were raised (cf. Barasch & James, 1994; Gass & Selinker, 1994; Gregg, 1984, 1986; McLaughlin, 1987; White, 1987). Because one of the major components deals with input, the model is briefly reviewed here. There are five basic hypotheses in this model, the acquisition-learning hypothesis, the natural order hypothesis, the monitor hypothesis, the input hypothesis, and the affective filter hypothesis.

3.3.1. The Acquisition–Learning Hypothesis

Krashen (1982) assumed that second language learners have two independent means of developing knowledge of a second language. One way is through what he called *acquisition* and the other is through *learning*.

> . . . *acquisition* [is] a process similar, if not identical to the way children develop ability in their first language. Language acquisition is a subconscious process; language acquirers are not usually aware of the fact that they are acquiring language, but are only aware of the fact that they are using the language for communication. The result of language acquisition, acquired competence, is also subconscious. We are generally not consciously aware of the rules of the languages we have acquired. Instead, we have a "feel" for correctness. Grammatical sentences "sound" right, or "feel" right, and errors feel wrong, even if we do not consciously know what rule was violated. (Krashen, 1982, p. 10)

Other ways of describing acquisition include implicit learning, informal learning, and natural learning. In nontechnical language, acquisition is *picking-up* a language.

> The second way to develop competence in a second language is by language *learning*. We will use the term "learning" henceforth to refer to conscious knowledge of a second language, knowing the rules, being aware of them, and being able to talk about them. In non-technical terms, learning is "knowing about" a language, known to most people as "grammar," or "rules." Some synonyms include formal knowledge of a language or explicit learning. (Krashen, 1982, p.10)

In Krashen's view, not only does learning take place in two different ways, but learners also use the language developed through these systems for different purposes. Thus, the knowledge acquired (in the nontechnical use of the term) through these means, remains internalized differently. Moreover, knowledge learned through one means (e.g., learning) cannot be internalized as knowledge of the other kind (e.g., acquisition).

How are these two knowledge types used differently? The acquired system is used to produce language. The acquisition system generates utterances because in producing language learners focus on meaning, not on form. The learned system serves as an inspector of the acquired system.

It checks to ensure the correctness of the utterance against the knowledge in the learned system.

3.3.2. Natural Order Hypothesis

This hypothesis states that elements of language (or language rules) are acquired in a predictable order. The order is the same regardless of instruction. The natural order was determined by a synthesis of the results of the morpheme order studies (see Gass & Selinker, 1994; Larsen-Freeman & Long, 1991, for summary) and is a result of the acquired system, without interference from the learned system.

3.3.3. Monitor Hypothesis

As mentioned earlier, only the acquired system is responsible for initiating speech. The learned system has a special function—to serve as a Monitor and, hence, to alter the output of the acquired system. However, the Monitor cannot be used at all times. There are three conditions that must be met, although Krashen claimed that while these are necessary conditions, they are not necessarily sufficient. The Monitor may not be activated even when all three conditions have been satisfied.

The three conditions for Monitor use are time, form, and rule knowledge. Learners need time to think about and use the rules available to them in their learned system. Although time may be basic, one must also be focused on form. A learner must be paying attention to how we are saying something, not just to what we are saying. Finally, in order to apply a rule, one has to know it. In other words, one has to have an appropriate learned system in order to apply it. Thus, the Monitor is intended to link the acquired and learned systems in a situation of language use. The time factor was eliminated after a study by Hulstijn and Hulstijn (1984) found that time without a focus on form did not lead learners to attend to correctness.

3.3.4. Input Hypothesis

The input hypothesis is central to Krashen's overall sketch of acquisition and is a supplement to the natural order hypothesis. If there is a natural order of acquisition, how is it that learners move from one point to another? In Krashen's view, the input hypothesis provides the answer. Second languages are acquired "by understanding messages, or by receiving 'comprehensible input'" (Krashen, 1985, p. 2).

Krashen defined *comprehensible input* in a particular way. Essentially, comprehensible input is that bit of language that is heard or read and that contains language slightly ahead of a learner's current state of grammatical knowledge. Language containing structures that a learner already knows essentially serves no purpose in acquisition. Similarly, language containing structures that are way ahead of a learner's current knowledge is not useful. A learner does not have the ability to do anything with those structures. Krashen (1985)defined a learner's current state of knowledge as i and the next stage as $i + 1$. Thus, the input to which a learner is exposed must be at the $i + 1$ level in order to be of use in terms of acquisition. "We move from i, our current level to $i + 1$, the next level along the natural order, by understanding input containing $i + 1$" (p. 2).

Krashen assumed a language acquisition device, that is, an innate mental structure capable of handling both first and second language acquisition. The input activates this innate structure, but only input of a very specific kind ($i + 1$) will be useful in altering a learner's grammar.

In Krashen's view, the input hypothesis is central to all of acquisition and also has implications for the classroom.

a) Speaking is a result of acquisition and not its cause. Speech cannot be taught directly but 'emerges' on its own as a result of building competence via comprehensible input.

b) If input is understood, and there is enough of it, the necessary grammar is automatically provided. The language teacher need not attempt deliberately to teach the next structure along the natural order—it will be provided in just the right quantities and automatically reviewed if the student receives a sufficient amount of comprehensible input. (Krashen, 1985, p. 2)

This leaves little for a teacher to do other than ensure that the students receive comprehensible input.

3.3.5. Affective Filter Hypothesis

It is well known that not everyone is successful in learning second languages. How can this be explained? In Krashen's view, one way would be to claim that they had not received comprehensible input in sufficient quantities; another would be to claim that an inappropriate affect was to blame. Affect here is intended to include things such as motivation, attitude, self-confidence, or anxiety. Krashen thus proposed an affective filter. If the filter is up, input is prevented from passing through; if input is prevented from passing through, there can be no acquisition. If, on the other hand, the filter is down or low, and if the input is comprehensible, the input will reach the acquisition device and acquisition will take place. The affective filter is responsible for individual variation in second language acquisition and differentiates child language from second language acquisition because the affective filter is not something that children have or use.

The affective filter hypothesis captures the relations between affective variables and the process of second language acquisition by positing that acquirers differ with respect to the strength or level of their affective filters. Those whose attitudes are not optimal for second language acquisition will not only tend to seek less input, but they will also have a high or strong affective filter—even if they understand the message, the input will not reach that part of the brain responsible for language acquisition. Those with attitudes more conducive to second language acquisition will not only seek and obtain more input, but they will also have a lower or weaker filter. They will be more open to the input, and it will strike "deeper" (Krashen, 1982, p. 31)

The affective filter hypothesis accounts for the failure of second language acquisition in one of two ways, insufficient input of the right sort or high affective filter.

Krashen also said (1982, p. 33), "In order to acquire, two conditions are necessary. The first is comprehensible (or even better comprehend*ed*) input containing $i + 1$, . . . and second, a low or weak affective filter to allow the input 'in.' " This is equivalent to saying that comprehensible input and the strength of the filter are the true causes of second language acquisition. In a later version Krashen (1985) stated

> We can summarize the five hypotheses with a single claim: People acquire second languages only if they obtain comprehensible input and if their affective filters are low enough to allow the input "in." When the filter is "down" and appropriate comprehensible input is presented (and comprehended), acquisition is inevitable. (p. 4)

In sum, according to Krashen, acquisition can be accounted for by two of the five hypotheses, the input hypothesis and the affective filter hypothesis, in addition to the acquisition device. Comprehensible input and a low affective filter are necessary and sufficient conditions. Clearly, we are not much further ahead; we are only told that if learners have low affective filters (e.g., a willingness to learn) and understand the input, learning will be automatic. We still know little about the mechanisms of learning. How does input get converted to intake?

I do not detail the criticisms of Krashen's model except to point out that understood input may be less beneficial than may at first appear. For example, White (1987) argued not against the input hypothesis per se but against Krashen's formulation of it. She made a number of arguments about the imprecision of Krashen's claims, but the one that I focus on here is the argument that there are times when specific negative evidence will be necessary.

> the role of correction or grammar teaching would not be merely to improve the monitoring abilities of the learner. Thus, for example, it might help the

learner to acquire the English adverbial system or the correct use of subject pronouns, if he or she is explicitly told that adverbs cannot go between verb and object, or that subjects are required in English. In these cases, where there are 'gaps' in the L2 input, it is unfortunately not enough to supply the correct form: One may actually have to draw the learner's attention to the gap. (p. 107)

To this I add that conversational interactions indeed serve a similar purpose. It is where the input is incomprehensible and where one interlocutor seeks clarification or confirmation that we can begin to consider how conversations may serve as negative evidence. This is the subject of chapter 5.

NOTES

1. In some sense the distinction between *input* and *interaction* is an artificial one because interaction is a form of input. The separation of these two topics into two different chapters is done not out of any belief that the distinction is real or rigid but out of the necessity of chunking words in a book into more manageable units, known as chapters.
2. A caveat is in order. It is often difficult to compare studies from culture to culture because the person(s) primarily responsible for child care may differ. In most studies of child language acquisition in industrialized societies, investigations centered on dyadic conversations (usually mother and child). In other cultures, it is frequently the case that children spend significant amounts of time with people other than parents (cf. Bavin, 1992; Nwokah, 1987; Ochs, 1985; Schieffelin, 1985).
3. Schieffelin (1985) reported that there is some restricted talk to children in the 6–12 month range. This is generally limited to imperatives, rhetorical questions, and greetings, none of which require a response. For example, Schieffelin cited the example of a rhetorical question such as, "Is it yours?" (meaning "it is not yours!"). These are used as negative comments when children reach for something they should not have. The only necessary response is the cessation of the action.
4. This is used to teach the social and pragmatic uses of language (e.g., teasing, shaming, requesting, challenging, reporting).
5. In the following section I take up this issue with regard to second language acquisition, where it is clear that the input fluctuates depending on the (perceived) level of proficiency or understanding of the learner.
6. Brown (1977) similarly pointed to a double role for child-directed speech: It facilitates comprehension, and it directs the child's attention to language, or certain parts of language.
7. The extent to which this role of questions is related to a certain socioeconomic class is in question (cf. Heath, 1983).
8. These categories of analysis are based on Farrar's (1992) study. The categories in his earlier study (1990) are slightly but not substantially different.
9. The desire to make a conversation run smoothly is particularly obvious when dealing with NNSs. This is illustrated by the frequent use of topic changes in discourse with non-natives, as in the following example (see also chapter 5, this volume).

   From Butterworth (1972), cited in Hatch (1983)
   NS: Who is the best player in Colombia?
   NNS: Colombia?
   NS: Does uh . . . who is *the* Colombian player?

    NNS: Me?
    NS: No, in Colombia, who is *the* player?
    NNS: In Colombia plays. Yah.
    NS: No, on your team. On the Millionarios.
    NNS: Ah yah, Millionarios.
    NS: No, on the Millionarios team.
    NNS: Millionarios play in Colombia. In Sud America. In Europa.
    NS: Do, do they have someone like Pele in Colombia?
    NNS: Pele? In Colombia? Pele?
    NS: In Colombia? Who is, who is Pele in Colombia? Do you have someone?
    NNS: In Bogota?
    NS: Yeah, who is the best player?
    NNS: In Santo de Brazil?
    NS: OK (gives up), and you are center forward?

The difficulty of engaging in conversations with nonfluent speakers has been noted anecdotally in my own collaborative work with Evangeline Varonis. In one instance, an American student informed the authors that if she saw a NNS friend at a time she was feeling tired, she would walk the other way so as to avoid what was likely to be a tiring conversation. In another situation in which the authors were faking a non-native accent and were asking for directions in a midwestern university town, one woman waved them away, indicating no desire to engage in a conversation with them. This situation can, of course, be used to one's advantage. On those occasions in which I have received obscene phone calls, I use this knowledge and start feigning a non-native accent: "What, you vant what? I don't understand; please speak more slowly." Inevitably, the caller hangs up, and on one occasion a caller even apologized. This can be used very effectively with annoying sales calls as well. And they say that there are no practical implications for second language acquisition research!

Chapter 4

Input and Second Language Acquisition Theories

4.0. INTRODUCTION

As discussed throughout the earlier chapters, not all input is created equal. Nonetheless, it is an incontrovertible fact that some sort of input is essential for language learning; clearly, languages are not and cannot be learned in a vacuum. What is controversial is the type and perhaps amount of input necessary for second language development and what additional information might also be necessary for the development of second language knowledge. Many ways of looking at second language acquisition are available in the short tradition of our field; each point of view looks at input from a slightly different angle and through a slightly different pair of glasses.

In this chapter, I consider diverse models of second language acquisition and the ways in which they conceptualize the role of input in learning. In so doing, I focus on four current (or at least major) approaches to second language acquisition, all of which treat input in a slightly different way: the input–interaction position (see chapters 3 and 5); the input hypothesis (see chapter 3); the UG approach (see chapter 2) and an information-processing perspective (see chapter 2, McLaughlin, 1987; and McLaughlin, Rossman, & McLeod, 1983). In the second part of this chapter I consider how input might differentially affect different kinds of linguistic information and how learners with different linguistic backgrounds might be differentially affected by the same input.

4.1. INPUT–INTERACTION PERSPECTIVE

As I argue in chapter 5, a crucial portion of the learning picture comes from the input–interaction perspective. Within this framework, the input to the learner coupled with the learner's manipulation of the input through interaction forms a basis of language development. With regard to input, there are two aspects to consider, the functions of simplified input in terms of language learning and the relation between simplifying speech and comprehension (see chapter 3). It is a given that without understanding, no learning can take place. Although understanding alone does not guarantee learning, it does set the scene for potential learning. With regard to comprehension, however, one must recognize that not all types of modified input are equally worthwhile. For example, Parker and Chaudron (1987) reviewed the literature and showed that simplifications resulting from discourse elaboration or modification of the conversational structure are more likely to result in comprehension than those simplifications at the linguistic level. This and other studies are reviewed by Yano, Long, and Ross (1994). In their study of comprehension of simplified versus elaborated texts, they argued that elaboration of input provides learners with information necessary for comprehension but has the added advantage of providing the "rich linguistic form [learners] need for further language learning" (p. 214). The main point concerns interaction. Through negotiation of meaning, learners gain additional information about the language and focus their attention on particular parts of the language. This attention primes language for integration into a developing interlinguistic system.

4.2. THE INPUT HYPOTHESIS

A second framework within which input plays a dominant role is the input hypothesis, developed by Krashen (1980, 1982, 1985) as part of the Monitor model (see chapter 3). He took a position slightly modified from the one just presented. In his view, acquisition takes place by means of a learner's access to comprehensible input. That is, only a certain portion of the input is useful for the development of linguistic knowledge: the input at an $i + 1$ level, or a little bit beyond the learner's current system. This is, of course, a simplification of Krashen's position as presented in chapter 3. The main points are that the input assumes a central role in his model of how second language acquisition takes place and that only a certain type of input is relevant.

4.3. UNIVERSAL GRAMMAR

Yet another position regarding the role of input comes from the Chomskyan school of linguistics (cf. chapter 2; Cook, 1988; White, 1989b, for detailed presentations of this position). This position is the most theoretically developed position and, hence, the easiest to test. As discussed in chapter 2, in this view learners start with what is known as UG. The theory underlying UG assumes that language consists of a set of abstract principles that characterize core grammars of all natural languages. If children have to learn a complex set of abstractions, there must be something in addition to the language input to which they are exposed in order for them to learn the target language with relative ease and speed. Univeral Grammar is postulated as an innate language faculty that specifies the limits of a possible language. The task for learning is greatly reduced if one is equipped with a set of innate structures that constrain possible grammar formation. Certain kinds of linguistic systems are ruled out a priori. (See chapter 2 for an extended discussion of the theoretical need for an innate language faculty.)

In chapter 2 the role of adverb placement (see section 2.1) in relation to acquisition was outlined. An even more complex problem exists in second language acquisition because not only is the input impoverished for first language acquisition, but also learners are influenced by their first language or other languages known (Trahey & White, 1993; White, 1991). To take a hypothetical example from SLA data, consider the following sentences from Italian.

1. Giovanni beve   lentamente il   caffè.
   John   drinks slowly   the coffee.
2. Lentamente Giovanni beve   il   caffè.
   Slowly   John   drinks the coffee.
3. Giovanni lentamente beve   il   caffè.
   John   slowly   drinks the coffee.
4. Giovanni beve   il   caffè lentamente.
   John   drinks the coffee slowly.

Italian, like French and many other languages, differs from English in the possible placement of adverbs. In English, adverb placement is more constrained. The English translation equivalents of Examples 2, 3, and 4 are possible, but Example 1 is not. For an Italian speaker learning English with no explicit pedagogical intervention, there is little from the input to inform our learner that Example 1 is not possible in English. The learner hears only sentence types 2, 3, and 4. There is no way of knowing that not hearing sentence 1 is not an accidental nonoccurrence as opposed to an overt indication of ungrammaticality. This is an important piece of information that we come to know about language, so the question is how we come to know it. A learning principle predicts that the learner's first choice is to assume a smaller grammar, that is, the grammar that is a subset of other possible grammars[1]; see Fig. 4.1. Thus, given a choice, a learner (either a child or an adult) will (unconsciously, of course) assume that the grammar that allows the more limited set of sentences is the correct one.

For English speakers learning Italian, if learners select the more restricted grammar (i.e., the English type), the evidence from the input alone (i.e., the full range of possible Italian sentences) would immediately allow these

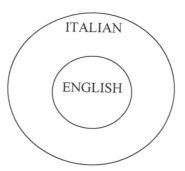

FIG. 4.1. Superset–subset relationship.

learners to modify their hypothesis because sentences in the superset would be heard. On the other hand, an Italian speaker learning English who assumes that Italian is like English will need explicit correction or instruction to change from an Italian adverb placement grammar to the English one. If a learner assumes the grammar from his or her native language, as in these instances, then the only way to come up with the correct English grammar is through some sort of intervention. The important point is that the input alone will not be sufficient.

There are other aspects of UG that are important to this discussion, such as the area of parameters. Recall from the discussion in chapter 2 that parameters represent clusters of properties. That is, if one is learned, they are all learned. Thus, in consideration of a parameter that assumes a clustering of grammatical structures, the input serves only as a catalyst to trigger certain changes in the learner's grammar. One could be exposed to input exemplifying one of the structures, and if the structures really stick together, the others will be learned as a consequence of learning the first, even in the absence of direct input. Even though no one has attempted to quantify how much input is needed for change to come about, theoretically only one instance is needed for parameters to be reset or for a change in the core parts of one's grammar to occur.

What is the role of correction, or interaction as a possible form of correction, in this view? Recall from chapter 2 that the assumption is that feedback or correction is not forthcoming. The counterargument is that direct (or indirect) intervention is indeed forthcoming and that one does not need innateness to explain language acquisition. This, of course, is an empirical issue and one that is in dispute, as was discussed in chapter 2 with regard to arguments presented by Bohannon and Stanowicz (1988) for first language acquisition. However, even if correction does exist and does exist with some frequency, it often provides information about the ungrammatical (or inappropriate) utterance but does not tell a learner what needs to be done to modify a current hypothesis. Furthermore, as every teacher knows, even with explicit correction, learners' grammars are often impervious to change.

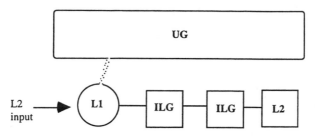

FIG. 4.2. The L2 initial state = the L1 final state (and UG has withered away). From *Proceedings of the Boston Conference on Language Development* (p. 4), by L. White, 1996, Sommerville, MA: Cascadilla Press. Copyright 1996 by Lydia White. Reprinted with permission.

However, the UG position is not a uniform one. White (1996b) pointed out that there are four current positions with regard to UG and, for the purposes of this chapter, with regard to the relation between input and UG.

One position maintains that the initial state of L2 is actually the final state of L1; that is, UG has atrophied, disappeared, or whatever metaphor one wants to use. This position was articulated by Bley-Vroman (1990) Schachter (1988), and Tsimpli and Roussou (1991), among others. White (1996b) argued that input plays the role shown in Fig. 4.2. The input feeds directly into the L2 system, which initially is essentially the L1 system. For learners who know more than one language, the system is clearly more complex with the L2 input feeding into L1, L2, L3, and so on.

A second position also assumes that the starting point for L2 acquisition is the final state of L1, but unlike the previous position, it assumes the availability of UG (e.g., Schwartz, in press; Schwartz & Sprouse, 1994; White, 1985, 1986, 1989a). Here the learner uses the L1 grammar as a basis but has full access to UG when L1 is deemed insufficient for the learning task at hand. As shown in White's diagram (see Fig. 4.3), this differs from the first position in that there is a direct line to UG and the L2 input feeds into both the initial state system (= L1) and UG.

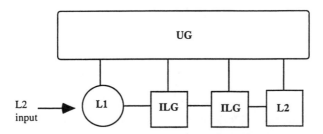

FIG. 4.3. The L2 initial state = the L1 final state (and UG is still available). From *Proceedings of the Boston Conference on Language Development* (p. 4), by L. White, 1996, Sommerville, MA: Cascadilla Press. Copyright 1996 by Lydia White. Reprinted with permission.

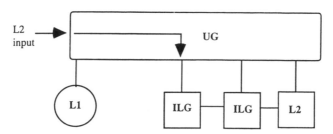

FIG. 4.4. The L2 initial state = the L2 initial state = UG. From *Proceedings of the Boston Conference on Language Development* (p. 5), by L. White, 1996, Sommerville, MA: Cascadilla Press. Copyright 1996 by Lydia White. Reprinted with permission.

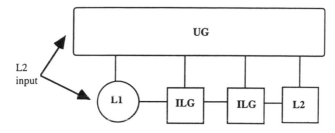

FIG. 4.5. Mixed positions. From *Proceedings of the Boston Conference on Language Development* (p. 6), by L. White, 1996, Sommerville, MA: Cascadilla Press. Copyright 1996 by Lydia White. Reprinted with permission.

A third position (see Fig. 4.4) maintains that the initial state of L2 is the same as the initial state for L1, that is, UG (see Epstein, Flynn, & Martohardjono, in press-a, in press-b). The input is mediated through UG and not through the L1, as in the previous two positions. Thus, UG serves as a filter through which the L2 input passes.

There is yet a fourth position (see Fig. 4.5), the compromise position. The L2 initial state is affected by both UG and L1. Certain aspects of the initial state are based on UG, and other aspects are based on the L1 (see Eubank, 1994a, 1994b; Vainikka & Young-Scholten, 1994; and White, 1996a). This model essentially has two filters, UG and L1.

4.4. INFORMATION PROCESSING

The fourth perspective to be discussed comes from the psycholinguistic literature and in particular the literature dealing with information processing. This position begins with the assumption that the human mind has a limited capacity for processing information. In one view, developed within a second language context by McLaughlin and his colleagues (cf. McLaughlin, 1990b), there are two dimensions of import for understanding language processing. One is automatic processing; the other is controlled processing. McLaughlin (1987) distinguished the two processes in the following way:

> *Automatic processing* involves the activation of certain nodes in memory every time the appropriate inputs are present. This activation is a learned response that has been built up through the consistent mapping of the same input to the same pattern of activation over many trials. Since an automatic process utilizes a relatively permanent set of associative connections in long-term storage, most automatic processes require an appreciable amount of training to develop fully. Once learned, an automatic process occurs rapidly and is difficult to suppress or alter. (McLaughlin, 1987, p. 134)

> *Controlled processing* is not a learned response, but a temporary activation of nodes in a sequence. This activation is under attentional control of the subject and, since attention is required, only one such sequence can normally be controlled at a time without interference. Controlled processes are thus tightly capacity-limited, and require more time for their activation. But controlled processes have the advantage of being relatively easy to set up, alter, and apply to novel situations. (McLaughlin, 1987, p. 135)

One can move from controlled processing to automatic processing through repeated performance. That is, a particular task that initially requires a significant amount of control and processing capacity (e.g., when one initially learns to drive a car) becomes through repeated trials so automatic that little attention and little processing capacity is involved.

In an information-processing account of second language acquisition, learners interact with the input as they focus attention on those parts of the input that have not been automatized. Thus, attentional demands are crucial in this framework. An underlying assumption is that in order to learn, a learner must first notice that there is something to be learned; that is, they must notice a gap between their interlanguage system and the target language system. This is done by drawing learners' attention to those parts of the input that do not coincide with their own internalized grammars (see Ellis, 1994; Faerch & Kasper, 1986; Sharwood Smith, 1986.

Yet another psycholinguistic model that has had some significance in the recent second language literature is the competition model (see chapter 2). Within this framework, the input also assumes an unspecified important role, serving both as evidence for hypotheses and as evidence against hypotheses.

I have presented a brief overview (see Table 4.1) of some of the characteristics of input and the function that input might have within different approaches to second language acquisition. To recap, the input–interaction framework attributes great importance to the input, but it does not differentiate among linguistic features. That is, input is input. Krashen's model also attributes a major role for input and specifies which input is important

TABLE 4.1
Overview of the Role of Input

	Input Is Specific	*Which Input?*	*How Important?*
Input/Interaction	No	All	Very
Krashen	Yes	Comprehensible Input	Very
UG	Yes	Parameters	Depends
Information Processing	No	All	Very

(comprehensible input), but the model does not say how we can determine which input is of value. In other words, although Krashen claimed that i + 1 is, needed, we have little way of being precise about what exactly level i is and hence we cannot determine what $i + 1$ is. The UG position attributes the least importance to input because from this framework input only serves as a catalyst or trigger for innate properties, but it is the most specific as to what kind of input is necessary. Finally, in the information-processing perspective, input serves the function of automatizing controlled knowledge and providing information necessary for restructuring. This is more an issue of quantity of input than of quality.

4.5. LEARNERS AND THE SELECTION OF INPUT

Most of the positions discussed in the preceding section fall in the middle portions of the model presented in chapter 1 (Fig. 1.1). That is, they are positions that operate independently of any specific learner. However, individual characteristics need to be taken into account when dealing with input. The question remains: What about the learners themselves and their role in the selection of input? Input selection is determined by the learner (in both the input–interaction and the information-processing perspectives) but is determined by linguistic facts in Krashen's model and the UG model.

There is yet another factor to consider in a discussion of input. Beebe (1985) argued that

> studies of input in second language acquisition must view non-native speakers not simply as passive recipients of comprehensible or incomprehensible input from native speakers, but as active participants in choosing the target language models they prefer and thus acquiring "the right stuff" according to their values. In other words, learners have "input preferences" (or "model preferences") in the sense that they consciously or unconsciously choose to attend to some target language models rather than others. (p. 404)

What does it mean to say that there are model preferences? Beebe intended this to mean the kinds of people who are providing the input. For example, is the input coming from friends or from nonfriends? Is it coming from a high-prestige group or a low-prestige group? Is it coming from teachers or from peers? Is it coming from NSs or NNSs? Is it coming from one's own social group or from another social group? She concluded that these are important considerations in understanding what input is even attended to. In her view, one must understand the feelings or motivations behind the preferences for or rejections of certain linguistic models. As she noted, this is a complex notion because the literature amply documents polar opposites of preferences. There are some, for example, who attend to input of their own social group, and there are others who attend to input from outside of their own social group. Such concepts as solidarity, ethnocentrism, feelings of identification, loyalty, social identity, and intergroup dynamics, as she pointed out, all deal with the concept of membership, and all have been shown to affect second language acquisition in one way or another (cf. Preston, 1989). The study of these sociolinguistic factors, however, has been largely in the domain of output. That is, how do these factors affect what a person produces? Assuming the correctness of Beebe's (1985) position, that learners accept input on the basis of some of these factors, then the study of these factors must take place much earlier in the process, that is, in relation to the input.

This view is clearly antithetical to the position that those advocating a UG framework take, or, if not antithetical, at least theoretically uninteresting because although it may be true that these factors are relevant, what is crucial to their theory is what type of input is necessary to trigger linguistic change or grammar modification. It is irrelevant to consider the person providing the input.

4.6. INPUT AND LINGUISTIC INFORMATION

It is generally assumed that input is equally relevant and equally valid for all areas of linguistic information. That is, equal importance is given to input in the sorting out of semantics, in learning the grammar of a language, and in learning the meanings of lexical items. However, certain parts of language are difficult to learn even with significant exposure to the language, whereas other parts are easier to learn (see chapter 3, this volume). For example, Olshtain and Cohen (1989) gave the following anecdote:

> One morning, Mrs. G, a native speaker of English now living in Israel, was doing her daily shopping at the local supermarket. As she was pushing her shopping cart she unintentionally bumped into Mr. Y, a native Israeli. Her natural reaction was to say "I'm sorry" (in Hebrew). Mr. Y turned to her and said, "Lady, you could at least apologize."

> On another occasion the very same Mr. Y arrived late for a meeting conducted by Mr. W (a native speaker of English) in English. As he walked

into the room he said, "The bus was late," and sat down. Mr. W, obviously annoyed, muttered to himself, "These Iraelis, why don't they ever apologize!" (p. 53)

Blum-Kulka and Olshtain (1986) also reported that after many years of living in a target language situation, certain pragmatic features (in their case, the amount of talk in speech acts) remain non-native-like. Thus, pragmatic knowledge is learned late (if ever). Another example underscores this point.

> An administrative officer of an English language program had telephoned the university dormitory to straighten out a problem that the English language students were having. The dormitory employee was a fluent non-native speaker. After a pleasant conversation the dormitory employee attempted to transfer the call to another individual. There were many clicks after which the employee realized that the English language program employee was still on the phone and said:
> Oh, it's still you!
> The English language program employee's instinctive reaction was "What did I do wrong?" He was somewhat offended at what initially seemed to him a comment that reflected the other's annoyance at what he had taken to be a pleasant conversation.

It appears that subtleties of pragmatics had not been learned despite (unless she really was annoyed with him) the fact that all other aspects of language appeared to have been. Thus, the input for a fluent non-native speaker appears to be sufficient for grammatical development but not, as these cases suggest, for pragmatic development. Additionally, reports such as that by Coppieters (1987) suggest that even with grammatical fluency and native-like abilities, linguistic intuitions are not native-like (but see Birdsong, 1992, for a different interpretation of similar data).

In most discussions concerning input, the amount of control that learners have over the learning process is not generally considered. In chapter 1 I differentiated between factors that are under the learner's control and factors that are not. Such aspects as personality and affect, under the learner's control to the greatest extent, are important for input. Their role is less significant at the levels of intake and grammatical restructuring, areas affected by pure linguistic and psycholinguistic factors devoid of cultural and social context. Finally, personality and affect once again emerge as important factors at the level of output. In other words, factors that are under learner's control to the greatest extent have the greatest effect only for initial input and for output. Importantly, the amount of control over what becomes relevant information for learners varies from individual to individual. Furthermore, the input that is necessary for grammar development varies according to different characteristics of language and individual learners' knowledge of language. To illustrate these differences I focus on the input necessary for different parts of one's grammar (section 4.6.1) and input requirements for different types of learners (section 4.6.2).

4.6.1. Input and Syntax/Semantics

Sorace (1993a, 1993b; 1995; Bard, Robertson, & Sorace, 1996) argued that two kinds of changes occur in learners' grammars, discontinuous and continuous. She considered in particular two kinds of verbs in Italian, verbs such as *andare* and *venire*, which mean "to go" and "to come," respectively, and verbs such as *camminare*, which means "to walk." Both *andare* and *venire* are intransitive verbs that require *essere* ("to be") as an auxiliary, whereas *camminare*, also an intransitive verb, requires *avere* ("to have"). She was particularly interested in how learners of Italian learn the appropriate auxiliary to use with these two types of verbs. That is, do they use the auxiliary *essere* or the auxiliary *avere*? Auxiliary choice is dependent on both syntactic and semantic factors. Some verbs are sensitive to both lexical–semantic distinctions as well as syntactic configurations. For example, there is a hierarchy such that verbs that take *essere* are most likely to be those that represent a change in location (i.e., "to come" or "to go"). Next on the hierarchy are those verbs that represent a change in condition (as for example, the verb *crescere*, "to grow"). Even less likely to use *essere* are those that represent a continuation of a condition (as *durare*, "to last," or *sopravvivere*, "to survive"). Finally, and least likely to require *essere*, are those verbs that express existence of a condition (as *essere* or *esistere*, "to exist"); see Table 4.2. Other choices are dependent on syntactic configurations. That is, it is truly the syntactic structure that dictates the auxiliary to be used. As an example, consider the following examples, which include obligatory AUX change with clitic-climbing.

> 6. Ho   dovuto andare.
>   have (I) had   to go.
>   'I had to go'

> 7. Ci   sono   dovuto andare
>   clitic am (I) had   to go
>   'I had to go'

TABLE 4.2
Hierarchy of Auxiliary Choice

Most likely to take *essere*	
⇩ change in location	*andare* 'to come'/*venire* 'to go'
⇩ change in condition	*crescere* 'to grow'
⇩ continuation of a condition	*durare* 'to last/*sopravvivere* 'to survive'
⇩ existence of a condition	*essere* 'to be'/*esistere* 'to exist'
Least likely to take *essere*	

Once the clitic *ci* is part of the sentence, there is an obligatory change from *avere* to *essere* with no meaning difference. Hence, the choice of auxiliary is entirely dependent on the syntactic form.

What Sorace found in looking at data from learners of Italian was a differentiation in terms of input use with regard to auxiliary selection. They were sensitive to the input with regard to lexical semantic properties of auxiliary selection (regardless of their L1), but they appeared to be impervious to the input with respect to some of the syntactic properties. Lexical–semantic properties were acquired incrementally, whereas syntactic properties, if they were acquired at all, developed in a discontinuous fashion (A. Sorace, personal communication, January 25, 1993).

Thus, it is possible for the input, or in Sorace's terms, the evidence available to learners, to have a varying effect depending on the part of the grammar to be affected—more so for lexical semantics and less so for syntax.

4.6.2. Input and Amount of Linguistic Knowledge

The preceding section discussed how input differentially affected integration of linguistic knowledge. I now turn to learner-internal factors and their effect on the potential conversion of input to intake. In particular, I consider prior linguistic background knowledge, not in terms of specific languages known (i.e., language transfer) but in terms of the amount of linguistic knowledge learners have. Zobl (1992) argued for differential effects of input dependent not on different parts of the grammar but on the amount of linguistic knowledge that a learner brings to the language learning situation. Specifically, he looked at unilinguals versus multilinguals. Unilinguals are learners who know only one language (i.e., their native language) when they begin learning a second language, and multilinguals are learners who know their native language plus one or more other languages. In making this distinction, he noted that adults create wider grammars than the L2 input would warrant. Within the context of the role of the native language, he meant simply that transfer from the NL leads learners to produce utterances that are possible in L1 but not in L2. If adult second language learners formulate wider grammars than the input data would warrant due to the well-established phenomenon of language transfer, then the more languages that an individual has to draw on, the greater the possibilities will be that their grammars will be even wider.

There are two pieces of evidence that Zobl (1992) used to differentiate multilingual from unilingual second language learners. One is anecdotal, the other empirical. Anecdotally, Zobl referred to reports (Larsen-Freeman, 1983) that multilinguals generally pick up languages with greater ease than do unilinguals. Assuming that this is true, how can it be accounted for? One possible explanation is that multilinguals are less conservative in their learning procedures and hence progress at a faster pace. That is, the hypotheses they formulate on the basis of the input are likely to be more liberal and based upon more slender evidence. For example, for multilinguals, few exemplars might be necessary for the creation of a (correct or incorrect) hypothesis. This could, of course, depend on the specific languages known. Consider a hypothetical and idealized learner who knows Spanish and Italian. The learner is now in the situation of learning Portuguese and obtains input that suggests that Portuguese is a prodrop language (see chapter 3). Because that learner already knows two prodrop languages, it will take little evidence to suggest the reasonableness of the hypothesis for Portuguese. This learner could be compared to another learner of Portuguese, a NS of English who knows only English. It might take many more instances of prodrop input before that learner reaches the same prodrop hypothesis. Consider again the first learner, who, being a fast learner, now knows Spanish, Italian, and Portuguese. This learner now wants to learn English and hears sentences like "Wanna go?" This learner, knowing three prodrop languages, on very slender evidence may now assume (incorrectly) that English is also a prodrop language. Fodor and Crain (1987), in fact, argued that conservative learning procedures progress at a slower rate because they only allow hypotheses that fit the input data.

Zobl's (1992) empirical evidence for his claim came from multilinguals' and unilinguals' performance on a cloze test and on a grammaticality judgment test. The results were not as clear-cut as Zobl would have liked; however, they do lend some support to the notion that unilinguals and multilinguals formulate different hypotheses on the basis of (presumably) the same input.

Table 4.3 is a summary table of his results from the grammaticality judgment task. The multilinguals recognized the ungrammaticality of the

TABLE 4.3
Results From Zobl (1992)

		Narrower Grammar	Wider Grammar	Difference
I.	Verb–Object Adjacency			
	a) V NP Adv NP			
	"*A waitress brought the woman quickly a menu."	UL	ML	19.2
	b) V Adv NP			
	"*She drank quickly the coffee."	UL	ML	10.0
	c) V PP NP			
	"*The girl was sending to her boyfriend a letter."	UL	ML	5.5

(Continued)

TABLE 4.3
(Continued)

		Narrower Grammar	Wider Grammar	Difference
II.	Passive From V NP NP			
	a) V NP t			
	"Mary was shown the new toy."	ML	UL	(1.6)
	b) V t NP			
	"*The new toy was shown Mary."	UL	ML	33.3
III.	Wh-movement From V NP NP			
	a) V NP t			
	"What will the children show Mary?"	UL	ML	16.8
	b) V t NP			
	"*Who will the children show the new toy?"	UL	ML	11.4
IV.	Wh- and Passive Movement From V NP NP	UL	ML	16.8
V.	Antecedent–Reflexive Binding			
	"John talked to Mary about herself."	UL	ML	27.8
VI.	Backward Anaphora			
	"John saw her while the girl ate lunch."	ML	UL	(18.8)
VII.	Null Subject/Object			
	a) Null Subject			
	"*Mary would never stay out late because must get up early"	ML	UL	(3.3)
	b) Null Object			
	"*The man bought flowers and gave to his wife."	UL	ML	13.9
VIII.	Deletion in COMP			
	"*The people live next door are very helpful."	ML	UL	(10.0)
IX.	Superiority Condition			
	"*I forget what who said during the meeting."		ML	23.3
X.	Wh-movement With Exceptional Case Marking Verbs			
	"Who is he expecting to marry Susan?"	UL	ML	16.6
XI.	Long Wh-movement			
	a) That-Trace			
	"*Which glass did John say that breaks easily?"	UL	ML	2.2
	b) "Who does the teacher think will probably pass the exam?"	ML	UL	(4.1)
XII.	Picture-Noun Extraction			
	a) From VP			
	"Who did the artist sell a picture of?"	ML	UL	(11.0)
	b) Spec. Subj.			
	"Who do they admire the artist's painting of?"	ML	UL	(11.0)
	c) Subject Condition			
	"What do pictures of scare children?"	UL	ML	2.3

Note. Language Transfer in Language Learning edited by S. Gass and L. Selinker. John Benjamins Publishing Company. Amsterdam/Philadelphia, 1992. Reprinted with permission.

sentence types less frequently than the unilinguals. That is, their grammars appear to be less conservative than the unilinguals' grammars. Of the 20 structures tested, the results from 13 suggest that the unilinguals (the ULs) have narrower grammars than the multilinguals. Of the remaining 7 structures, the differences on 6 can be accounted for by looking at the groups of subjects who did versus those who did not know Chinese. In general, there is some support, albeit not statistically significant, for the fact that multilinguals have wider grammars.

In relating this to input, one must also consider what type of evidence is necessary for a learner to recognize that certain sentences are indeed ungrammatical in English. In many instances, the input is not sufficient to make a learner aware that these sentences are ungrammatical in English, for the learner only hears grammatical sentences.[2] There is no way for learners to know a priori why they have not heard ungrammatical sentences. One possibility is that the sentences are ungrammatical and therefore not available through the input, but another possibility is that the learner just hasn't heard the sentences and that it is a matter of time before these sentences surface in the input. The only way to change one's grammar is through negative evidence. It is clear that both groups of Zobl's learners need negative evidence, but the claim I make is that the two groups will differ in how they respond to the input. That is (and this may depend on the languages the learners know), there may be more converging information for multilinguals than for unilinguals, leading multilinguals to believe that sentences that are ungrammatical in English are actually grammatical. It would therefore take at least more frequent and direct negative evidence to disabuse multilinguals of their faulty hypotheses. I return to this notion in the Epilogue in the discussion of classroom implications.

4.7. WHEN AND WHAT DO LEARNERS NEED?

The final point to consider in a discussion of input is what learners need and when they need it. Not all of the positions considered here are explicit on this point. Krashen was perhaps the most explicit in stating that the only relevant input is input at the $i + 1$ level. However, he gave us little indication of how we can know whether specific input is indeed at the $i + 1$ level or at the $i + 23$ level.

The information-processing perspective provides no greater help because there is no theoretical determination of when input will or will not be utilized. However, all input is potentially important for building up through experience the automatic processes necessary to deal with fluent language. Gass (1988a) and Schmidt (1990) argued that noticing features in the input is important (or in Schmidt's work, essential) to grammar change (see also Tomlin & Villa, 1994). Although both suggested features that might lead input to be noticed, neither study was explicit in stating when input will or will not be noticed. I argue, however, that it is impossible to make this determination on the basis of linguistic information alone. Rather, the determination can only come by viewing the learners as they interact with the input.

The input–interaction view must take the position that noticing is crucial. In negotiation the learner is focusing on linguistic form, and that focus, or specific attention paid to linguistic form, is the first step toward grammar change.

The UG position is in some ways clearer about when and what sort of input is necessary. With regard to adverb placement, reduction of one's grammar from a superset to a subset position can only take place with negative evidence or explicit correction. That is, when dealing with superset–subset relations, input is only useful in those instances when a learner is moving from a subset to a superset.

I have reviewed the role of input within various frameworks and have shown that they make different predictions about input. Some emphasize the quantitative aspect (such as the information-processing view), whereas others, such as the UG perspective and perhaps Krashen's model, emphasize qualitative aspects of the input. I have also shown how sociolinguistic factors, linguistic factors, and psycholinguistic factors all feed into an understanding of input.

We are all familiar with ways in which the same event can be interpreted very differently depending on the perspective that one brings to the interpretation. This is illustrated by the following story based on the many disputations between Jews and Christians in Medieval Europe (Novak & Waldoks, 1981, pp. 88–89).

In a small town during the Middle Ages, there lived a priest who hated the Jews. As was the common occurrence, the priest announced that there would be a disputation between the Jews and the Catholics. But this disputation was not merely for the sake of God and truth, for if the Jews lost, they would be banished from the town. If they won, they would be allowed to remain in peace.

The debate, the priest announced, would take place in one week's time and would be conducted entirely in sign language, so as to avoid the loud shouting matches that were typical of these disputations. The Jews were to appoint a member of their community to debate against the priest, who would, of course, represent the Catholics.

The Jews in the town were greatly distressed. Even the rabbi was reluctant to debate against the priest, for although he was a learned man, what did he know of sign language?

In the entire community only one man stood willing to debate against the priest, and that was Yankele the poultry dealer. "Are you a fool?" his wife asked. "What do you know of theological matters? Wiser men than you have declined this dubious honor."

"My dear woman," replied Yankele, "there is simply no choice. Who else is willing to perform this task? And if nobody comes forward, we will be banished at once."

On the afternoon of the disputation, the entire town gathered in the marketplace. The Catholics stood on one side, the Jews on the other. In the middle of the town square stood the priest, with Yankele beside him.

Finally, the disputation began. The priest stepped forward and in the air he drew a large, lofty circle. When he had finished, Yankele stepped forward and stamped his foot on the ground. The priest looked worried, and the Catholics, noting the priest's worried look, began to murmur that all was not well.

A moment later, the priest had recovered his calm, and mumbling a few words to himself, stepped forward and held three fingers in the air. Yankele then stepped forward and held up his middle finger.

Once again, looking disturbed, the priest hesitated. Then he fumbled in his garments and drew out a chalice of wine and a loaf of bread. He bit off a piece of bread from the loaf, took a sip of wine from the cup, and then stepped back, smug and satisfied.

When he had finished, Yankele stepped forward. In his hand was an apple, and he took a big bite from it. At this point the priest threw up his arms in despair. "I give up," he cried. "Let the Jews live here in peace!"

There was great rejoicing among the Jews, and great amazement and consternation among the Catholics, who crowded around their leader. "O Holy Father," they said, "tell us the meaning of these symbols."

"My children," said the priest, "I began by describing an arc, reminding the Jew that God is everywhere. Then he stamped on the ground, reminding me that God was right here. Then I raised three fingers to indicate the Holy Trinity; he raised one finger to show that God was One and indivisible. Finally, I took out the holy bread of eternal life and the cup of everlasting salvation, representing the body and the blood of our Savior. But then the Jew brought out the apple, reminding me of original sin, and I knew that our argument had ended. It was over, he had won. I had to keep to my promise and let the Jews remain here in peace."

Meanwhile, on the other side of town, Yankele was surrounded by a delirious mob. "You are truly a great and wise man," the rabbi said. "And now tell us the meaning of what we have witnessed."

"Certainly," said Yankele. "First the priest pointed far away, meaning that the Jews had to leave this town and find another place to live. No, I replied stepping on the ground, we were going to stay right here! Then he tried to tell me that we had three days in which to leave; I held up one finger, meaning that he could get screwed because not a single one of us was leaving. Finally, he gave up, because he took out his lunch—and so I took out mine!"

And so too with input. How we view its importance depends on our own theoretical orientation. Is it the major contributing factor to learning, or does it represent only the yeast that makes the dough rise, resulting eventually in a loaf of bread?

NOTES

1. I provided this example to show how such principles might operate in second language acquisition. It is imperative to note that the status of principles in second language acquisition research is far from clear. There is substantial evidence that principles, hypothesized as necessary for L1 learning, do not operate in an L2 context (see Broselow & Finer, 1991; Hirakawa, 1990; White, 1989b). If learners do not have access to the subset principle, for example, then the only way of disabusing a learner of the faulty hypothesis that sentence 1 is possible in English or retreating from an overgeneralized grammar is through some sort of explicit intervention (e.g., correction, overt explanation).
2. This assumes an ideal situation in which learners hear only grammatical sentences, "junky" (i.e., ungrammatical input) data being nonexistent. But, of course, life is not ideal.

Chapter 5

The Role of Interaction[1]

5.0. INTRODUCTION

The notion of *miscommunication* conjures up negative images—images of basic information exchange gone awry. It is the premise of this chapter that certain types of miscommunication, notably those that require conversational negotiation either of meaning or of form, are beneficial from the standpoint of learning.

Even though the importance of conversation to second language acquisition has long been recognized, only recently has it been the major focus of analysis. An earlier view of acquisition held that learners learned grammatical rules and then practiced these rules within a conversational setting; classroom drills, classroom interactions, daily interactions with native speakers, and so forth were considered only as a means of reinforcing the grammatical rules somehow acquired by a learner. Beginning more than two decades ago with work by Wagner-Gough and Hatch (1975) and developed in the following years by many researchers (see, for example, Gass & Varonis, 1985b, 1989; Long, 1980, 1981, 1983a; Pica, 1987, 1988; Pica & Doughty, 1985; Pica, Doughty, & Young, 1986; Pica, Young, & Doughty, 1987; Varonis & Gass, 1985b), L2 research has emphasized the role played by negotiated interaction between NSs and NNSs and between two NNSs[2] in the development of a second language. Within the current orthodoxy, conversation is not only a medium of practice; it is also the means by which learning takes place. In other words, conversational interaction in a second language forms the basis for the development of syntax; it is not merely a forum for practice of grammatical structures. In this chapter I take this view as a starting point and examine the form and function of conversational interaction.

5.1. MISCOMMUNICATION

As noted by Coupland, Wiemann, and Giles (1991), "communication problems [have been] treated as aberrant behavior which should be eliminated" (p. 1). When talking about communication, it is assumed that communication flows smoothly, but as Coupland et al. noted, "in the ethno-methodological tradition, language use, the making of meaning and its reconstruction, has been viewed as inherently problematic, strategic, and effortful" (p. 5). They further referred to "Garfinkel's (1967) perspective on talk as 'accomplishment' which acknowledges the probability of communicative inadequacy and incompleteness" (p. 5). Of course, this theoretical discussion of communication focuses on communication among and between native speakers. The problem becomes more complex when dealing with non-native speakers where miscommunication abounds and where communication in general is doubly problematic and effortful. As Collins (1985) reminded us:

> A few years ago a sketch on television's *Monty Python's Flying Circus* featured a misleading Hungarian phrasebook. "Can I have a box of matches?" was mistranslated into English along the lines of "I would like to feel your beautiful thighs." The appropriate rebuff in English was mistranslated into Hungarian as "Your eyes are like liquid pools." The phrasebook turned what should have been a routine exchange between a large Hungarian and a meek tobacconist into a violent brawl. The phrasebook introduced disorder into what the participants expected to be routine orderly interaction. (p. 5)

It is clear to anyone with even minimal exposure to conversation with a non-native speaker of a language (including oneself in a foreign culture), communication with non-native speakers involves many difficulties. I schematize types of miscommunication in Fig. 5.1.

Following Milroy (1984), miscommunication is defined as instances in which there is a mismatch between a speaker's intention and a hearer's interpretation. Gass and Varonis (1991) distinguished between a misunderstanding and incomplete understanding. In the former, there is a "simple disparity between the speaker's and hearer's semantic analysis of a given utterance" (Milroy, 1984, p. 15), whereas in the latter "one or more participants perceive that something has gone wrong" (p. 15). To illustrate a misunderstanding, consider the following example. The conversation occurred between a South African woman (native speaker of English) and a French woman. They had both had a lengthy day of traveling from London

MISCOMMUNICATION

ビ   ↘

misunderstanding   incomplete understanding

ビ   ↘

nonunderstanding   partial understanding

FIG. 5.1. Types of miscommunication. Adapted from E. Varonis and S. Gass, *Language in Society, 14,* 121–145. Copyright © 1985 by Sage Publications, Inc. Reprinted by permission of Sage Publications, Inc.

and were on a train in Calais bound for Paris. The two did not know each other but had been part of a large number of people who had left London for Dover by train early in the morning. Because of fog in Dover, they had had a layover of many hours while they waited to take a boat across the English channel. This conversation occurred immediately after they had boarded the train in Calais. They settled into their seats, facing one another:

1. From Varonis and Gass (1985a)
   NS: When I get to Paris, I'm going to sleep for one whole day. I'm so tired.
   NNS: What?
   NS: I'm going to sleep for one whole day.
   NNS: One hour a day?
   NS: Yes.
   NNS: Why?
   NS: Because I'm so tired.

The two lapsed into silence, presumably puzzled by the comments of the other; they did not exchange a word for the remainder of the journey. Of course, misunderstandings as defined here can also occur between two native speakers, as in the following example. Two NSs were standing in a dormitory lounge where a TV was on loudly. The first one (not listening to the TV) referred to an upcoming political rally he had read about:

2. NS1:   When is the rally, Saturday?

The second responded with an apparent nonsequitur (although most likely was prompted by something on the television):

3. NS2:   Do you know what arrested development is?
   NS1:   What, the rally?

NS2: Oh, is it a rally?

What differentiates these two types of miscommunication is the perception that a problem exists. Even though both miscommunication and incomplete understandings occur in non-native discourse, what is of interest here is the latter type since it is claimed that these interaction types are useful for acquisition due to the lengthy negotiation that takes place in resolving perceived problems.

By far the largest number of communicative events of incomplete understandings are those in which there is some sort of negotiation to resolve the difficulty. *Negotiation* refers to communication in which participants' attention is focused on resolving a communication problem as opposed to communication in which there is a free-flowing exchange of information. Negotiated communication includes, then, both negotiation of form and negotiation of meaning, although clearly these two are not always easily separable. The following conversation exemplifies the extent to which negotiation of form and meaning are intertwined.

4. From Gass and Varonis (1985a)

NNS: There has been a lot of talk lately about additives and preservatives in food. How—

NS: —A a a lot, a lot of talk about what?

NNS: Uh. There has been a lot of talk lately about additives and preservatives in food.

NS: Now just a minute. I can hear you—everything except the important words. You say there's been a lot of talk lately about what [inaudible]?

NNS: —additive, additive, and preservative, in food—

NS: Could you spell one of those words for me, please?

NNS: A D D I T I V E.

NS: Just a minute. This is strange to me.

NNS: H h . . .

NS: Uh . . .

NNS: 'N other word is P R E S E R V A . . .

NS: —Oh, preserves.

NNS: Preservative and additive.

NS: Preservatives, yes, okay. And what was that—what was that first word I didn't understand?

NNS: Okay in—

NS: —additives?

NNS: Okay.

NS: —additives and preservatives.

NNS: Yes.

NS: Ooh right . . .

In this example, the participants focused their attention on that part of the discourse (additives and preservatives) that was causing one of the participants difficulty. In many instances, particularly in conversations involving NNSs, the difficulties, even when recognized, never get resolved, as in the following example from Butterworth (1972), cited by Hatch (1983) and repeated here from chapter 3, note 10.

5. NS: Who is the best player in Colombia?
   NNS: Colombia?
   NS: Does uh . . . who is *the* Colombian player?
   NNS: Me?
   NS: No, in Colombia.
   NNS: In Colombia plays. Yah.
   NS: No, on your team. On the Millionarios.
   NNS: Ah yah, Millionarios.
   NS: No, on the Millionarios team.
   NNS: Millionarios play in Colombia. In Sud America. In Europa.
   NS: Do, do they have someone like Pele in Colombia?
   NNS: Pele? In Colombia? Pele?
   NS: In Colombia? Who is, who is "Pele" in Colombia? Do you have someone?
   NNS: In Bogota?
   NS: Yeah, who is the best player?
   NNS: In Santo de Brazil?
   NS: OK (gives up), and you are center forward?

In sum, negotiation occurs when there is some recognized asymmetry between message transmission and reception and when both participants are willing to attempt a resolution of the difficulty (see Varonis & Gass, 1985a, for a description of means of resolution).

5.2. INCOMPLETE UNDERSTANDINGS AS TRIGGERS FOR NEGOTIATION

As discussed in the preceding section, a lack of full communication is the result of asymmetries between what one interlocutor intends to say and what another understands. As noted earlier, this can be a partial understanding, as in Examples 4 and 5, or it can be a total lack of any understanding, as was presumably the case in Example 1.

There are a number of ways in which a conversational incongruity can be handled. It can be ignored, possibly because a comment could be perceived as rude or as face threatening to one's interlocutor (due to the implication of poor language abilities as the cause of the lack of understanding). It can be put into storage, with a hope of later understanding, either during the course of the conversation when more information becomes available or later upon further reflection of what the conversational partner could have meant. With particular importance for non-native speakers, it can also be commented on with the hope of clarification. It is this type of exchange that is labeled negotiation, and this type of exchange has significance for second language acquisition.

Varonis and Gass (1985b) operationally defined *nonunderstanding routines* (essentially negotiation routines) as "those exchanges in which there is some overt indication that understanding between participants has not been complete" (p. 73).[3] As Varonis and Gass (1985b) stated, "the *sine qua non* of a non-understanding routine is that within the exchange there are embeddings of one or more clarifications" (p. 73). The term *nonunderstanding routine* is somewhat inaccurate because the stimulus for a routine of this sort may be an instance of nonunderstanding, partial understanding, or even no understanding. Pica's (1994) characterization of the stimulus is conceptually similar: "the modification and restructuring of interaction that occurs when learners and their interlocutors anticipate, perceive, or experience difficulties in message comprehensibility" (p. 494). What is important to note in this definition is that even though Pica's immediate concern was second language learning, the kinds of routines found among non-natives are also found among native speakers, although they occur with greater complexity and frequency when NNSs are involved (cf. Long, 1980).

These routines occur not only in adult discourse but also in child L2 discourse, as seen in Examples 6 and 7. In these examples, two 8-year-olds, Angel, a native speaker of Spanish, and Joe, a native speaker of English, are playing.

6. From Peck (1980, p. 161)
   J: That's like on—Ernie and Bert—(roar)
   A: No, like a crazy boy! (laugh)
   J: (laugh) That's more like it. (high pitch) What?
   A: (chuckling) Like a crazy boy!
   J: Like a mazy—like a—a—
   A: *Crazy!*
   J: I—I mean—li' li' (pretending to stutter) I mean—I—I—I mean—I mean—I mean—I mean—I mean—(normal voice) I mean a crazy?
   A: A crazy.
   J: A crazy what, a crazy daisy?
   A: No, a crazy you.
   J: Oh! Oh! Oh!
   A: You are
       [   ]

J: Oh!
A: Crazy.
J: Oh! (10x)

As Peck (1980) pointed out, the original " 'No, like a crazy boy' became 'A crazy,' then 'No, a crazy you,' and last, 'You are crazy' " (p. 161), the latter of course being grammatical.

    7. From Peck (1980, p. 157)
      A: That is mine—pieces
      J: (laugh)
      A: Oooh. That very simple
      J: Got it.
            [   ]
      A: That very simple
      J: (mockingly, slowly) That—is—very—/simpəl/ What /simpəl/ mean? /ʃ/
      A: /simpəl/!
      J: /impəl/!
      A: Silly! (laugh)
            [   ]
      J: You're   silly
      A: Your are.
      J: Your *are.*
      A: (frustrated) Oooh!
      J: Oooh!
      A: Only one piece.
      J: Only one /piʃ/ /piʃ/ /piʃ/ /piʃ/ I can't stop
                           [   ]
                       This a old   piece. Piece.
      J: /piʃ/ /piʃ/. You like /piʃəs/?
      A: No, I like pieces.
      J: What. Whatta you mean—you like /piʃəz/? I like /piʃəs/
                                   [ ]
      A: pizza
      A: I like pieces, pizzas.
      J: /pɛpsiʃ/?
      A: (sing-song) Pepsi Coli—yeah.
      J: /pɛpʃi koliʃ / (laugh) /pɛpʃi koliʃ/ /pɛpʃi/ cola? /pɛpʃi/ cola!

These two examples show that the kind of negotiation described here is not limited to adult discourse. Rather, there are similarities in the language play of children. Like adults, children focus on parts of the discourse that the NNS needs to modify. Unlike adults, children may do this in a mocking or teasing fashion, thus making the resolution or NNS modification more urgent.[4] The function, though, is the same: Language per se is the focus of attention as opposed to the meaning as the focus. The NNS can work out the appropriate form by matching it against, in this case, a NS model. Oliver (1995) similarly noted that negative evidence serves a similar function when provided to children: It is incorporated into their developing second language systems. Her study consisted of NS–NNS child dyads involved in one-way and two-way tasks. Following are two examples that show how negative evidence in the form of negotiation results in corrected forms from the NNS.

8. From Oliver (1995)
   NS: Where do you put the saucepan?
   NNS: Saucepan? (pause) Um under the, the first *to cook . . . the food.*
   NS: Under the *cooker?*
   NNS: Yep.
   NS: *On the* floor?
   NNS: No, in the cooker. *On the* cooker.

9. Data from Oliver (1995)
   NNS: [Drawer one]
   NS: Hm?
   NNS: Drawer. That one. *Drawer.*
   NS: *Drawers.*
   NNS: Yer, *drawers.* On drawers.

As can be seen, the child in these examples appears to have used the discourse as a learning device. The negotiation per se has provided usable information that is then used to make appropriate modifications. Although the play that was seen in the Peck (1980) examples is not present here (probably because the context was a specific task rather than a play situation), the same types of negotiation routines that are seen in adult discourse, and arguably their functions, are indeed present.

To model this kind of conversational interaction, Varonis and Gass (1985b) proposed the model in Fig. 5.2. Essentially, there are two parts to this model, a trigger and a resolution. The trigger is the stimulus for the

FIG. 5.2. Model of negotiation of meaning. From "Non-native/Non-native Conversations: A Model for Negotiation of Meaning," by E. Varonis and S. Gass, 1985, *Applied Linguistics, 6,* p. 74. Copyright 1985 by *Applied Linguistics.* By permission of Oxford University Press.

negotiation that ensues. The resolution, then, is an attempt to resolve the perceived difficulty. Within the resolution, there is an indicator (I) that alerts an interlocutor that a problem exists. For example, consider the following:

10. NNS1:   Yeah. How long . . . will you be? Will you be staying?
    NNS2:   I will four months.
→   NNS1:   Four months?
    NNS2:   Stay four months here until April.

In this exchange there was apparently a lack of understanding on the part of NNS1 of NNS2's "four months."[5] NNS1 questions it (I), thereby seeking clarification, by using rising intonation. The indicator halts the normal flow of the conversation, in essence putting the topic of conversation on hold while clarification of a particular part is worked out. Following an indicator, there is generally a response (R) through which the original speaker acknowledges the difficulty. A response can take a number of forms, including some attempt at modification, as seen when NNS2 added a verb as well as additional information. Following a response, Varonis and Gass' model includes a reaction to the response (RR) in which there is some further acknowledgment that the parties are engaged in a negotiation routine. This can be illustrated in Example 11.

11. From Pica (1994)
    NNS: The windows are crozed.   T
    NS: The windows have what?   I
    NNS: Closed.   R/T
    NS: Crossed? I'm not sure what you're saying here.   I
    NNS: Windows are closed.   R
    NS: Oh, the windows are closed, oh, OK, sorry.   RR

In line 1, the NNS talks about the windows being "crozed," which the NS, not surprisingly, has difficulty understanding. Thus, the indicator, "the windows have what?" indicates to the NNS that there is a problem; the NNS responds with a reformulation, "closed." Once again, the NS does not understand and indicates so by saying "crossed?" followed by an overt statement to that effect. The NNS responds one more time, this time with correct punctuation, "windows are closed." The NS finally closes the negotiation routine with a reaction to the response, and, in this case, apologizes for the interaction, "Oh, the windows are closed, oh, OK, sorry."

What is perhaps most interesting about conversations involving non-native speakers is the complexity of these negotiation routines. In particular, one clarification may often be the trigger for another negotiation. This is schematized in Fig. 5.3 with the preceding conversation.

The windows are crozed

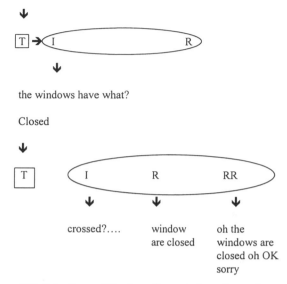

FIG. 5.3. Exemplification of negotiation of meaning.

Pica, Holliday, Lewis, Berducci, and Newman (1991) used the term *signal* rather than *indicator* because the latter, they argued, assumed that the researcher understood the intentions of the speaker. Regardless of the specific terminology used, the main point remains that through message clarification and elaboration, NNSs receive more useable input in their quest to understand the L2, and further, this new or elaborated input draws attention to interlanguage features that diverge from the L2. This information is the catalyst for restructuring. This has been referred to in the recent literature as enhanced input. Sharwood Smith (1991) provided the following diagram (Fig. 5.4) to illustrate this concept. Negotiation, along with certain classroom activities, such as teacher explanation and drills (yes, even drills!), can bring certain forms to a learner's attention, forms that might otherwise go unnoticed, thus enhancing the input and making it more salient—serving in a sense a predigestive function.

5.3. THE QUESTION OF NEGATIVE EVIDENCE

In this section I discuss the various ways in which corrective feedback (i.e., negative evidence) occurs, focusing primarily on two main areas: indirect feedback, as when an interlocutor says, "What?", "I didn't understand you," or "Could you say that again?" and direct feedback, as is often found in classrooms: "No, that isn't right, it should be . . ." or "What would the correct form be?" After a discussion in which I describe corrective feedback, I examine the function these corrections have. This discussion approaches the issue from a theoretical as well as an empirical standpoint.

FIG. 5.4. Input enhancement (examples). From "Speaking to Many Minds: On the Relevance of Different Types of Language Information for the L2 Learner," by M. Sharwood Smith, 1991, *Second Language Research, 7*, p. 121. Copyright 1991 by *Second Language Research*. Reprinted with permission.

In looking at feedback and in conversational structures in general, a number of variables will be considered, among them task type, status, ethnicity, proficiency level, gender, and topic knowledge. I argue that in these conversations learners receive a significant amount of feedback about the correctness or incorrectness of forms (i.e., phonological, syntactic, semantic).

In chapter 2, the concept of negative evidence was discussed with the argument that, at least with regard to second language learning, it is necessary to effect change, even though the evidence might be limited in its explicitness. In Fig. 5.5 I have characterized the kinds of feedback along two continua ranging from explicit to inexplicit and direct to indirect. Examples of these various types are given below:

explicit direct	**direct**	**explicit**
	That's wrong.	You should say . . .
explicit indirect	**indirect**	**explicit**
	Pardon me?	Do you mean . . . ?
inexplicit direct	**direct**	**inexplicit**
	That's wrong.	repetition or nothing
inexplicit indirect	**indirect**	**inexplicit**
	Pardon me?	nothing

In chapter 1 (see section 1.4.3), I pointed out that some input may serve no learning purpose. Rather, time or conversational pressures may be such that the input occurs with little attention being paid to it. The

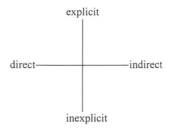

FIG. 5.5. Types of feedback.

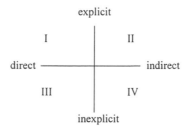

FIG. 5.6. Types of feedback revisited.

same can be said for negotiation. Often individuals are so absorbed by the goal of extracting meaning from what another is saying that they can put no time or effort into the form of a conversation. That is, the conversational trouble is glossed over rather quickly and serves only the immediate function of interpreting another's intention. This is most likely to be the case when the clarification is of the inexplicit and indirect type (see Fig. 5.6, type IV). On the other hand, when the indicator is explicit and direct, there is a greater likelihood that change will result. It is also the case that types I and II are the least frequently occurring types outside the classroom, given the social awkwardness of directly stating that someone is wrong.

Long (1980) was the first to point out that conversations involving non-native speakers exhibit forms that do not appear to any significant degree when only native speakers are involved. This is not to say that these same conversational structures are absent in NS–NS speech, only that they occur to a much lesser degree. For example, confirmation checks (e.g., "Is this what you mean?"), comprehension checks (e.g., "Do you understand?" "Do you follow me?"), and clarification requests (e.g., "What?" "Huh?") are peppered throughout conversations in which there is a non-proficient non-native speaker participant. Some examples follow.

Comprehension check

12. NNS: I was born in Nagasaki. Do you know Nagasaki?

13. NNS1:   And your family have some ingress.

    NNS2: yes ah, OK, OK.
    NNS1: more or less OK?

Confirmation check

14. NNS1: When can you go to visit me?
    NNS2: visit?

Clarification request

15. NNS1: . . . research
    NNS2: Research, I don't know the meaning.

In addition to these negotiation features, different kinds of questions are asked, often with the answer suggested by the native speaker immediately after the question is asked. Example 16 includes two native speakers of English; Example 17 shows a NS and a NNS.

16. NS1: What do you think of Michigan?
    NS2: It's nice, but I haven't gotten used to the cold weather yet.

17. From Hatch (1983)
    NS: What does he make in Colombia? Do you like California?
    NNS: Hnnn?
    NS: In Colombia, what does your father make? In Buena Ventura?
    NNS: In Buena Ventura?
    NS: Yeh, your father.
    NNS: No.
    NS: Oh well . . . (gives up) Yeah, I like it.

In Example 16, the conversation precedes in stepwise fashion; in the second, there is an indication of nonunderstanding ("Hnnn?"), with the result being a narrowing down of the topic (from Colombia to Buena Ventura) accompanied by a more explicit repetition of the original question ("your father" rather than "he"). These conversational tactics provide the NNS with as much information as possible as she attempts to ascribe meaning to the NS's stream of sounds.

In Example 18 the native speaker asks an or-choice question. That is, the native speaker not only asks a question but provides the non-native speaker with a range of possible answers.

18. From Long (1983a)
    NS: Well, what are you doing in the United States? Are you just studying or do you have a job? Or . . .

NNS: No. I have job.

A similar example occurs when the native speaker gives a single answer rather than a range of answers.

19. From Long (1980)
    NS: When do you take the break? At ten-thirty?

In all of the examples discussed in this section, the effect of NS and NNS modifications (whether intentional or not) is to aid the NNS in understanding. This reduces the burden for the NNS in that he or she is assisted by others in understanding and in producing language appropriate to the situation. However, outward signs of negotiation and resolution of that negotiation may only be strategies to show solidarity, rather than true indications of meaning negotiation (Aston, 1986; Hawkins, 1985). As mentioned in note 5, one must be careful in analyzing negotiation sequences as exchanges involving either the negotiation of meaning or negotiation of form because there are instances where negotiation of discourse structure is at issue.

5.3.1. Factors Affecting Negotiation

It would be too simplistic to assume that these integral parts of negotiation sequences occur without influence from the context in which they appear. To the contrary, many factors affect the structure of conversation. In the next few sections I consider task type, background knowledge and status differences, familiarity, gender, and proficiency.

5.3.1.1. Task Type. Much recent literature has focused on the notion of task and its importance in syllabus design and in second language learning. It is not my intent in this chapter to review this literature, but I show how the notion of task type might affect second language learners.

Duff (1986) investigated the effect of task type on the input to learners and the interactions in which they are engaged. To consider this question, she set up two types of task. A problem-solving task, which she called a convergent task, required individuals to come to some sort of agreement. The second was a debate, which she referred to as a divergent task because no agreement was required or even desired. This is different from the notion of one-way and two-way task distinction developed by Long (1981), which refers to participants' control over information. The subjects were same gender Japanese–Chinese pairs, who performed two problem-solving tasks and two debate tasks. To determine the differences in the structure of conversations between the two task types, various quantitative and qualitative measures were used. Duff found in the problem-solving task more turn taking, questions, and *c-units*, a minimal unit of communication that incorporated some notion of meaning. On the other hand, in the debate task were more instances of longer turns, extended discourse, and complex syntax. In general, she noted that in the problem-solving tasks there was greater interaction of the type described in this chapter. Duff was careful to point out that the two tasks produce different types of language, perhaps complementary when considering the function they serve in language acquisition. I return to this point in section 5.4.1.4, on gender differences.

Gass and Varonis (1985a) examined questions similar to those raised by Duff, although they specifically investigated one-way versus two-way tasks. One-way tasks involved giving information from one participant to another, whereas two-way tasks involved exchanges of information, with each participant holding information crucial to the resolution of the task. In the one-way task, one member of a dyad described a picture in such a way that the second member of the pair could draw it. In the two-way task, each member listened to a different tape in which a detective interviewed two robbery suspects. Only by putting together the information about the four suspects could the true robber be identified. The results were analyzed according to the model of negotiation routines described in section 5.2. The differences between the two task types were not significant, contrary to Long's (1983a) predictions that more modified interaction in two-way tasks would occur, as opposed to one-way tasks. It should be noted, however, that negotiation within the framework discussed in this chapter is a narrower concept than modified interaction, with the latter including some conversational features such as the use of or-choice questions or topic shifts.

Doughty and Pica (1986) reported the results of a study that more closely approximated the predictions of Long (1983a). In this and other research (e.g., Pica & Doughty, 1985), they referred to the exchange type as a difference between required information exchange and optional information exchange. In their 1986 study, which looked at participation patterns (i.e., teacher fronted, small group, dyadic), they used a required information exchange that involved boards with different arrangements of flowers and trees. In order to come up with one complete board with a picture of an entire garden, individuals had to exchange information. In their 1985 study, an optional information exchange task (i.e., a problem-solving task) was used. In general, as predicted by Long's (1983a) initial hypothesis, the amount of interaction was greater in the required information exchange condition than in the optional information exchange condition. Furthermore, task effect interacted with the participation pattern type. More interaction occurred in the group and dyadic conditions than in the teacher-fronted condition, but no significant difference emerged between group and dyadic conditions.[6] This study, then, appears to corroborate Long's (1983a) earlier predictions regarding the importance of task type.

Pica (1987) compared teacher-fronted activity with student–student participation on two tasks, a decision-making task and an information exchange task. She considered the quantity of interactional moves (i.e., comprehension checks, confirmation checks, clarification requests) in four conditions (in the student–student tasks, the teacher was either present or not). In the teacher-fronted decision making task, there were few opportunities for interaction, as the following example from Pica's data shows.

20. From Pica (1987, pp. 14–15)

Teacher	Students
All right, which family do you think	
i—which families are too old to have	
children? Which families are right—	
are old enough or a good age to have	
children?	
	S1: Number one.
All right, so the first one . . .	
what's good about them is they're	
the right age and also?	
	S2: The Health.
The health. They're in good health.	
All right. Who else should we con-	
sider? All right. So family one's	
strong—strongest points are	
they're a good age for having	
children and also their health is—	
you know good health. All right.	
Who else should we consider?	
	S3: Number three.

TABLE 5.1
Comprehension and Confirmation Checks and Clarification
Requests in Decision-Making Discussion and
Information-Gap Task, Adapted From Pica (1987)

	Version			
	Teacher-Fronted		Student–Student	
Activity	r	%	n	%
Decision-making discussion	79	11	23	6
Information-exchange task	127	15	145	24

Note. "Second Language Acquistion, Social Interaction and the Classroom," by T. Pica, 1987, Applied Linguistics, 8, p. 14. Copyright 1987 by Applied Linguistics. By permission of Oxford University Press.

In contrast, the information exchange task without a teacher present elicited many more examples of interactional exchanges (see Table 5.1). These data suggest that at least two variables are significant in understanding the opportunities for modificational interaction: task type and teacher presence. Tasks that require students to participate in such a way that a single resolution of a task is necessary are most likely to bring about the kinds of interaction that facilitate acquisition.

Brock, Crookes, Day, and Long (1986) observed non-native speakers incorporating examples of native speaker corrective feedback following errors when communication took place in the context of communication games. In other words, learners' grammars may be quickly destabilized if they give sufficient attention to the area in question, with the assumption that they would pay more attention in the context of a game with a definite goal or outcome, as opposed to free conversation.

The importance of task is further supported by Crookes and Rulon (1985), who examined native–non-native dyads. They considered the incorporation of corrective feedback in three situations, one free conversation and two two-way communication tasks. Feedback was defined as the correct usage of a word by a NS immediately following a non-native incorrect utterance. They found significantly more feedback in task-related conversation than in free conversation and suggested that for maximum grammatical destabilization, linguistic material should be slightly familiar to the non-native speaker and the structure of the task should require the maximum use of this material by both parties. Pica, Young, and Doughty (1987), using a picture arrangement task in which input to the learner was either premodified or interactionally modified, found that comprehension (as measured by task completion) was superior when the negotiation was allowed as opposed to when it was not. Knox (1992) extended this observation to naturalistic conversation, suggesting that form-focusing and subsequent non-native speaker modification occurs in certain types of constrained settings, such as a structured interview or service encounter.

Finally, in a study of gender differences (see section 5.3.1.4), Pica, Holliday, Lewis, Berducci, and Newman (1991) found that the amount of interaction in both cross-gender and same-gender dyads depended on task type. In particular, negotiation was greatest in a picture description task in which one individual described a picture for another to draw. There was less negotiation in an information exchange task (i.e., putting pictures into their proper sequence) and an opinion exchange task (i.e., focused conversation). They concluded that, in general, negotiation is greater when all of the information needed for a resolution is in the hands of a single individual as opposed to being shared by two individuals. Thus, the kind and amount of negotiation, or opportunities for input enhancement, may depend to some extent on the type of language use, either inside or outside of the classroom.

Aston (1986), taking a different position, argued that tasks that promote negotiation often result in language that is frustrating to produce and as a result is error-laden. This contention is contrary to the conclusions drawn from the studies reported here as well as others, which fail to indicate that the language produced in negotiating the setting has more errors than language in non-negotiated situations. The issue of frustration may in fact be real, although few studies have opted to look at that issue within the context of negotiation. Aston was correct in claiming that negotiation does not always result in correct forms and that, in fact, it may result in pidginized varieties, as shown in the following examples. He was incorrect in assuming that this vitiates the input–interaction argument because the argument is that negotiation allows for opportunities to obtain comprehensible, usable input, not that that language always result in comprehension or that it is always used.

The data in the following example come from two Italian women engaged in a drawing task.

21. From Aston (1986)
    NNS1: What have you drawn?
    NNS2: It's a hm (.) we are: er in the country, there is a: (.) a house, with a lot—with some: trees and:
    NNS1: Er we are: in a country.
    NNS2: In the country.
    NNS1: We aren't I the centre of the—this country. We are: where
    NNS2: Er (.) Ah, it's not country, er I mean—
    NNS1: It's a town.
    NNS2: Nein. No.
    NNS1: No.
    NNS2: I mean—
    NNS1: It's a field.
    NNS2: Yes. Yes.
    NNS1: It's a field.
    NNS2: Yes.

Aston argued that the negotiation of the meaning of *country* (which was correct when NNS1 began) resulted in an incorrect meaning (compounded by a similar homonymy in Italian of the word *paese*) of the word *country*, due in part to a switch by NNS2 to an indefinite article. That this can and does happen is not in dispute; what is claimed is that this is not the norm, as argued by Gass and Varonis (1989, 1994) and further supported by the results of Oliver (1995).

5.3.1.2. Background Knowledge and Status Differences.
Differences in status are likely to determine to some extent the amount, if not kind, of negotiation that will take place. For example, it is unlikely that negotiation (at

least that initiated by the NNS) is frequent between individuals whose status difference (or power relationship) is quite different. We have little experimental evidence on this point with regard to non-native speakers,[7] but the following anecdote serves to illustrate the point, even though it occurred between two native speakers. NS1 (a full professor) is talking about the research of a third person.

22. From Varonis and Gass (1985b):
    NS1: Do you think his research is monolithic?
    NS2 (a graduate student): Well, it's hard to say.

In reality she was hoping (or should we say praying?) for more information that would reveal the meaning of *monolithic* in this particular context; all she could conjure in her mind were the large monoliths at Stonehenge in England. It would have been embarrassing to admit her ignorance and begin a negotiation routine. In another example, in a classroom context, a teacher is talking to a student.

23. From Varonis and Gass (1985b):
    T: Compare the openings of *Absalom Absalom* and *A Farewell to Arms*.
        In, *Absalom Absalom* there is a greater use of hypotaxis.
    S (having no idea what hypotaxis means): Hypotaxis?

Great status differences may inhibit negotiation, especially in those instances in which the NS is of a higher status than the NNS (e.g., a professor and student).

In the second language literature there have been few recent studies on the role of status and background knowledge in determining the shape of conversation. It is often assumed that being a NS confers status on an individual and that the NS therefore dominates a conversation (e.g., Beebe & Giles, 1984; Scarcella, 1983, 1992) with a NNS. Zuengler (1989b), referring to Levinson (1987), correctly pointed out that dominating a conversation limits the nondominant party's right to talk. If so, and if talking plays an important interactional role in learning, then the role of dominance is a crucial issue to consider (see also section 5.3.1.4 on gender differences). The mere fact of being a NS, however, does not seem always to be significant in determining who will dominate a conversation. Zuengler (1989a) looked at interrupting behavior as evidence of dominance and argued that the concept of control often has less to do with nativeness versus non-nativeness than with the amount of knowledge that the individuals have about the subject matter. In other words, the discourse domain (Selinker & Douglas, 1985) is more of a determinant than is linguistic knowledge. Zuengler's (1989a) study did not deal with real topic knowledge differences because participants were only induced to believe that the partner knew more about a topic; however, in follow-up work Zuengler

(1989b) sought to remedy this by conducting a study in which individuals (NS and NNS pairs) could truly be said to have a different knowledge source. The results were not clear. Conversations in which the NNS was more advanced academically showed no evidence of dominant interrupting behavior on the part of the NNS. However, in that same situation, there was evidence of dominance in terms of greater amount of talk. Although the studies did not examine negotiation routines per se, one can perhaps interpret these results to suggest the possible role of status differences in amount of negotiation: the greater the status difference, the fewer the negotiations. This interpretation would be consistent with the claims made by Varonis and Gass (1985b) concerning the relation between comfort in a conversation and negotiation (see section 5.3.1.4).

Further support for status differences affecting conversational structure come from Woken and Swales (1989). In a clever design, non-native speakers with expertise in computer science instructed native speakers in the use of a particular word-processing system with which the NSs were not familiar. The analysis of these conversations consisted of many measures; the measure that is most relevant to the issue of negotiation is that of other-corrections. In their data, Woken and Swales found no examples of a NS correcting a NNS even in areas of grammatical misuse. In other words, there was no NS-initiated negotiation of form. All the correction was content correction on the part of the NNS. Hence, once again, status or knowledge-based differences appears to deter the use of frequent negotiation routines.

5.3.1.3. Familiarity.

In the preceding section I considered the interpersonal concept of status difference. There is yet another interpersonal variable that may be relevant: familiarity. Most studies control for familiarity by ensuring that participants either do or do not know one another before actual data collection. An exception to this practice is a study by Plough and Gass (1993), in which subjects performed two tasks, an information gap task and a discussion task in which participants had to come to an agreement about an issue. The dyads were comprised of NNS–NNS pairs; half had known one another before the data collection, whereas the other half had met only at the time of the experiment. The unfamiliar pairs exhibited fewer instances of nonunderstanding; that is there was less evidence of negotiation. Additionally, more conversational continuers (e.g., echoing a previous utterance with the intent of ensuring the smooth flow of the conversation) were produced by unfamiliar pairs. This result suggests that when individuals are not familiar with one another, they are more concerned that the conversation proceed in a smooth fashion; a breakdown is a greater threat to face than it is when individuals know one another. Breakdowns occur when negotiation takes place and is inhibited by frequent echoes used to keep the conversation moving.

A study by Gass and Varonis (1984) supports the notion of familiarity as a relevant variable even though that study dealt only with comprehension. They found that the greater the familiarity with an individual speaker (or other speakers of the same language), the more likely listeners were to understand.

5.3.1.4. Gender.   The study of male–female differences in talk has received considerable attention in the public arena due to the work of Tannen (e.g., 1990). Within the input–interaction framework, the interest has been only slight. Gass and Varonis (1986) first looked at this issue in a paper that focused on negotiation styles in three groups of non-native speakers: male–male, female–male, and female–female. Each dyad (all native speakers of Japanese) participated in one free conversation task and two picture description tasks. The results showed more negotiation in same gender dyads than in mixed gender dyads. When looking at who initiated the negotiation (i.e., in the model discussed in section 5.2, at who provided the indicator), in the mixed gender dyads, women provided the indicator almost twice as frequently as men.

Another important difference was noted in the male–female conversations: Men talked more, as evidenced by a word count. This was the case in three of the four male–female dyads; men talked 60% to 77% of the time. In contrast, in the same gender dyads, no individual spoke more than 58.3% of the time. On the other hand, the number of conversational turns that each participant took was approximately the same for men as for women. These results suggest that men, when they have a turn, hold it for a longer period of time. Although the opportunities for talk time are more or less equal, men and women do not utilize these opportunities in the same way (the issue of practice in talking, or output, is discussed in chapter 6).

It is clear that there are differences (among others discussed by Gass and Varonis, 1986) in male–female conversational behavior, and these differences may have a role in acquisition. Women, by initiating negotiation sequences (i.e., asking for conversational help when something is unclear), may be making it possible to obtain more input that is usable in acquisition. Men, on the other hand, by producing more, may be using the conversation for hypothesis testing. These results were corroborated by Pica, Holliday, Lewis, and Morgenthaler (1989), although their findings were the result of a post hoc analysis and not a particular research design. Furthermore, the comparisons were made between male and female NNSs, all interacting with a female interlocutor.

A study with a larger database (the Gass and Varonis study had only 10 dyads) was that of Pica et al. (1991). Their study (32 dyads) departed from the research design of Gass and Varonis in that the dyads were native–

non-native pairs. Each dyad performed four tasks, two picture description tasks (like the Gass and Varonis study), a jigsaw task in which each interlocutor held a piece of information that was crucial to the task (i.e., creating a sequence of pictures), and an opinion exchange task. This latter task was a more focused version of the Gass and Varonis free conversation task.

At first glance, their results seem in part to contradict those of Gass and Varonis (1986). For example, the negotiation sequences in cross-gender and same-gender dyads were nearly the same. However, as Pica et al. (1991) pointed out, the major factor contributing to the lack of negotiation in cross-gender dyads came from the male native speaker–female non-native speaker pairs. This is consistent with the sociolinguistic literature and also earlier work by Varonis and Gass (1982, 1985b), who argued that conversations between native and non-native speakers are often fraught with difficulty because of the discomfort of conversing with a noncommunicative partner. Even though nonunderstandings are frequent, it is uncomfortable to be responsible for continuous interruptions in the form of some sort of indicator.

An important difference between the Pica et al. (1991) study and the Gass and Varonis (1986) study is that the former dealt with native–nonnative speakers pairs, whereas the latter consisted of non-native–non-native speaker pairs. It may be that the former situation inhibits negotiation given the status difference vis-á-vis language between the partners. Varonis and Gass (1985b) argued that "a greater amount of negotiation work takes place in NNS–NNS discourse than in either NS–NS or NNS–NS discourse. . . . non-native speakers, in conversations with other non-native speakers, may feel that as learners they have little to lose by indicating a non-understanding, because they recognize their 'shared incompetence' " (p. 84). Their study consisted of native–non-native dyads as well as exclusively non-native dyads. Non-natives in dyads with other non-natives, but not those in dyads with natives, frequently acknowledged their lack of English proficiency. Varonis and Gass (1985b) argued that a shared incompetence allowed participants to feel comfortable enough to "put the conversation on hold" and negotiate particular forms or meanings.

> non-native speakers do not lose face by negotiating meaning in the same way they might with native speakers. [Learners in an intensive English program] had nothing invested in trying to come across as totally competent speakers of English. We might predict that non-native speakers who did not consider themselves language students might be less willing, given equivalent language ability, to admit a language difficulty. (p. 85)

Thus, the fact that the studies differed in the dyad structure makes a comparison difficult if not unreliable.

In general, the research on variables affecting negotiation shows that a gap in background knowledge (linguistic or content) between participants leads to more frequent opportunities for negotiation. Whether these opportunities are seized depends in part on interpersonal as well as personal characteristics. I return to this concept in the Epilogue in the discussion of the classroom.

5.4. INTERACTION AND DEVELOPMENT

Many studies in the second language acquisition literature have been influential in their descriptions of what occurs in negotiation routines; many were summarized and synthesized in the preceding sections. Few, however, have established a link between actual negotiation and subsequent learning, operationally defined as change in linguistic knowledge. This is, of course, a crucial question, if not the crux of the issue, as noted by Schachter (1986). The main reason for the dearth of studies is the difficulty, if not impossibility, of getting reliable data. Short of taping all input that learners receive, every negotiation in which they engage, and every bit of subsequent output, there is little way of knowing just what the source of change is.

An exception was an important study by Sato (1986, 1990) early in the history of input–interaction studies. She questioned a direct positive relation between interaction and language development. She examined the English of two Vietnamese boys, finding that neither the NS input to the boys nor the naturalistic interaction between them and their native speaker interlocutor resulted in increased language proficiency. Her study, focusing on the marking of past time reference, did not suggest that grammatical encoding of such reference increased as a function of proficiency. Instead, the NNSs relied on the situational or discourse context to establish a time frame. Because past tense was for the most part recoverable from context, there was an insignificant interactional burden on the part of participants. Furthermore, past tense marking in English is often not phonologically salient, reducing the learner's opportunities to utilize relevant information. Thus, at least in the case of past tense marking, there is little necessity and little opportunity to obtain or provide linguistic information in the conversation. However, given the boys' relatively rudimentary knowledge of English, the situation might have been different if Sato's subjects had been at a different stage of development, a stage at which they were ready to learn past tense forms (Pienemann, 1992).

Sato's (1986, 1990) findings have been corroborated by other studies that also focus on native speaker–non-native speaker naturalistic conversations. Chun, Day, Chenoweth, and Luppescu (1982) reported relatively little explicit feedback in free conversations between native and non-native speakers and therefore questioned the value of correction as an integral part of successful acquisition. In another study, Day, Chenoweth, Chun, and Luppescu (1984) further questioned the role of error correction in second language acquisition, noting that of 1,595 student errors in their corpus, only 117 (7.3%) were singled out for corrective feedback by native speaker interlocutors.

A follow-up study by Brock, Crookes, Day, and Long (1986) suggested that the effect of conversational interactions on acquisition may be influenced in part by task. They investigated a broader range of negative feedback in native–non-native free conversations, examining short-term effects of such input on the NNS's language development. They found surprisingly little change in learner forms, with only 26 of 152 instances (17.1%) in which learners clearly responded by incorporating the native speaker's corrective feedback into their next turns. However, as mentioned earlier, they pointed out the possibility of an effect of the task.

Incorporation of corrective feedback, albeit in this case between two non-native speakers was noted by Gass and Varonis (1989). Particularly interesting in the context of non-native–non-native conversations is the way changes are made. By this I mean the direction of the change. Theoretically, when two individuals are conversing and they produce different forms, and if one accommodates to the other's speech, the change could be in the direction of a correct or an incorrect form. However, it appears that in the vast majority of cases, change occurs in the direction of the target language form and not in the direction of an incorrect form (see Gass & Varonis, 1994).

It is clear that for all researchers working in this area, a major difficulty occurs in the determination of change as distinguishable from an echoed response in the next turn. Most research has considered immediate destabilization of an incorrect form, as evidenced by a correct form in a turn subsequent to the corrective feedback. However, it may be difficult, if not impossible, to determine longer range effects. An exception was found by Gass and Varonis (1989), who noted instances of incorporation of target-like forms in stretches of discourse considerably after the corrective feedback. There seemed to be some sort of permeation or thinking time during which a learner may have contemplated the effects of an earlier negotiation, incorporating a correct form after a considerable stretch of discourse. Two such examples follow (see also section 6.2.1.2).

24. From Gass and Varonis (1989)
    NNS1: ... woman has a [dək]
    NNS2: Duck? (surprised)
    NNS1: [dɔk]
    NNS2: [dɔk] Ah, I see—

NNS1: A [dək]
NNS2: What kind of dog?
(eight turns)
NNS1: The dog wear s–some clothe. . . .

25. From Gass and Varonis (1989, p. 78)
NNS1: Uh holding the [kəp]
NNS2: Holding the cup?
NNS1: Hmm hmmm . . .
(seventeen turns)
NNS2: Holding a cup
NNS1: Yes
NNS2: Coffee cup?
NNS1: Coffee? Oh yeah, tea, coffee cup, teacup.
NNS2: Hm hm.

As mentioned earlier, most of the work discussed thus far forms the basis of the input–interaction hypothesis but unfortunately failed to show a direct link between input, interaction, and acquisition. More recent work has begun to focus on the establishment of a more direct relation between interaction and subsequent production or learning.[8]

Loschky (1994) investigated the acquisition of two locative expressions in Japanese by native speakers of English. This study included three conditions: One group of second language learners received unmodified input (i.e., control group), a second group received premodified input, and the third group was involved in negotiating input. The task was to identify pictured objects from spoken descriptions. The study focused on the effects of comprehensible input and interaction on vocabulary retention and comprehension. Negotiation had a positive effect on comprehension, but no positive effect was noted for the acquisition of vocabulary items or on the acquisition of the locative constructions he was investigating, as determined through an immediate posttest including two vocabulary recognition tests and a sentence verification task. In comparison to the control group, the negotiation group performed better, but the premodified group did not. A delayed posttest one day later showed no significantly greater retention of lexis or morphosyntax by the negotiation group, although all groups did make pretest–posttest gains.

Gass and Varonis (1994) were similarly concerned with a delayed effect of interaction, in other words, an effect that appeared to last longer than one subsequent turn. They compared the effects of modified input, unmodified input, interactionally modified input, and noninteractional input on the comprehension of instructions and on the later production of instructions. Not surprising was their finding that negotiated interaction and modified input aided comprehension, as evidenced by the NNS's ability to follow instructions appropriately. Furthermore, and relevant to the present discussion, when negotiated interaction was allowed during the time an NS was giving instructions to the NNS, that same NNS was better able to perform in a direction-giving task than were NNSs not provided with the opportunity of negotiated interaction when receiving instructions on a prior task. It was not clear what about the prior negotiation facilitated later accurate instruction giving by the NNS. As in the Loschky (1994) study, there did not appear to be evidence of newly acquired vocabulary resulting from negotiation. What did appear were better discourse organizational strategies.

Ellis, Tanaka, and Yamazaki (1994) also considered the role of vocabulary learning as a result of negotiation. In their study, input that was interactionally modified yielded better comprehension rates than did premodified input (as in the Gass and Varonis, 1994, study) and resulted in the acquisition of more word order meaning but not greater vocabulary acquisition (as in the Gass and Varonis study). They argued that the "cornerstone of the interaction hypothesis . . . is alive and well" (p. 481). They further claimed that a "causative relationship" exists (p. 482), at the same time acknowledging the limitation of this claim to the focus of their study—vocabulary.

A factor that makes it difficult to claim that interaction per se is crucial was provided by Ellis et al. (1994) and Pica (1991, 1992). In those studies there was no learning advantage for those actually involved in interaction as opposed to those who just listened to an interaction. Although this may appear to argue against the necessity of interaction, I argue that it does so only partially. If what is crucial about interaction is the fact that input becomes salient in some way (i.e., enhanced), then it matters little how salience comes about—whether through a teacher's self-modification, one's own request for clarification, or observation of another's request for clarification. The crucial point is that input becomes available for attentional resources and attention is focused on a particular form or meaning. When learners are in an active interactional mode, they can focus on what is necessary for them—that is, their own attention can drive the interaction. When one is only an observer, one may or may not serve the same linguistic needs as the actual interactant. This interpretation is corroborated by Pica (1991).

Mackey (1995) also set out to establish the extent to which a relation could be found between conversational interaction and L2 development. She looked at the acquisition of question formation, building on the developmental model by Pienemann and Johnston (1987). In their model, originally developed to account for the acquisition of German word order by second language speakers, there were discernible and ordered stages of acquisition, each governed by processing mechanisms that constrained the movement from one stage to the next. Although a detailed discussion of the model is not relevant to the present discussion (see Ellis, 1994; Larsen-Freeman & Long, 1991, for details), a brief explanation will help in putting Mackey's work in context. The model makes a strong prediction of word order development in that a learner will start off (apart from single words or chunks) with canonical order, such as SVO (e.g., "I like Sydney," "You are student?"). A second stage involves some movement, but movement that does not interrupt the canonical order (e.g., "In Vietnam, I am teacher"; "Do you have apartment"; "Why you no eat?"). In the next stage, canonical order is interrupted (e.g., "Have you job?" "I like to eat my friend's house"). In this stage one can see the beginnings of syntactic development. In the fourth stage, movement entails the recognition that the moved elements are part of grammatical categories. For example, in "Why did you go?" the learner needs to know that the AUX must be in second position and that tense is marked on the AUX. Finally, learners recognize substrings and learn that grammatical operations can operate across the substrings (e.g., "He didn't leave, did he?"). Because this model makes a prediction about development and because conversational interaction within an input–interaction framework is hypothesized to influence development, the model makes a fertile testing ground for both the Pienemann and Johnston (1987) model and for the interaction hypothesis.

Mackey (1995) conducted research in which learners of English were engaged in communicative tasks with questions as the targeted structure and with opportunities for interaction between participants. Mackey noted a positive relation between interaction and development such that learners who were involved in structure-focused interaction moved along a developmental path more rapidly than learners who did not. As she noted, interaction was able to "step up the pace" (p. 5) of development but was not able to push learners beyond a developmental stage.[9] In other words, developmental stages could not be skipped. In conditions in which learners received only premodified input but in which no opportunities were allowed for interaction, development was not noted. Interesting was the finding that evidence for more developmentally advanced structures was noted in delayed posttests rather than immediately. This supports the claim made throughout this book that interaction is a priming device, allowing learners to focus attention on areas that they are working on. In many instances, thinking time is needed before change takes place. It is further noteworthy that in Mackey's study the delayed effect is found more often in more advanced structures, where it is reasonable to assume that more thinking time is needed before a learner is able to figure out what changes to make and how to make them.

Tarone and Liu (1995) argued, on the basis of interactional data in three settings, that a learner's involvement "in different kinds of interaction can differentially affect the rate and route of the acquisition process" (p. 108). The data come from a Chinese native speaker learning English in Australia. At the onset of data collection, the child was almost 5; at the end, he was almost 7 years old. Data were collected in three situations: in interactions with teachers, in interactions with peers, and in interactions with the researcher (in English, although the researcher was a NS of Chinese). As in Mackey's (1995) study, the focus of attention was Pienemann and Johnston's (1987) developmental sequence of interrogatives, specifically on both the rate and route of acquisition. With regard to rate, Tarone and Liu (1995) argued that new forms nearly always emerge in one context (i.e., interaction with the researcher) and then spread to the context with peers and then to interactions with teachers. What is important, however, is that new forms emerge from interactions themselves, and the differential demands of each interaction differentially allow for the emergence of new forms. In other words, different contexts push the learner to produce new forms to a greater extent than other contexts (see also Selinker & Douglas, 1985).

Interesting is Tarone and Liu's (1995) finding regarding the route of acquisition. Although their findings were similar to those of Mackey (1995) with regard to the rate, they diverged with regard to the route. They found that the route could be altered depending on the context. For example, later stage interrogatives occurred in interactions with the researcher before the appearance of earlier stages. Liu (1991) suggested that the explanation for this discrepancy lies in the context of the interaction itself, in which there were significant amounts of input of later stage questions. An additional factor may be that the question forms that appeared to be absent from the child's speech were ungrammatical in English, with presumably no input (e.g., "Why you do that?"). Thus, it may be that later stages stemming from an input flood of grammatical utterances can be induced when earlier stages are ungrammatical and hence devoid of external input.

5.5. CONCLUSION

In this chapter, I have presented some of the literature on interaction, focusing in particular on the role of interaction in second language acquisition. I have argued that negotiation is a means of drawing attention to linguistic form, making it salient and thereby creating a readiness for learning. It is furthermore a way in which learners receive feedback on their own production. When something is not produced according to the standards of the target language, speakers will often receive an indication through an indicator that initiates a negotiation sequence. The claim is not that negotiation causes learning nor that there is a theory of learning based on interaction. Rather, negotiation is a facilitator of learning; it is one means but not the only means of drawing attention to areas of needed change. It is one means by which input can become comprehensible and manageable. To return to the concepts raised in chapter 2, it is a form of negative evidence (or can be taken as such by the learner), although the extent to which it provides actual correction is questionable, depending in large part on individual learners. White (1987), in fact, argued that what is necessary for learners is not comprehensible input but incomprehensible input. By this she meant that negotiation (triggered by something incomprehensible) becomes the impetus for learners to recognize the inadequacy of their own rule system.

An eventual theory of second language acquisition will need to account *inter alia* for the nature of linguistic knowledge (i.e., competence in the theoretical sense) that L2 learners attain and how that knowledge is attained. Attention, accomplished in part through negotiation, is one of the crucial mechanisms in this process.

NOTES

1. Many of the ideas expressed in this chapter were developed in collaboration with Evangeline Marlos Varonis.
2. Most of the research in second language acquisition within this framework has considered dyads rather than large groups of conversational participants. This is, in some sense, an accident of research design or more likely due to the ease with which dyadic conversational data can be gathered. This limitation does not imply that conversations with more than two individuals do not serve the same purpose as dyadic conversations. Rather, larger groups engaged in conversations have not been investigated to any significant extent in the L2 literature.
3. The literature is replete with terminology to refer to essentially the same phenomenon: interactional modification, conversational interaction, negotiation of meaning, negotiation, negotiated interaction, interactional adjustments, conversational work, negotiation work (Gass & Varonis, 1984; Long, 1980, 1983a, 1983b, 1985; Long & Porter, 1985; Loschky, 1994; Mackey, 1995; Pica, 1994; Pica et al., 1989; Pica et al., 1987; Scarcella & Higa, 1981; Varonis & Gass, 1985b; and others).
4. I thank Elaine Tarone for bringing this example to my attention and an unknown member of the 1996 Second Language Acquisition (Teachers of English to Speakers of Other Languages) breakfast seminar audience for pointing out the urgency involved in the resolution.
5. To attribute a function to this type of discourse can be tricky at times. For example, Houck and Gass (1996) presented the following example:

> NS: Okay, so we're just gonna give our opinions about these. Uhm, do you have an overall opinion?
> NNS: Do I have a overall (one)? Uhm. (longish pause—head movement and smile)

They argued that this was not a language difficulty despite the superficial similarity to negotiation routines. Rather, the NNS appears to be thrown by the abruptness of the question. In Japanese discussions of this sort, it is typical for initial discussion to focus on the procedures necessary to carry out the task at hand. That is, Japanese groups tend to require more time to get into the heart of the discussion. For Americans, "Okay" is a common opener, after which they launch right in (Watanabe, 1993), much as the NS did when she said, "Okay, so we're just gonna give our opinions about these. Uhm, do you have an overall opinion?" Hence, by taking a more global look at the situation, including knowledge of this individual's linguistic background and proficiency (which was very high), her performance in other parts of the discourse, and other factors, one can easily become convinced that the problem was a global discourse one and not a local linguistic one. This difference in perspectives, of course, is similar to the situation in chapter 4 in which the Jews and Christians were in dispute.

6. It should be noted that although there was no significant difference between the group and dyadic conditions, in all three of the classes selected for study, the dyadic condition was greater than the group condition. In one group of students there was a relatively large difference and in another a very small difference.

7. An exception to this is the collaborative work of Bardovi-Harlig and Hartford (e.g., Bardovi-Harlig & Hartford, 1993, 1996), who examined advising sessions between NSs and NNSs, focusing in particular on the speech acts of rejections and suggestions. Their work was not carried out within an input–interaction framework, but they suggest an explanation for a NNS's inability to readily conform to native speaker pragmatic norms (despite their linguistic sophistication, which is sufficient to allow admission to a U.S. university): a lack of negative evidence about the form that a particular speech act should take.

8. Clearly, I do not intend to equate production with acquisition but rather wish to suggest that production of forms is one piece of evidence that can be used to suggest that those forms are part of a learner's grammar.

9. This is in some sense reminiscent of early work by Zobl (1982), who, in discussions of the role of the native language, noted that native language background affects the speed at which certain developmental stages are transversed.

Comprehension, Output, and the Creation of Learner Systems

6.0. INTRODUCTION

The crucial consideration in any study of second language acquisition is an understanding of the nature of learner systems and how those learner systems come to be. The previous chapters have provided an account of ways in which these systems may come about. I have argued that interaction, with its attentional resources being forced on particular parts of grammatical systems, is one crucial aspect. I have also argued that as a first step to learning, a learner must be aware of a need to learn. That is, a knowledge gap must be recognized. Negotiation of the sort that takes place in conversation is a means to focus a learner's attention on just those areas of language that do not match those of the target language.

Two further aspects of the picture are discussed in this chapter: comprehension and output. In this discussion I also refer to the concept of intake, which received mention in chapter 1.

6.1. COMPREHENSION

Most models of second language acquisition assume comprehension as a major component. In some models (e.g., the monitor model), comprehension is stated as central; in fact, it is the *sine qua non* of acquisition. It drives acquisition in some inexplicable way. In other models (e.g., UG), although it is not stated explicitly, one assumes that in order to determine if input is relevant, one must decode the input in some understandable way (i.e., the input must be comprehended). In the model presented in chapter 1, the emphasis is not on comprehensible but on comprehended input. Input must be decoded and processed before it is usable for the development of learner systems, and different ways or levels of comprehension include comprehension for meaning as well as comprehension of syntactic relations or patterns. For example, as mentioned in chapter 1, one might understand that *apple juice* is something to drink; one might also understand the morphological relation between the two parts. This latter understanding provides a deeper analysis, which in turn allows for more productive use of the language (e.g., *guava juice*). Similarly, one might understand that "It's hot in here" is a statement of the temperature; one might also have a deeper understanding of the pragmatic force of the utterance, enabling learners to do more with language (i.e., use declarative statements as subtle requests—"This room is messy" might mean "Clean up the room"). Hence, comprehension involves many levels of comprehended language.

Further support for the existence of semantic and syntactic levels of comprehension and the independence of these levels comes from a study by Doughty (1991; also discussed in chapter 1, section 1.4.2). In her study of the rate of acquisition of English relativization, two experimental groups, one focusing on meaning and one focusing on rules, made gains on a pretest–posttest format over a control group that had an exposure-only format. Both groups were able to internalize structural aspects of the instructional input; however, the rule-focused group was not as successful on meaning-comprehension as the meaning-focused group. Thus, structural comprehension and internalization did not seem to depend on meaning comprehension. The meaning-focused group internalized the structural aspects of the input (i.e., relative clauses) and comprehended the input in the sense of meaning. Thus, structural internalization was not compromised by comprehension at the level of meaning.

6.1.1. Input Processing

An area that has received attention in recent years is input processing, which has to do with presentation and timing of input in a pedagogical framework. In particular, it deals with the conversion of input to intake and specifically focuses on form–meaning relations (VanPatten, 1995; VanPatten & Cadierno, 1993; VanPatten & Sanz, 1995). VanPatten and his colleagues presented a model for instructional intervention that relies heavily on the notion of attention to form and the crucial role it plays as a learner moves from input to intake and finally to output. They compared two instructional models, one in which input was practiced as a form of output manipulation (i.e., traditional grammar instruction in which information is presented to the learner and then practiced) and the other in which the attempt is to

change the way input is perceived and processed (i.e., processing instruction; see Figs. 6.1 and 6.2). Rather than allow an internalized system to (begin to) develop, one attempts to influence the way that input is processed and hence the way the system develops. The results of experiments (both sentence-level and discourse related) suggest a positive effect for processing instruction. Subjects in the processing instruction group were better able to understand and produce the target structure (in this case, direct object pronouns in Spanish) than were the traditional instruction group (VanPatten & Cadierno, 1993; VanPatten & Sanz, 1995).

Other studies that consider the role of input processing, albeit in a slightly different manner, are the studies known as the "Garden Path" studies (Tomasello & Herron, 1988, 1989), in which input in the form of corrective feedback (i.e., exceptions to a general rule) was provided either before a faulty generalization was made (in the VanPatten framework, this is akin to the input processing mode in which the focus is on processing input before internalization of that input) or after learners had been led down the garden path and induced to make an overgeneralization. The corrective feedback was more meaningful after learners had been induced to produce an error than when the goal was preventing an error.[1]

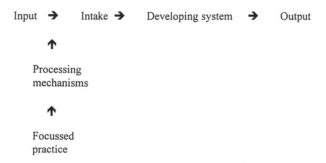

It is clear from these studies and others discussed in this book that some sort of comprehension must take place before we can begin to talk about intake and acquisition. This, of course, begs the question of what is meant by comprehension. As noted earlier, comprehension can range from "an inferential process based on the perception of cues" (Rost, 1990, p. 33) to a detailed structural analysis. Thus, both top–down processing relying on prior knowledge and contextual cues (e.g., visual, oral, etc.) as well as bottom–up processing to which attention to form is crucial are relevant to understand understanding. However, *comprehension* and *acquisition* are not synonymous (see also Sharwood Smith, 1986). Some input will be utilized for meaning, and other input will be utilized to further grammar development. The former precedes the latter: Semantic comprehension, is a prerequisite to syntactic comprehension, and syntactic comprehension is a prerequisite to acquisition.[2] None guarantees the following step. In other words, semantic comprehension is necessary for syntactic comprehension, but it does not guarantee it.

Swain (1995) cited work of Clark and Clark (1977), who pointed to the difference between the two types of comprehension.

> Listeners usually know a lot about what a speaker is going to say. They can make shrewd guesses from what has been said and from the situation being described. They can also be confident that the speaker will make sense, be relevant, provide given and new information appropriately, and in general be cooperative. Listeners almost certainly use this sort of information to select among alternative parses of a sentence, to anticipate words and phrases, and sometimes even to circumvent syntactic analyses altogether. (p. 72)

Assuming the validity of this notion, it follows that comprehension (in the usual sense of the word) may serve little purpose in helping learners understand the syntax of the language, which is an[3] ultimate goal of language learning. Cook (1996, p. 76) similarly noted that the ability to decode language for meaning—"processing language to get the 'message' "— is not the same as code breaking, which refers to the determination of the nature of the linguistic systems used for conveying meaning, that is, "processing language to get the 'rules' " (p. 76).

6.1.2. Intake

As mentioned in chapter 1, I view intake as the process of assimilating linguistic material. Intake is the component of mental activity that takes learners from the input to their interlanguage grammars. This, for course, suggests that intake is not merely a subset of input. In the intake component, psycholinguistic processing takes place. This definition finds support in much of the L2 learning literature, from the early use of the word by

Corder (1967): "input is what goes in not what is *available* for going in, and we may reasonably suppose that it is the learner who controls this input, or more properly his intake" (p. 165) to the most detailed study of intake by Chaudron (1985), who defined *intake* as "the mediating process between the target language available to learners as input and the learners' internalized set of L2 rules and strategies for second language development" (p. 1) to a study by Loew (1993), who noted that "intake is distinct from input and is usually defined as an intermediate process between the exposure to input and actual language acquisition" (p. 334).

Kumaravadivelu (1994) argued that intake factors include individual characteristics (e.g., age, anxiety), negotiation, tactical abilities (e.g., learning and communication strategies), affective variables (e.g., attitudes, motivation), knowledge (e.g., linguistic, metalinguistic), and environmental conditions (e.g., social and educational context). He also described intake processes, including grammaticalization, transfer, inferencing, structuring, and restructuring. In his view, all must work together for optimal conversion of input to intake. This is clearly not a linear conversion; rather, these conditions and processes occur interactively. As Kumaravidelu (1994) stated, "the entire operation is seen as interactive and parallel, responding simultaneously to all available factors and processes at a given point of time. In other words, none of the intake factors by itself seems to be a *prerequisite* for another to be activated, but all are considered *corequisites*" (p. 61). Thus, intake is where information is culled from the environment, synthesized, and digested in preparation for integration into a developing system.

6.2. OUTPUT

Input alone is not sufficient for acquisition; as discussed in section 6.1, when one hears language, one can often interpret the meaning without the use of syntax. For example, if one hears only the words *dog, bit, girl*, regardless of the order in which those words occur, it is likely that the meaning "the dog bit the girl" is assumed. Little knowledge, other than the meanings of the words and something about real-world events, is needed. This is not the case with production, for which one is forced to put the words into some syntactic structure (see also section 1.1.5). Production then "may force the learner to move from semantic processing to syntactic processing" (Swain, 1985, p. 249). In fact, the impetus for Swain's original study was the lack of L2 development by immersion children even after years of academic study in that second language. Swain studied children learning French in an immersion context, hypothesizing that what was lacking in their development as native-like speakers of French was the opportunity to use language productively as opposed to using language merely for comprehension. She compared results on a number of different grammatical, discourse, and sociolinguistic measures of sixth-grade children in a French immersion setting with sixth-grade native French-speaking children. The lack of proficiency of the immersion children coupled with their apparent lack of productive use of French led her to suggest the crucial role of output in the development of a second language.

It is trivial to state that there is no better way to test the extent of one's knowledge (linguistic or otherwise) than to have to use that knowledge in some productive way—whether it be explaining a concept to someone (i.e., teaching), writing a computer program, or, in the case of language learning, getting even a simple idea across. However, output has generally been seen not as a way of creating knowledge but as a way of practicing already-existing knowledge. In other words, output, or production, has traditionally been viewed as a way of practicing what has previously been learned. Figure 6.1 shows that with regard to teaching practices, output and the manipulation of output is viewed as a forum for practicing rules that have already been presented to learners and as a way of aiding learners in internalizing the rules in some not precisely clear way. This was certainly the thrust behind early methods of language teaching in which the presentation–practice (i.e., drill and repetition) mode was in vogue. A second more traditional role for output was as a method by which additional (and perhaps richer) input could be elicited (see Krashen, 1989)—the keep-them-talking model. The idea that output or language use could be part of the learning mechanism itself was not seriously contemplated prior to Swain's (1985) important paper, in which she introduced the notion of comprehensible or "pushed" output: Learners are pushed or stretched in their production as a necessary part of making themselves understood. In so doing, they might modify a previous utterance or they might try forms that they hadn't used before.

Comprehensible output thus refers to the need for a learner to be "pushed toward the delivery of a message that is not only conveyed, but that is conveyed precisely, coherently, and appropriately" (Swain, 1985, p. 249). In a more recent explication of the concept, Swain (1995) claimed "output may stimulate learners to move from the semantic, open-ended, nondeterministic, strategic processing prevalent in comprehension to the complete grammatical processing needed for accurate production. Output, thus, would seem to have a potentially significant role in the development of syntax and morphology" (p. 128).

The question becomes the following: In what ways can output function as a central role in the learning process? In the next sections I discuss four possible ways in which output may provide learners with a forum for important language learning functions: testing hypotheses about the structures and meanings of the target language; receiving crucial feedback for the verification of these hypotheses; developing automaticity in interlanguage production; and forcing a shift from meaning-based processing of the second language to a syntactic mode.

6.2.1. Hypothesis Testing

The notion of hypothesis testing has been central to research in second language acquisition for a number of years (cf. Schachter, 1983, 1992). I argue in this section that output, in particular when part of a negotiation sequence, is a way of testing a hypothesis. This is not to say that hypotheses are being consciously tested every time a second language speaker produces an utterance. However, through negotiation and through feedback learners can be made aware of the hypotheses that they are entertaining as they produce language. That is, the activity of using language helps create a proficiency at analysis that allows learners to think about language.[4] I argued earlier, with regard to comprehension, that greater analysis (in this case focusing on surface form) leads to more possibilities for acquisition. Many questions remain unanswered. Are learners on their own, without any intervention, analytical about language as they put utterances together into a text? Do learners perform some rapid-fire mental analysis using whatever resources they may have at hand as they produce language? One important result (Cumming, 1990) suggests that adults are in fact analytical as they create interlanguage spoken text.

6.2.1.1. Talking About Form. Swain (1995) suggested that learners are in fact involved in testing hypotheses and that they use the forum of interaction to work through them. In support of this position, Swain presented the following example from two L2 learners (age 13) in attendance at an immersion program in Canada. The teacher had just read aloud a text and the students, having taken notes on the reading, worked in pairs to reconstruct the text as closely as possible in terms of both content and form. The sentence they were working on in this example is: *En ce qui concerne l'environment, il y a beaucoup de problemes qui nous tracassent* ("as far as the environment is concerned, there are many problems that face us").

From Swain (1995, pp. 133–134; translation, pp. 143–144)

K = student
G = student
T = teacher

K: Wait a minute! No, I need a Bescherelle (verb reference book). Please open the Bescherelle at the page with, OK, at the last page (i.e., the index). OK look for *tracasse*, one page two pages.

G: *Tra, tra, tracer.*

K: *Tracasser* page six. Look for it please.

G: No problem.

K: It's on page

G: Verb <on page> six. OK, it's the same as *aimer*, (i.e., it is conjugated in the same way and *aimer* is given as the standard example for all verbs with this pattern of conjugation).

K: Let me see it please (reading from the page). *Le passé simple, nous tracasse* (Keith is trying to find a first person plural version of the verb which sounds like *tracasse* the word he has written in his notes, but is unable to find one).

G: Perhaps it's here.

K: No, it's just *nous aime* (pause) ah, the present. *Tracasse. Aimons,* isn't it *tracasse* (to teacher who has just arrived)? It's not *nous tracasse* (what he has written down in his notes). It's *nous tracassons?*

T: It's the *problems* that are worrying us (deliberately not directly giving the answer).

K: *Nous tracassons*

G: <u>Oh</u> (beginning to realize what is happening).

K: Yeah? (So what?)

G: The problems which are worrying us. Like the (pause). It's the problems (pause) like, that concerns us.

K: Yes, but *tracasse* isn't it <u><o-n-s></u>

G: *Tracasse.* It's not a, it's not a (pause), yeah, I dunno (unable to articulate what he has discovered).

K: OK, it says the problems which worry us. Therefore, is *tracasse* a verb? That you have to conjugate?

T: Uh huh.

K: So is it *tracassons?*

T: It's the **problems** which are worrying us.

G: Us, it's it's not, yeah, it's the problems, it's *not, it's not us.*

K: <u>Ah! E-n-t</u> (3rd person plural ending), OK. OK.

As Swain explained, the question here relates to the morphology of the French verb and the use of a relative clause. The difficulty lies in the fact that student K had taken the French phrase *nous tracasse* without taking into consideration that the entire constituent was *qui nous tracasse* ("that we are faced with"). In the first instance it appears that *nous,* "we," is the subject and that the verb should therefore be *tracassons* to agree with the first person plural subject. In actuality, *nous tracasse* is part of the relative clause *qui nous tracasse* with *qui,* "that," as the third person singular subject. The entire dialogue is one in which student K is at first puzzled, then verbalizes the problem and then works to understand the syntax and hence the morphology. In sum, through discourse this child is able to come to a correct conclusion after an initial faulty hypothesis.

6.2.1.2. Self-Correction. Another piece of evidence for the fact that learners test hypotheses through production is the very simple fact of self-correction. As discussed throughout this book, negotiation sequences produce many instances of corrective feedback to learners, from native speakers and non-native speakers alike. These instances appear to have, in some instances, long-lasting effects on language development. In the following examples, it appears that Hiroko is ready to accept a correction. Her quick and easy acceptance of Izumi's *at* suggests a tentativeness that bespeaks of hypothesis testing rather than a conviction of the correctness of her utterance.

2. From Gass and Varonis (1989, pp. 80–81)

   Hiroko: Ah, the dog is barking to—
   Izumi: at
   Hiroko: at the woman.

3. Hiroko: A man is uh drinking c-coffee or tea uh with uh the saucer of the uh uh coffee set is uh in his uh knee.
   Izumi: in him knee
   Hiroko: uh on his knee
   Izumi: yeah
   Hiroko: On his knee.
   Izumi: So sorry. On his knee.

In this negotiation, it appears that both Hiroko and Izumi are tentative and are in a sense fishing for the right form. This interpretation is supported by Hiroko's frequent hesitations in her initial utterance and by Izumi's apology at the end. Other examples (also discussed in chapter 5) suggest the longer term retention that results from these negotiations.

4. From Gass and Varonis (1989, p. 78).

   Atsuko: Uh holding the [kəp].
   Toshi: Holding the cup?
   Atsuko: Hmm hmmm . . .
   (17 turns)
   Toshi: Holding a cup.
   Atsuko: Yes.
   Toshi: Coffee cup?

> Atsuko: Coffee? Oh yeah, tea, coffee cup teacup.
> Toshi: Hm hm.

In this example, the initial clarification request for Toshi (an indicator) suggests to Atsuko that something is wrong with her pronunciation of the word [kəp]. The initial indicator caused her to notice something in her pronunciation that did not match the expectation of her partner, and the remainder of the dialogue was one of hypothesis testing in which she matched her phonetic formulation against that of her partner's. However, Pica (1988) did not find a large number of instances of corrections following feedback, leading her to suggest that "it was not evident from the data that the NNSs were *testing hypotheses* during negotiated interactions" (p. 68). In contrast, a later study by Pica et al. (1989) showed that clarification requests yield modifications in learner output; learners "test hypotheses about the second language, experiment with new structures and forms, and expand and exploit their interlanguage resources in creative ways" (p. 64). I return to this discussion in the next section. That Pica (1988) only considered immediate responses to feedback suggests only that the interaction did not result in immediate change, not that it did not stimulate change.

6.2.2. Feedback

In chapter 2 I discussed the role of negative evidence (i.e., information that a particular utterance is deviant vis-à-vis target language norms) and pointed out that with regard to children, it cannot be a necessary condition for acquisition. What, then, about second language learning? It is undoubtedly the case that adults (at least those in formal learning situations) receive more correction than children, and it may further be the case that adults must have negative evidence (i.e., that it is a necessary condition) in order to accomplish the goal of learning a second language (Birdsong, 1989; Bley-Vroman 1989; Gass, 1988a; Schachter, 1988). Although this research has been based primarily on theoretical arguments, some empirical evidence suggests that negative evidence is in some instances necessary for second language acquisition.

White (1991) considered the development of adverb placement by French children learning English. She was interested in the question of how learners learn not to do something that is present in the native language. In particular, French learners of English have to learn that English allows subject–adverb–verb (SAV) order (e.g., *He always runs*) and that it does not allow subject–verb–adverb–object (SVAO) order (e.g., **He drinks always coffee*). White's study consisted of five classes of French native speakers learning English as a second language (two classes at Grade 5 and three classes at Grade 6) and one control group of monolingual native speakers of English. One Grade 5 group and two Grade 6 groups were given explicit instruction as well as exercises and correction on adverb placement; the other groups were given instruction on questions using the same type of exercises but no explicit instruction on adverbs. The classroom treatment lasted two weeks. All children were given pretests, posttests immediately following the treatment sessions, a second posttest five weeks later, and a follow-up test one year later. The tests consisted of grammaticality judgment tasks (with correction), preference tasks, and a sentence manipulation task. Comparing the groups' performance, White showed that negative evidence indeed promoted the learning of adverb placement but that the effects of the treatment were not as long-lived as anticipated; the two groups did not differ on their performance one year following the treatment.

Throughout this book I have argued that negotiation, because of the focus on incorrect forms, serves as a catalyst for change. Learners who are provided with information about incorrect forms are able to search for additional confirmatory or nonconfirmatory evidence. If negotiation as a form of negative evidence serves to initiate change, the factors that determine whether the initiated change results in permanent restructuring of linguistic knowledge must be identified. As with any type of learning, there needs to be reinforcement of what is being learned. These concepts are schematized in Fig. 6.3. If additional input is not available, learners do not have the opportunity to obtain confirmatory or disconfirmatory evidence. Without additional focused evidence, it is not surprising that the learners in White's (1991) study did not retain knowledge of English adverb

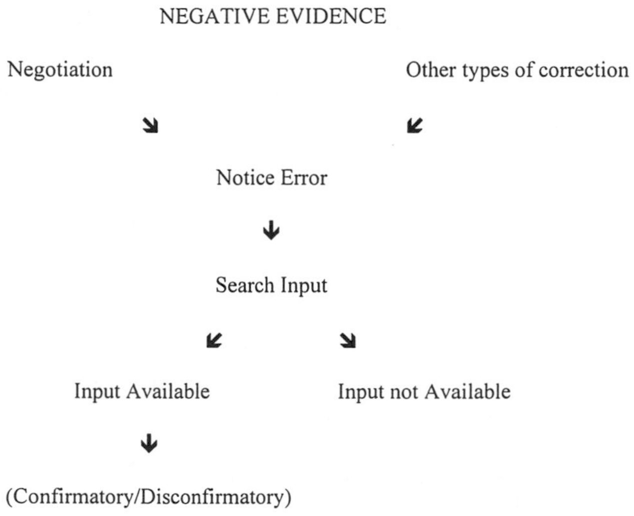

NEGATIVE EVIDENCE

Negotiation   Other types of correction

↘   ↙

Notice Error

↓

Search Input

↙   ↘

Input Available   Input not Available

↓

(Confirmatory/Disconfirmatory)

FIG. 6.3. The function of negative evidence.

placement. In other words, acquisition appears to be gradual and, simplistically, takes time and often requires numerous doses of evidence. That is, there is an incubation period beginning with the time of the initial input (negative or positive) to the final stage of restructuring and output.

Although White's (1991) study importantly shows that negative evidence may be necessary to trigger a permanent change in one's grammar, it does not show that positive evidence alone (i.e., input alone) is insufficient. (In fact, the question group in White's study received little information about adverbs from the naturalistic classroom data to which they were exposed). Trahey and White (1993) did a follow-up study to determine the effect of positive evidence. Their study consisted of two Grade 5 classes of French students learning English. Both classes were given an input flood of English adverbs (i.e., positive evidence only) over a 2-week period. The same timetable as in the White (1991) study was used with the exception of 3-week rather than five-week follow-up testing and no testing one year later. They found that input was sufficient for learners to notice that SAV order is possible in English but that it was not sufficient to detect the ungrammaticality of SVAO sentences. Thus, taken together, these two experiments show that positive evidence can reveal to learners the presence of information in the L2 that is different from their native language but that it takes negative evidence to show L2 ungrammaticality when the L1 counterpart is grammatical.

Other studies have also suggested that feedback serves a corrective function (e.g., Gass & Varonis, 1989; Pica, Holliday, Lewis, & Morgenthaler, 1989). The Pica et al. study is interesting in that the authors provided the first systematic evidence that learners respond differentially to different types of feedback. In their study one important focus was on different types of native speaker signals to non-native errors. They found that the greatest amount of modification comes in response to clarification requests, as in the following example (Nobuyoshi & Ellis, 1993),

5. NNS: He pass his house.
   NS: Sorry?
   NNS: He passed, he passed, ah, his sign.

as opposed to modeling. That the non-native speaker is forced to make the actual correction, as opposed to hearing and perhaps thinking about the correct form, is in itself a facilitator to acquisition. Again, however, longer term retention is not known.

Nobuyoshi and Ellis (1993) conducted a study that suggests longer term retention after focused attention. Learners had to describe a series of pictures that depicted events that had happened the previous weekend and the previous day. The experimental group received feedback through clarification requests that focused on past tense forms. The control group did not receive focused feedback. The results can only be considered suggestive due to a very small sample size, but, in the experimental group, two of three subjects were able to reformulate the correct forms after feedback and were able to maintain the correct forms at a subsequent administration one week later. In the control group, none of the subjects showed an accuracy gain.

Similarly, Lightbown (1992) compared corrective feedback provided by teachers immediately after the occurrence of an error in a communicative activity to feedback on audio-lingual drills or pure practice activities. She found that in both cases learners were able to self-correct, but only in the first case was the self-correction incorporated into their second language systems, as evidenced by use of the targeted form outside the classroom.

Takashima (1995), in a study of Japanese learners of English, investigated the effects of feedback that was focused on particular morphological form (e.g., past tense and plural[5]) versus feedback that was communication oriented. The focused feedback was in the form of clarification requests ("Sorry?" "What did you say?"). Groups of students had to work together to make up a story based on a sequence of pictures, of which each student in the group had only one. One student was then nominated to tell the story to the class. This was the actual feedback session, for the teacher provided either focused morphological feedback or content feedback. The accuracy rate for past tense increased at a faster rate during the time of the study (11 weeks) in the focused morphological correction group as opposed to the content correction group. Furthermore, the magnitude of the difference increased as a function of time. Improved accuracy was noted for the particular student who was corrected (in front of the class) as well as for those students who were in the class observing the interaction. Interestingly, when considering the actual reformulations, there was no correlation between the reformulated utterances and improvement in accuracy. This finding suggests, as stated earlier in this book, that the actual interaction does not constitute change itself but is only a catalyst for later change. Illustrative of this is the following excerpt from Takashima (1995) in which the first clarification request appears to fall short of the mark in that the student makes no change, but as the storytelling continues, the student seems to be more sensitive to the past tense forms, even self-correcting in the last turn.

   6. From Takashima (1995, p. 77)
      S = Student; T = Teacher
      S: One day, the fairy, sting the magic wand to Cinderalla.
      T: Sorry?
      S: One day, the fairy sting the magic wand to Cinderalla.

T: OK.
S: Cinde, ah, Cinderaella changed into, the beautiful girl. (Laugh) Ah, and, the, Cin, Cinderella wen Cinderella went to the palace by coach. The, the prince fall in love at a first glance.
T: Sorry?
S: Ah, the prince fall in, falled falled in love Cinderella at a first glance. And they dance, they danced . . . Ah, Cin, Cinderella have, Cinderella have to go home.

The input has been enhanced through clarification requests, and the output has similarly been enhanced (Takashima's term), apparently as a function of the input enhancement.

Carroll, Roberge, and Swain (1992) found some support for the role of corrective feedback but not in aiding learners in the development of generalizations based on the input data. Their study concerned French suffixation. In particular, English subjects were trained on two forms of French suffixes, -*age* and -*ment*. One group then received corrective feedback when errors occurred, whereas the control group received no such correction. The results suggested that corrective feedback helped learners memorize those individual words on which corrective feedback was provided, but did not help learners restructure their grammars. Learners did not move to the next step of generalizing the correction to novel forms.

I now turn to an examination of the function that negative evidence might have. One could argue that when errors are made and when, as a result, there is feedback, this feedback provides the learner with information that an utterance is deviant, that is, feedback to a faulty hypothesis. In an ideal situation, a learner's grammar is then modified. There are obvious limitations to this view. First, corrections cannot occur with all incorrect forms. Second, many so-called errors are errors of interpretation for which there may be no evidence that an error has even occurred. In other words, if a learner interprets an utterance with the incorrect syntactic configuration, there is no way of knowing that misinterpretation has occurred and therefore no way of correcting the misinterpretation. As an example, consider reflexivization. If a learner of English interprets the sentence *John is afraid that Bill will cut himself* as if the *himself* referred to John (as is possible in some languages), there is no immediate way of disconfirming that hypothesis.

A third and perhaps more important limitation is that error acknowledgment, such as expressions of nonunderstanding (e.g., *huh?*), does not provide information that is sufficiently specific to inform learners where exactly an error has been made. That is, is the failure in communication the result of incorrect syntax, phonology, morphology, or vocabulary? Error acknowledgment also does not indicate what to do to correct the error.

6.2.3. Automaticity

A third function of output is the development of fluency and automaticity of processing. As discussed in chapters 1 and 4, the human mind is a limited processing system. Certain processes are deliberate, requiring a significant amount of time and space. Others are routine and automatic, occupying less time and space. McLaughlin (1987) claimed that automatization involves "a learned response that has been built up through the consistent mapping of the same input to the same pattern of activation over many trials" (p. 134). I extend this notion to output: The consistent and successful mapping (i.e., practice) of grammar to output results in automatic processing (see also Loschky & Bley-Vroman, 1993).

6.2.4. Meaning-Based to Grammatically Based Processing

In some sense this is where the study of output began. Swain's (1985) initial hypothesis stated that output "may force the learner to move from semantic processing to syntactic processing" (p. 249). This notion has been discussed throughout the book, and I do not reelaborate here. Suffice it to say that processing language only at the level of meaning will not and cannot serve the purpose of understanding the syntax of the language, a level of knowledge that is essential to production of language.[6]

In sum, output provides learners the opportunity to produce language and gain feedback, which, by focusing learners' attention on certain local aspects of their speech, may lead them to notice either a mismatch between their speech and that of an interlocutor (particularly if as part of the feedback a linguistic model is provided) or a deficiency in their output. Noticing, then, leads to reassessment, which may be an on-the-spot reassessment or longer term complex thinking about the issue. The latter may be bolstered by gathering additional information through a variety of sources (e.g., input, direct questioning, grammar books, dictionaries). This, in essence, is the process of learning (see also Swain & Lapkin, 1995).

NOTES

1. Criticisms have been allayed against the Tomasello and Herron (1988, 1989) methodology and analysis (see Beck & Eubank, 1991, and the response by Tomasello & Herron, 1991).
2. Whether or not this is the case for all parts of language is questionable. For example, Sheldon and Strange (1982) and Gass (1984) noted that accurate speech production of particular sounds often precedes the perception of those sounds.
3. I use *an* rather than *the* because it is clear that there are important aspects of language to be learned beyond syntax (e.g., pragmatics, phonology). I argue, however, that the focus on these aspects at a detailed level of analysis is also a prerequisite to their acquisition. For example, within the realm of pragmatics, it is not sufficient to understand that someone

is being polite (akin to understanding at the level of meaning); rather, it is necessary to understand the means by which politeness takes place (akin to understanding at the level of syntax).

4. The relevance of metalinguistic knowledge to acquisition has been discussed by many (e.g., Bialystok, 1987; Birdsong, 1989). Metalinguistic ability refers to one's capability to consider language not just as a means of expressing ideas or communicating with others but as an object of inquiry. Thus, making puns suggests an ability to think about language as opposed to using it only for expressive purposes. Similarly, judging whether a given sentence is grammatical in one's language or translating from one language to another requires a person to think about language as opposed to engaging in pure use of it.

5. In actuality, only the past tense part of the study could be analyzed due to the paucity of examples of plural markers that could be corrected.

6. I am not including so-called *reading knowledge* of a language, necessary for many graduate degree programs. In those instances it may indeed be possible to know little of the syntax (perhaps other than basic word order phenomena) and to rely only on lexical knowledge and knowledge of the subject matter as decoding cues. It is often the case that individuals who have a reading knowledge are incapable of encoding that language or of decoding that language in anything but a written format.

Chapter 7

Epilogue: Classroom
Implications and Applications

7.0. INTRODUCTION

This book, a book about second language acquisition, has not dealt with the area of pedagogy, nor is it my intent to do so, for a whole new book would be spawned. Nevertheless, because L2 pedagogy must be grounded, at least to some extent, in learning and how learning takes place, it is appropriate to attempt to make a link between the two. In this regard, the question to be raised is how the information gleaned from a study of input, interaction, and output contributes to decisions about the classroom.

Often a great deal is required of the field of second language acquisition with regard to expectations of the way it should inform second language pedagogy. Considerations of this sort may be misguided or at least premature (cf. Lightbown, 1985). Knowledge of the way acquisition takes place does not necessarily provide definitive guidelines about classrooms but rather provides information about how we might think about the learners in our classrooms.

None of the models or approaches I have discussed provide THE answer to classroom decisions. Some are perhaps more theoretically sound than others, but each has something to contribute to our understanding of the classroom. For example, some aspects of an information processing view do not necessarily stand in contradiction to a UG view. Each emphasizes different aspects of the learning process. Both conceptions of the input must be taken into account.

The classroom is a means to enhance the input, to use a term coined by Sharwood Smith (1991, 1993). By input enhancement, Sharwood Smith (1991) referred to the "process by which language input becomes salient to the learner" (p. 118). Input enhancement is similar (although not identical) to the concept of input noticing or apperceived input, discussed earlier. A major difference is that input enhancement can be learner generated or externally generated, whereas input noticing or apperception refers only to learner internal processes. Of course, not all externally created salience results in noticed input, for students may be asleep, may be thinking about a girlfriend or boyfriend, or may just not realize that anything is being emphasized. However, input enhancement is a special and, as argued in the earlier chapters of this book, a necessary part of language learning. It is a supplement to naturalistic evidence, one that is inherent to classroom learning. Externally induced input is what the classroom can bring to the learning process. It is likely that learners reach a point where differences between their own learner systems and the target language are imperceptible. At this point, enhanced input is necessary to prevent the cessation of language development.

From an information-processing perspective, input is necessary for greater automaticity (see section 6.3). That is, many exemplars will lead to automatic processing. This does not rule out the possibility that some innate structure such as UG forms an integral part of the learning process. We need to understand that input enhancement, perhaps through explicit correction or some other form of negative evidence or explicit grammatical instruction, is necessary for certain types of grammar change. Figure 6.1 shows that enhancement may need to be followed with numerous examples in an effort to restructure and automatize a learner's use.

Just as it is inappropriate to conceptualize input as a monolithic phenomenon, neither should the classroom be seen as a place where learners all progress at the same rate and with similar needs; nor must input be of only one type. Whether we want to have large doses of input or whether we want explicit grammatical instruction should never be put as yes–no questions; the answer is not just "yes" or "no," but "yes and no." We need to ascertain when the answer is "yes" and when the answer is "no." Considerations of language proficiency are also relevant. Is the input type or output requirement the same for all levels of proficiency? Evidence from empirical research suggests that differences exist (Pica, 1988; Pica et al. 1989; Swain & Lapkin, 1995).

In the remainder of this epilogue, I sketch a view of language teaching that is consistent with what has been discussed in this book. In particular, I focus on the notion of task to lay out issues related to language classrooms.

7.1. LANGUAGE CLASSROOMS

How we organize language courses and language lessons within those courses is of major importance in the field of L2 pedagogy. Before being able to talk about the organization of a language lesson, however, we need first to determine what our unit of organization is. Throughout the history of language teaching, we have seen different principles espoused for language classrooms. Predominant among them has been the structural syllabus, which takes grammatical structures as the basic unit of analysis. An instructor or textbook then puts them in some order, depending on a variety of factors, and students move from one structure to another. This, of course, says nothing about how these structures are taught (i.e., through explicit grammatical instruction or through presentation of input); it only says that these structures are ordered. More recently other guiding principles have emerged, such as language functions or language notions or situations in which learners are likely to find themselves.

7.1.1. Tasks

A relatively recent arrival on the scene of language teaching is the notion of task.[1] As Nunan (1989) pointed out, the discussion of tasks belongs to both syllabus design and methodology. In fact, it is a means by which these hitherto separate aspects of language teaching can be united. In his words, "if we see curriculum planning as an integrated set of processes involving, among other things, the specification of both what and how, then the argument over whether the design and development of tasks belongs to syllabus design or to methodology becomes unimportant" (p. 1). Tasks are the building blocks of all lessons because they specify what we do and how we do it. They are in some sense independent of the syllabus type adopted in a classroom in that one can have tasks that are perfectly compatible with a structural syllabus or with a notional–functional syllabus. They are in another sense dependent on syllabus type in that the actual focus of a particular lesson (which depends on the syllabus) dictates the type of task to be used.

Defining a task is by no means easy. For the present purposes, I view a classroom task as a piece of work that must be completed.[2] I also restrict the discussion to tasks that involve some oral exchange among or between learners. Clearly, there are other definitions of task, some of which differ somewhat from my own (e.g., Breen 1987; Long, 1985; Long & Crookes, 1992; Richards, Platt, & Weber, 1986; Skehan, 1996).

As Nunan (1989) pointed out, most definitions focus on meaning as opposed to language form. Skehan (1996) made a similar point in his own definition when he noted that "for present purposes a task is taken to be an activity in which: meaning is primary" (p. 39). However, it is imperative to point out that approaches to teaching that use a task as primary are not necessarily incompatible with a structural syllabus, for one can have an underlying grammatical organization without having a focus on form. Nunan made this specific point in his definition of task: "as a piece of classroom work which involves learners in comprehending, manipulating, producing or interacting in the target language while their attention is principally focused on meaning rather than form" (p. 10). Although I agree to some extent with earlier meaning-based definitions, I do not agree that a lack of focus on form is a necessary part of task-based learning. To the contrary, a focus on form when it is appropriately determined and appropriately timed is an essential part of the learning process.

7.1.2. Tasks and Learning Correlates

In preceding chapters I have taken the position that language learning (and, it follows, a theory of language learning) cannot depend on a single conceptualization of language. Often the literature is replete with presumed dichotomies, dichotomies, which appear on the surface to be contradictory and incompatible (e.g., arguments regarding competence as found in Eckman, 1994; Ellis, 1990; Gregg, 1990; Tarone, 1990). Within the cognitive psychology literature, one also finds arguments for structure-based learning that results in restructuring (e.g., McLaughlin, 1990b) and arguments for an exemplar-based approach to learning (cf. Carr & Curran, 1994). As Skehan (1996) pointed out, "The former [the restructuring approach] regards development in terms of the growth and complexity of the underlying system involved, while the latter [exemplar learning] is more concerned with the accumulation of exemplars, and their utility in performance" (p. 42). Consistent with earlier discussions is Skehan's (1996) contention that findings in general are "consistent with a dual-mode of processing, in which there is evidence for both structured learning and exemplar-based learning, but with the operation of both modes combining in a synergistic manner to yield results, and degrees of learning, that are more than simply the sum of the parts" (p. 43).

The importance of structural learning combined with meaning-based input that provides numerous exemplars or chunks is clear. I thus return to the issue of the necessity of form-focused instruction. The controversy over form-focused instruction (which includes grammar instruction and error correction) has been raging for a number of years (cf. Hulstijn, 1995; Larsen-Freeman, 1995; VanPatten, 1993; VanPatten & Cadierno, 1993). In order to come to an understanding of this issue, it is important to examine the learning correlates of form-focused instruction.

It is well known that earlier language teaching methodologies were based on grammar-translation. Within grammar-translation, a method that has as its basis the assumption that language learning involves the acquisition of conscious knowledge, specific grammatical points are explained in metalinguistic terms. On the other hand, many current approaches to language teaching leave little room for explicit grammatical instruction (see, for example, Krashen & Terrell, 1983). Those who argue against the need for explicit grammatical instruction (whether within a grammar-translation framework or not) typically invoke the argument that L1 and L2 acquisition are similar processes and that, after all, explicit instruction or explanation is not involved in L1 acquisition. In fact, it is commonplace now to avoid form-focused instruction as well as explicit error correction, with the concomitant argument that what is needed for acquisition to take place is sufficient quantities of input. Required within this view is the creation of as natural an environment as possible in order for learners to have significant opportunities to express meaning through their second language. Of course, what is natural is not always efficient (Widdowson, 1991), yet despite these objections, many teachers continue to rely on explicit presentation of grammatical rules, and many students continue to expect rule presentation.

Pedagogical descriptions may aid the learner to internalize parts of the target language but do not necessarily represent what the learner has internalized. Therefore, it is important to understand how we might in fact aid the learner. Returning to the notions of attention and the creation of noticeable gaps, we can see that instruction focused on grammatical (intended broadly) form can bring mismatches to a learner's attention.

7.2. PUTTING THEORY TO PRACTICE AND PRACTICE TO THEORY

7.2.1. Selective Attention

What then is the role of the classroom, and how does it relate to selective attention? What goes on in the classroom facilitates student awareness of target language forms and meanings and of the discrepancies between what they have themselves construct for their second language and the system that becomes apparent to them (through instruction) from the target language data they confront. In other words, the classroom acts as a selective attention device (i.e., it is an input enhancer, to use Sharwood Smith's [1991, 1993] terms). Put differently, the object of instruction is self-discovery on the part of the learner. Thus, the role of the classroom is to aid the learner in making efficient use of the resources at hand to facilitate self-discovery (Rutherford & Sharwood Smith, 1985; Sharwood Smith, 1981).

7.2.2. Enhancing the Input

Focused instruction, as I have argued, is a first step in the modification of one's grammar. This is of course an oversimplification of the significance of instruction because attention is in the eye of the beholder (Sharwood Smith, 1991). A teacher can draw attention to something, but the learner must do something with that input. In Sharwood Smith's (1991) words,

> . . . colouring instances of particular morphological inflections green, or embedding instances of a particular grammatical rule or principle in a meta-linguistic explanation, as in the giving of rules for using the subjunctive in French, could all be construed as attempts to put 'flags' in the input, that is, to direct the learner's attention to particular properties of the input in the hope that they can use these flags to develop their own internal mental flags. (p. 120)

My remarks thus far should not be construed as a plea to return to grammar-translation classrooms. This is a plea, however, to attempt to understand why form-focused instruction is important, if not necessary, for acquisition.

How can form-focused instruction be related to task-based learning? What is necessary is the creation of tasks that can themselves drive attention to form. Consider the more typical means of presenting new grammatical structures, with a presentation of structure (with explanation) followed by practice of the structure in a controlled way and then in a less controlled way. Structuring our syllabi around tasks gives greater latitude in teaching and allows a way out of this relatively unsuccessful and meaningless means of having students combine a focus on form and a focus on meaning. Samuda (1993) presented a scheme for developing the "need to mean" in students. As she stated, "task(s) create a 'need to mean,' which brings students to the threshold of actively recognizing a 'gap' in their knowledge which needs to be bridged in order to complete the task successfully. The teacher's role is to bring to consciousness an awareness of how the language works as the students need it."

In this view, there are various ways of presenting data. In most tasks there is initially some sort of input to the task, such as a description of a room after a murder, a list of items found in an individual's pocket (or the presentation of the actual items), or a picture. A second part of a task is the actual task operation—a discussion in which students attempt to determine who murdered whom, a description of the individual whose pocket items have been presented, or a description of a picture. Finally, there might be some resolution to the task in terms of the outcome.

An example from an actual textbook may be illustrative (Riggenbach & Samuda, 1993). Students are initially presented with the following figure (Fig. 7.1). Their task is to write in the name of each person in this pho-

THE LEFT   THE RIGHT

NAME	LIKES	AGE	HAIR	OCCU-PATION	EYES	HEIGHT
Linda	football	75	red	doctor	green	5' 9½"
Bob	beer	19	brown	student	blue	5' 9½"
Susan	music	25	blonde	student	green	5' 1"
Frank	cats	43	gray	artist	brown	6' 4"
Carla	food	28	black	singer	blue	5' 5"
George	movies	44	bald	writer	brown	5' 10"
Diana	opera	58	brown	engineer	gray	5' 10"

CLUES

1. The oldest person is behind the youngest woman
2. The tallest woman is behind someone who is thirty years younger than her.
3. The shortest person is in front of someone with green eyes.
4. The tallest man is next to the tallest woman.
5. The person who likes beer is not quit as tall as the person next to him on the right.
6. The man who is on the right of the youngest person is behind the tallest person.
7. The youngest person is as tall as the person next to him on the left.
8. The 28-year-old singer is not next to anybody.

FIG. 7.1. Silhouettes and identification task. From *Dimensions of Grammar: Form, Meaning and Use, Book Two* (pp. 46–47), by H. Riggenbach and V. Samuda, 1993, Boston, MA: Heinle & Heinle. Copyright 1993 by Heinle & Heinle. Reprinted with permission.

tograph. Relative clauses are needed to interpret the information and to express the various physical relationships. In fact, in this example the targeted structure is in the input. But where does presentation of language material fit in? Samuda (1993) outlined the sequence of events presented in Fig. 7.2.

In this scheme, the language presentation would most likely take place after the students had performed an initial task in which students had been brought to the threshold of "needing to mean" (i.e., noticing the gap), after

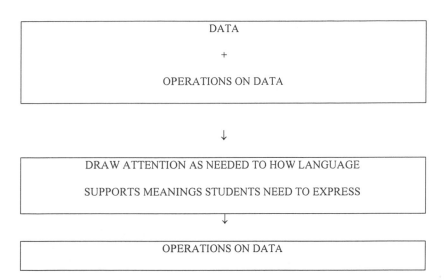

FIG. 7.2.   Sequence of events in structure-based tasks. From *Grammar Tasks: Creating a Need to Mean*, by V. Samuda 1993, October. Paper presented for the English Language Center Colloquium, Michigan State University. Copyright 1993 by V. Samuda. Reprinted with permission.

their attention had been drawn, through a task, to a particular grammatical form. I refer to this as surreptitious focus on form, which can of course be followed by more typical language exercises (i.e., the operation on data part). In this model one moves away from a present, practice, produce mode and am using tasks to reorder this sequence into a form of practice, presentation, production.

To return to the discussion of language learning, if the goal is to get students to notice the gap while doing language work that is both meaningful and engaging, then using tasks in the way described here achieves that end. In thinking about the role of tasks in the language classroom, however, it is not sufficient to consider only the task itself. We need also to consider the way learners relate to the task in a classroom setting. What happens during a task?

7.2.3. The Role of Tasks

7.2.3.1. Negotiation. As discussed in chapter 5, negotiation refers to those instances in conversation in which participants need to interrupt the flow of the conversation in order for both parties to understand what the conversation is about. One function of these conversations is to bring gaps to a learner's attention. A second function is metalinguistic awareness (see chapter 6).

7.2.3.2. Metalinguistic Awareness. Non-native speakers in a classroom setting often spend more time on metalinguistic activities rather than on activities of pure use. These activities include, for example, studying rules of grammar and memorizing vocabulary words. The ability to think about language is often associated with increased ability to learn a language. In fact, bilingual children seem to have greater metalinguistic awareness than monolingual children (Bialystok, 1987).

In early language teaching methodologies much classroom activity engaged learners in just this type of consciousness raising. These methodologies provided a direct means of alerting learners to the language but at the expense of spending classroom time in practice activities. However, increased metalinguistic awareness can take place in other ways. Learners are made aware of errors in their speech (whether in grammar, pronunciation, content, or discourse) through the questioning and clarification that often takes place in negotiation. In other words, negotiation makes learners aware of incongruity between the forms they are using and the forms used by the native-speaking community. In order to respond to an inquiry of nonunderstanding, non-native speakers must modify output, as discussed in chapters 5 and 6. For this modification to take place, the learner must become aware of a problem and seek to resolve it. Hence, the more the learner is made aware of unacceptable speech, the greater the opportunity for the learner to make appropriate modifications. Although there is limited evidence as to the long-range effects of these modifications, one can presume that negotiation, because it leads to heightened awareness, ultimately leads to increased knowledge of the second language. For example, in the following exchange, even though the NNS never produces the correct form, she becomes aware of a pronunciation problem through the indications of nonunderstanding.

1. From Pica (1987, p. 6)
   NNS: And they have the chwach there.
   NS: The what?
   NNS: The chwach—I know someone that—
   NS: What does it mean?
   NNS: Like um like American people they always go there every Sunday.
   NS: Yes?
   NNS: You know—every morning that there pr-that—the American people get dressed up to got to um chwach.
   NS: Oh to church—I see.

To return to the discussion of task-based learning, it is the task itself that can create the opportunities for extended negotiation. Thus, the task designer's responsibility is to develop task types to force the kind of distance needed between participants to allow extended negotiation. An examination of the language of these tasks is needed to understand which tasks are more beneficial to which learners and when. Do we want our tasks to be of a familiar type (Plough & Gass, 1993)? Do we want the learners to be of the same nationality (Varonis & Gass, 1985b) or of the same gender (Gass & Varonis, 1986; see discussion in chapter 5)? All these questions are relevant and significant for the entire issue of tasks and how to approach the creation and formation of tasks for the language classroom.

7.2.3.3. Automaticity and Restructuring. Before concluding this discussion I point out one other area where it is important to examine the function of tasks closely. In the cognitive psychology literature (cf. McLaughlin, 1987, 1990b) two important learning processes are noted (see chapter 4): automaticity and restructuring. As noted earlier, automatic processes are those that have become routinized. Little effort is required to execute an automatic process (e.g., the steps involved in getting into a car and starting it are relatively automatized). Automatic processes come about as a result of "consistent mapping of the same input to the same pattern of activation over many trials" (McLaughlin, 1987, p. 134). The other important concept is that of restructuring. Restructuring involves change in one's underlying knowledge (McLaughlin, 1990b).

If restructuring and automatization are important aspects of the learning process, and if tasks are components or organizing principles of the language classroom, then it becomes necessary to examine how tasks contribute to these cognitive domains. Loschky and Bley-Vroman (1993) presented a model in which they talk about task types and their relative contribution to automatization and restructuring. Their main claim has to do with the necessity or likelihood of a targeted structure being part of a particular task. They divided tasks along a continuum from essential tasks to useful tasks to natural tasks, dimensions marked by the involvement of a particular structure in a task. In essential tasks, the targeted structure will in all cases appear; in useful tasks, the targeted structure is useful to the completion of the task but not essential; in natural tasks, the targeted structure appears frequently.

How does this relate to automaticity and restructuring? Figure 7.3 is a diagram taken from Loschky and Bley-Vroman (1993). Tasks that are at the essential end of the continuum will involve more restructuring because the task designer has more control over the output that will be produced and, hence, more control over where a learner's attention will be placed. At the other end of the continuum are the natural tasks. Recall the definition of automatization: a consistent mapping of input to activation, or in other words, practice. If natural tasks by nature have large numbers of tokens of a particular structure, both in the input to the task and in the execution of the task, then they are suited for practice and hence autom-

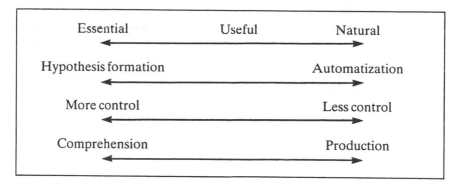

FIG. 7.3. Relationships among four basic dimensions of structure-based tasks. From *Tasks and Language Learning: Integrating Theory and Practice* (p. 142), by G. Crookes and S. Gass (Eds.), 1993, Clevedon: Multilingual Matters. Copyright 1993 by Multilingual Matters. Reprinted with permission.

atization. In looking at a scheme such as the one presented here, one has first to determine at what stage the learners in our classroom find themselves vis-à-vis a particular structure. Do they need to incorporate it into their grammars? That is, is restructuring necessary? Or do they just need to become more adept and automatic in using the structure? A determination of task type follows the answers to these questions. Preliminary research by Delk, Evart, and Helling (1993) suggests that the distinction of task types and the resultant learning outcomes may in fact be valid.

7.3. CONCLUSION

In this epilogue I have presented some of the considerations involved in task-based learning. In particular, I have presented a means and justification for task-based learning to be used in conjunction with a focus on form as well as a focus on meaning. Perhaps most important is the idea that regardless of what we ultimately adopt as a classroom methodology or means of syllabus organization, it is essential that we work in tandem with research on language learning that provides the ultimate justification for classroom teaching.

In many ways the field of second language acquisition appears to be one of great contradictions, and in many cases practitioners appear to want to portray it in that way. On the one hand, some claim that there is an innate linguistic system, to which second language learners have access and by which they construct their second language systems. On the other hand, others say that language acquisition cannot be investigated without considering the context within which it is used. For these individuals, language acquisition is guided by the interactions in which learners are involved. The feedback given in such interactions is crucial to learners as they hypothesis-test their way from no knowledge to a reasonably developed second language system.

Having done work in language universals, I am of the fundamental belief that second language acquisition is shaped by the nature of language (although the extent to which innateness plays a role is still a question). Having done work in input and interaction, I am of the fundamental belief that second language acquisition is shaped by the input one receives and by the interactions in which one engages. At first blush these appear to be contradictory, but I have never seen them in that light. I see nothing incompatible with arguments that language is constrained by universals (innate or otherwise) and that language is shaped by interactions. Although universals provide learners with the basic shape of language, there is still the factor of the native language. Beyond that, it is perhaps appropriate to think of universals not so much as informing learners about what they can do but of restricting their choices (see Schachter, 1983, 1992). From that basket of choices, learners must select; interactions and input help them with that task. The model outlined in chapter 1 is designed to capture that fact. It is intended to show that universals play one part of the dynamic picture of second language acquisition; our task as second language researchers is to determine the precise nature of the significance of universals and the extent to which they are (or are not) innate. The model is also intended to show that input and interaction have a role in understanding how second languages are learned; our task as second language researchers is to determine with precision the nature of that role. This book, I hope, has made inroads in that latter goal. The situation is reminiscent of a (well-known) anecdote cited by Nelson, Bonvillian, Denninger, Kaplan, and Baker (1984):

> There was a judge sitting with an apprentice as first a man came to tell his tale of injustice at the hands of a woman, and then the woman came to tell her opposite account. To each the judge said, "Yes, I understand. Your views are entirely correct." The apprentice paused after the second interview, frowned deeply, and burst out: "But they can't both be correct in their views!" And the judge replied, "Yes, yes you are right." (pp. 31–32)

NOTES

1. For research on ways of relating tasks and syllabus design, see Robinson (1996).
2. It is interesting to note that the word *task* originally comes from a word meaning *tax*. Hence, it is not inappropriate to think of a task as a difficult or challenging piece of work.

References

Allport, A. (1988). What concept of consciousness? In A. J. Marcel & E. Bisiach (Eds.), *Consciousness in contemporary science* (pp. 159–182). London: Clarendon.

Archibald, J. (1993, October). *Indirect negative evidence and blame assignment in L2 parameter setting.* Paper presented at the 22nd University of Wisconsin–Milwaukee Linguistics Symposium, Milwaukee, WI.

Arthur, B., Weiner, R., Culver, M., Lee, Y. J., & Thomas, D. (1980). The register of impersonal discourse to foreigners: Verbal adjustments to foreign accents. In D. Larsen-Freeman (Ed.), *Discourse analysis in second language research* (pp. 111–124). Rowley, MA: Newbury House.

Aston, G. (1986). Trouble-shooting in interaction with learners: The more the merrier? *Applied Linguistics, 7,* 128–143.

Bailey, N., Madden, C., & Krashen, S. (1974). Is there a "natural sequence" in adult second language learning? *Language Learning, 24,* 235–243.

Barasch, R., & James, C. (Eds.). (1994). *Beyond the monitor model: Current theory and practice in second language acquisition.* Boston, MA: Heinle & Heinle.

Bard, E., Robertson, D., & Sorace, A. (1996). Magnitude estimation of linguistic acceptability. *Language, 72,* 32–68.

Bardovi-Harlig, K. (1987). Markedness and salience in second-language acquisition. *Language Learning, 37,* 385–407.

Bardovi-Harlig, K., & Hartford, B. (1993). Learning the rules of academic talk: A longitudinal study of pragmatic development. *Studies in Second Language Acquisition, 15,* 279–304.

Bardovi-Harlig, K., & Hartford, B. (1996). Input in an institutional setting. *Studies in Second Language Acquisition, 18,* 171–188.

Barton, M., & Tomasello, M. (1994). The rest of the family: The role of fathers and siblings in early language development. In C. Gallaway & B. Richards (Eds.), *Input and interaction in language acquisition* (pp. 109–134). Cambridge, England: Cambridge University Press.

Bates, E., & MacWhinney, B. (1982). Functionalist approach to grammar. In E. Wanner & L. Gleitman (Eds.), *Language acquisition: The state of the art* (pp. 173–218). New York: Cambridge University Press.

162

Bates, E., & MacWhinney, B. (1989). Functionalism and the competition model. In B. MacWhinney & E. Bates (Eds.), *The cross-linguistic study of sentence processing* (pp. 3–73). Cambridge, England: Cambridge University Press.

Bavin, E. (1992). The acquisition of Walpiri. In D. Slobin (Ed.), *The crosslinguistic study of language acquisition* (pp. 309–372). Hillsdale, NJ: Lawrence Erlbaum Associates.

Bayley, R. (1994). Interlanguage variation and the quantitative paradigm: Past-tense marking in Chinese English. In E. Tarone, S. Gass, & A. Cohen (Eds.), *Research methodology in second language acquisition* (pp. 157–181). Hillsdale, NJ: Lawrence Erlbaum Associates.

Beck, M., & Eubank, L. (1991). Acquisition theory and experimental design: A critique of Tomasello and Herron. *Studies in Second Language Acquisition, 13,* 73–76.

Beebe, L. (1985). Input: Choosing the right stuff. In S. Gass & C. Madden (Eds.), *Input in second language acquisition* (pp. 404–414). Rowley, MA: Newbury House.

Beebe, L., & Giles, H. (1984). Speech-accommodation theories: A discussion in terms of second-language acquisition. *International Journal of the Sociology of Language, 46,* 5–32.

Bialystok, E. (1987). Words as things: Development of word concept by bilingual children. *Studies in Second Language Acquisition, 9,* 133–140.

Birdsong, D. (1989). *Metalinguistic performance and interlinguistic competence.* Berlin: Springer-Verlag.

Birdsong, D. (1992). Ultimate attainment in second language acquisition. *Language, 68,* 706–755.

Bley-Vroman, R. (1989). The logical problem of second language learning. In S. Gass & J. Schachter (Eds.), *Linguistic perspectives on second language acquisition* (pp. 41–68). Cambridge, England: Cambridge University Press.

Bley-Vroman, R. (1990). The logical problem of foreign language learning. *Linguistic Analysis, 20,* 3–49.

Bloomfield, L. (1933). *Language.* New York: Holt, Rinehart & Winston.

Blum-Kulka, S., & Olshtain, E. (1984). Requests and apologies: A cross-cultural study of speech act realization patterns. *Applied Linguistics, 5,* 196–213.

Blum-Kulka, S., & Olshtain, E. (1986). Too many words: Length of utterances and pragmatic failure. *Journal of Pragmatics, 8,* 47–61.

Bohannon, J., & Stanowicz, L. (1988). The issue of negative evidence: Adult responses to children's language errors. *Developmental Psychology, 24,* 684–689.

Bohannon, J., MacWhinney, B., & Snow, C. (1990). No negative evidence revisited: Beyond learnability or who has to prove what to whom. *Developmental Psychology, 26,* 221–226.

Breen, M. (1987). Learner contributions to task design. In C. Candlin & D. Murphy (Eds.), *Language learning tasks* (pp. 23–46). Englewood Cliffs, NJ: Prentice-Hall.

Brock, C., Crookes, G., Day, R., & Long, M. (1986). The differential effects of corrective feedback in native speaker–non-native speaker conversation. In R. Day (Ed.), *Talking to learn* (pp. 229–236). Rowley, MA: Newbury House.

Broselow, E., & Finer, D. (1991). Parameter setting in second language phonology and syntax. *Second Language Research, 7,* 35–59.

Brown, R., & Hanlon, C. (1970). Derivational complexity and order of acquisition in child speech. In J. R. Hayes (Ed.), *Cognition and the development of language* (pp. 11–53). New York: Wiley.

Brown, R. (1977). Introduction. In C. E. Snow & C. A. Ferguson (Eds.), *Talking to children: Language input and acquisition* (pp. 1–27). Cambridge, England: Cambridge University Press.

Bullemer, P. T., & Nissen, M. J. (1990). *On the relationship between attention and memory systems: The nature of expectancies underlying the expression of skill.* Unpublished manuscript, University of Minnesota, Minneapolis.

Call, M. (1985). Auditory short-term memory, listening comprehension, and the input hypothesis. *TESOL Quarterly, 19,* 765–781.

Carr, T., & Curran, T. (1994). Cognitive factors in learning about structured sequences: Applications to syntax. *Studies in Second Language Acquisition, 16,* 205–230.

Carroll, S., Roberge, Y., & Swain, M. (1992). The role of feedback in adult second language acquisition, error correction, and morphological generalizations. *Applied Psycholinguistics, 13,* 173–198.

Cazden, C. (1972). *Child language and education.* New York: Holt, Rinehart & Winston.

Cazden, C., Cancino, H., Rosansky, E., & Schumann, J. (1975). *Second language acquisition sequences in children, adolescents and adults.* Washington, DC: U.S. Department of Health, Education and Welfare, National Institute of Education Office of Research Grants.

Chaudron, C. (1985). Intake: On models and methods for discovering learners' processing of input. *Studies in Second Language Acquisition, 7,* 1–14.

Cheesman. J., & Merikle, P. M. (1985). Word recognition and consciousness. In D. Besner, T. G. Waller, & G. E. MacKinnon (Eds.), *Reading research: Advances in theory and practice* (Vol. 5, pp. 311–352). Orlando, FL: Academic Press.

Cheesman J., & Merikle, P. M. (1986). Distinguishing conscious from unconscious perceptual processes. *Canadian Journal of Psychology, 40,* 343–367.

Chomsky, N. (1959). Review of *Verbal Behavior* by B. F. Skinner. *Language, 35,* 26–58.

Chomsky, N. (1965). *Aspects of the theory of syntax.* Cambridge, MA: MIT Press.

Chomsky, N. (1975). *Reflections on language.* New York: Pantheon.

Chomsky, N. (1981). *Lectures on government and binding.* Dordrecht: Foris.

Chomsky, N. (1987). *Kyoto lectures.* Unpublished manuscript.

Chun, A., Day, R., Chenoweth, A., & Luppescu, S. (1982). Errors, interaction, and correction: A study of non-native conversations. *TESOL Quarterly, 16,* 537–547.

Clahsen, H., Meisel, J., & Pienemann, M. (1983). *Deutsch als Zweitsprache: Der Spracherwerb ausländischer Arbeiter* [German as a second language: Language acquisition by foreign workers]. Tübingen: Gunter Narr.

Clark, H., & Clark, E. (1977). *Psychology and language: An introduction to psycholinguistics.* New York: Harcourt Brace.

Clyne, M. (1977). Multilingualism and pidginization in Australian industry. *Ethnic Studies, 1,* 40–55.

Cohen, A., Ivry, R. I., & Keele, S. W. (1990). Attention and structure in sequence learning. *Journal of Experimental Psychology: Learning, Memory, and Cognition, 16,* 17–30.

Collins, H. M. (1985). *Changing order.* London: Sage.

Comrie, B., & Keenan, E. (1979). Noun phrase accessibility revisited. *Language, 55,* 649–664.

Cook, V. (1988). *Chomsky's Universal Grammar.* Oxford: Basil Blackwell.

Cook, V. (1994). The metaphor of access to universal grammar. In N. Ellis (Ed.), *Implicit and explicit learning of languages* (pp. 477–502). London: Academic Press.

Cook, V. (1996). *Second language learning and language teaching* (2nd ed.). London: Edward Arnold.

Coppieters, R. (1987). Competence differences between native and non-native speakers. *Language, 63,* 544–573.

Corder, S. P. (1967). The significance of learner's errors. *International Review of Applied Linguistics, 5,* 161–170.

Coupland, N., Wiemann, J., & Giles, H. (1991). Talk as "problem" and communication as "miscommunication": An integrative analysis. In N. Coupland, H. Giles, & J. Wiemann (Eds.), *"Miscommunication" and problematic talk* (pp. 1–17). Newbury Park, CA: Sage.

Crookes, G., & Rulon, K. (1985). *Incorporation of corrective feedback in native speaker/nonnative speaker conversations* (Tech. Rep. No. 3). Honolulu: University of Hawaii, Social Science Research Institute, Center for Second Language Classroom Research.

Cumming, A. (1990). Metalinguistic and ideational thinking in second language composing. *Written Communication, 7,* 482–511.

Curran, T., & Keele, S. W. (1993). Attentional and nonattentional froms of sequence learning. *Journal of Experimental Psychology: Learning, Memory, and Cognition, 19,* 189–202.

Day, R., Chenoweth, A., Chun, A., & Luppescu, S. (1984). Corrective feedback in native-nonnative discourse. *Language Learning, 34,* 19–45.

Delk, C., Evart, K., & Helling, S. (1993, October). *From renting an apartment to restructuring your grammar: The effects of task types on the language learning process.* Paper presented at the 22nd UWM Linguistics Symposium, Milwaukee, WI.

Demetras, M. J., Post, K., & Snow, C. (1986). Feedback to first language learners: The role of repetitions and clarification questions. *Journal of Child Language, 13,* 275–292.

Doughty, C. (1991). Second language instruction does make a difference: Evidence from an empirical study of SL relativization. *Studies in Second Language Acquisition, 13,* 431–469.

Doughty, C., & Pica, T. (1986). "Information Gap" tasks: Do they facilitate second language acquisition? *TESOL Quarterly, 20,* 305–325.

Duff, P. (1986). Another look at interlanguage talk: Taking task to task. In R. Day (Ed.), *Talking to learn: Conversation in second language acquisition* (pp. 147–181). Rowley, MA: Newbury House.

Dulay, H., & Burt, M. (1973). Should we teach children syntax? *Language Learning, 23,* 245–258.

Dulay, H., & Burt, M. (1974a). Natural sequences in child second language acquisition. *Language Learning, 24,* 37–53.

Dulay, H., & Burt, M. (1974b). You can't learn without goofing. In J. Richards (Ed.), *Error analysis: Perspectives on second language acquisition* (pp. 95–123). New York: Longman.

Dulay, H., & Burt, M. (1975). Creative construction in second language learning and teaching. In M. Burt & H. Dulay (Eds.), *On TESOL '75: New directions in second language learning* (pp. 21–32). Washington, DC: TESOL.

Eckman, F. (1994). The competence–performance issue in second-language acquisition theory: A debate. In E. Tarone, S. Gass, & A. Cohen (Eds.), *Research methodology in second-language acquisition* (pp. 3–15). Hillsdale, NJ: Lawrence Erlbaum Associates.

Eckman, F. (1996). On evaluating arguments for special nativism in second language acquisition theory. *Second Language Research, 12,* 398–419.

Eckman, F., Bell, L., & Nelson, D. (1988). On the generalization of relative clause instruction in the acquisition of English as a second language. *Applied Linguistics, 9,* 1–20.

Ellis, R. (1990). A response to Gregg. *Applied Linguistics, 11,* 118–131.

Ellis, R. (1994). *The study of second language acquisition.* Oxford: Oxford University Press.

Ellis, R., Tanaka, Y., & Yamazaki, A. (1994). Classroom interaction, comprehension, and the acquisition of L2 word meanings. *Language Learning, 44,* 449–491.

Epstein, S., Flynn, S., & Martohardjono, G. (in press-a). Second language acquisition: Theoretical and experimental issues in contemporary research. *Brain and Behavioral Sciences.*

Epstein, S., Flynn, S., & Martohardjono, G. (in press-b). The strong continuity hypothesis in adult L2 acquisition of functional categories. In S. Flynn, G. Martohardjono, & W. O'Neil (Eds.), *The generative study of second language acquisition.* Mahwah, NJ: Lawrence Erlbaum Associates.

Eubank, L. (1994a). Optionality and the initial state in L2 development. In T. Hoekstra & B. Schwartz (Eds.), *Language acquisition studies in generative grammar* (pp. 369–388). Amsterdam: John Benjamins.

Eubank, L. (1994b). Towards an explanation for the late acquisition of agreement in L2 English. *Second Language Research, 10,* 84–93.

Faerch, C., & Kasper, G. (1980). Processes in foreign language learning and communication. *Interlanguage Studies Bulletin, 5,* 47–118.

Faerch, C., & Kasper, G. (1986). The role of comprehension in second language learning. *Applied Linguistics, 7,* 257–274.

Farrar, J. (1990). Discourse and the acquisition of grammatical morphemes. *Journal of Child Language, 17,* 607–624.

Farrar, J. (1992). Negative evidence and grammatical morpheme acquisition. *Developmental Psychology, 28,* 91–99.

Farthing, G. W. (1992). *The psychology of consciousness.* Englewood Cliffs, NJ: Prentice-Hall.

Ferguson, C. (1971). Absence of copula and the notion of simplicity: A study of normal speech, baby talk, foreigner talk and pidgins. In D. Hymes (Ed.), *Pidginization and creolization of languages* (pp. 141–150). Cambridge, England: Cambridge University Press.

Ferguson, C. (1975). Towards a characterization of English foreigner talk. *Anthropological Linguistics, 17,* 1–14.

Fodor, J. D., & Crain, S. (1987). Simplicity and generality of rules in language acquisition. In B. MacWhinney (Ed.), *Mechanisms of language acquisition* (pp. 35–63). Hillsdale, NJ: Lawrence Erlbaum Associates.

Foster-Cohen, S. (1993). Directions of influence in first and second language acquisition research. *Second Language Research, 9,* 140–152.

Furrow, D., & Nelson, K. (1986). A further look at the motherese hypothesis: A reply to Gleitman, Newport & Gleitman. *Journal of Child Language, 13,* 163–176.

Furrow, D., Nelson, K., & Benedict, H. (1979). Mothers' speech to children and syntactic development: Some simple relationships. *Journal of Child Language, 6,* 423–442.

Gaies, S. (1979). Linguistic input in first and second language learning. In F. Eckman & A. Hastings (Eds.), *Studies in first and second language acquisition* (pp. 185–193). Rowley, MA: Newbury House.

Garfinkel, H. (1967). *Studies in ethnomethodology.* Englewood Cliffs, NJ: Prentice-Hall.

Gass, S. (1979a). *An investigation of syntactic transfer in adult second language acquisition.* Unpublished doctoral dissertation, Indiana University, Bloomington.

Gass, S. (1979b). Language transfer and universal grammatical relations. *Language Learning, 29,* 327–344.

Gass, S. (1982). From theory to practice. In M. Hines & W. Rutherford (Eds.), *On TESOL '81* (pp. 129–139). Washington, DC: Teachers of English to Speakers of Other Languages.

Gass, S. (1984). Development of speech perception and speech production abilities in adult second language learners. *Applied Psycholinguistics, 5,* 51–74.

Gass, S. (1988a). Integrating research areas: A framework for second language studies. *Applied Linguistics, 9,* 198–217.

Gass, S. (1988b). Second language vocabulary acquisition. *Annual Review of Applied Linguistics, 9,* 92–106.

Gass, S., & Lakshmanan, U. (1991). Accounting for interlanguage subject pronouns. *Second Language Research, 7,* 181–203.

Gass, S., & Selinker, L. (1994). *Second language acquisition: An introductory course.* Hillsdale, NJ: Lawrence Erlbaum Associates.

Gass, S., & Varonis, E. (1984). The effect of familiarity on the comprehensibility of nonnative speech. *Language Learning, 34,* 65–89.

Gass, S., & Varonis, E. (1985a). Task variation and nonnative/nonnative negotiation of meaning. In S. Gass & C. Madden (Eds.), *Input in second language acquisition* (pp. 149–161). Rowley, MA: Newbury House.

Gass, S., & Varonis, E. (1985b). Variation in native speaker speech modification to non-native speakers. *Studies in Second Language Acquisition, 7,* 37–57.

Gass, S., & Varonis, E. (1986). Sex differences in nonnative speaker–nonnative speaker interactions. In R. Day (Ed.), *Talking to learn: Conversation in second language acquisition* (pp. 327–351). Rowley, MA: Newbury House.

Gass, S., & Varonis, E. (1989). Incorporated repairs in NNS discourse. In M. Eisenstein (Ed.), *The dynamic interlanguage* (pp. 71–86). New York: Plenum.

Gass, S., & Varonis, E. (1991). Miscommunication in nonnative speaker discourse. In N. Coupland, H. Giles, & J. Wiemann (Eds.), *"Miscommunication" and problemtic talk* (pp. 121–145). Newbury Park, CA: Sage.

Gass, S., & Varonis, E. (1994). Input, interaction and second language production. *Studies in Second Language Acquisition Research, 16,* 283–302.

Giles, H., & Smith, P. (1979). Accommodation theory: Optimal levels of convergence. In H. Giles & R. N. St. Clair (Eds.), *Language and social psychology.* Baltimore, MD: University Park Press.

Gleitman, L., Newport, E., & Gleitman, H. (1984). The current status of the motherese hypothesis. *Journal of Child Language, 11,* 43–79.

Gordon, P. (1990). Learnability and feedback. *Developmental Psychology, 26,* 217–220.

Gregg, K. (1984). Krashen's monitor and Occam's razor. *Applied Linguistics, 5,* 79–100.

Gregg, K. (1986). Review of Krashen (1985). *TESOL Quarterly, 20,* 116–122.

Gregg, K. (1990). The variable competence model of second language acquisition, and why it isn't? *Applied Linguistics, 11,* 365–383.

Hakulinen, A. (1993). The grammar of opening routines. In S. Shore & M. Vilkuna (Eds.), *1993 Yearbook of the Linguistic Association of Finland.* Helsinki: Suomen kielitieteelinen yhdistys.

Hakuta, K. (1974). Prefabricated patterns and the emergence of structure in second language acquisition. *Language Learning, 24,* 287–297.

Halliday, M. A. K. (1975). *Learning how to mean: Explorations in development of language.* New York: Elsevier.

Halmari, H. (1993). Intercultural business telephone conversations: A case of Finns vs. Anglo-Americans. *Applied Linguistics, 14,* 408–430.

Halmari, H. (1995, February). *On the importance of communicative competence in the L2.* Paper presented at Michigan State University.

Hatch, E. (1983). *Psycholinguistics: A second language perspective.* Rowley, MA: Newbury House.

Hawkins, B. (1985). Is the appropriate response always so appropriate. In S. Gass & C. Madden (Eds.), *Input in second language acquisition* (pp. 162–178). Rowley, MA: Newbury House.

Heath, S. B. (1983). *Ways with words: Language, life, and work in communities and classrooms.* Cambridge, England: Cambridge University Press.

Hilles, S. (1986). Interlanguage in the PRO-drop parameter. *Second Language Research, 2,* 33–52.

Hiraike-Okawara, M., & Sakamoto, T. (1990). Japanese foreigner register in the use of vocabulary. In O. Kamada & W. Jacobsen (Eds.), *On Japanese and how to teach it* (pp. 211–223). Tokyo: Japan Times.

Hirakawa, M. (1990). A study of the L2 acquisition of English reflexives. *Second Language Research, 6,* 60–85.

Hirsh-Pasek, K., & Treiman, R. (1982). Doggerel: Motherese in a new context. *Journal of Child Language, 9,* 229–237.

Hirsh-Pasek, K., Treiman, R., & Schneiderman, E. (1984). Brown and Hanlon revisited: Mother's sensitivity to ungrammatical forms. *Journal of Child Language, 11,* 81–88.

Hoff-Ginsberg, E. (1985). Some contributions of mother's speech to their children's syntactic growth. *Journal of Child Language, 12,* 367–386.

Holender, D. (1986). Semantic activation without conscious identification in dichotic listening, parafoveal vision, and visual masking: A survey and appraisal. *The Behavioural and Brain Sciences, 9,* 1–66.

Houck, N., & Gass, S. (1996, March). *The pragmatics of disagreement.* Paper presented at the Sociolinguistics Colloquium, TESOL, Chicago, IL.

Horgan, J. (1994, July). Can science explain consciousness? *Scientific American,* 88–94.

Hulstijn, J. (1995). Not all grammar rules are equal: Giving grammar instruction its proper place in foreign language teaching. In R. Schmidt (Ed.), *Attention and awareness in foreign language learning* (pp. 359–386). Honolulu: University of Hawaii Press.

Hulstijn, J., & Hulstijn, W. (1984). Grammatical errors as a function of processing constraints and explicit knowledge. *Language Learning, 34,* 23–43.

Hunt, W. (1970). Syntactic maturity in school-children and adults. *Monographs of the Society for Research in Child Development, 35* (1, Serial No. 134).

Hyams, N. (1986). *Language acquisition and the theory of parameters.* Dordrecht: Reidel.

Issidorides, D. (1988). The discovery of a miniature linguistic system: Function words and comprehension of an unfamiliar language. *Journal of Psycholinguistic Research, 17,* 317–339.

Issidorides, D. (1991). *A rose by any other name . . . : An experimental psycholinguistic study of Dutch sentence comprehension by adult non-native listeners.* Unpublished doctoral dissertation, Free University, Amsterdam.

Issidorides, D., & Hulstijn, J. (1992). Comprehension of grammatically modified and non-modified sentences by second language learners. *Applied Psycholinguistics, 13,* 147–172.

James, W. (1890). *The principles of psychology.* New York: Holt, Rinehart & Winston.

Keenan, E., & Comrie, B. (1977). Noun phrase accessibility and universal grammar. *Linguistic Inquiry, 8,* 63–99.

Kelch, K. (1985). Modified input as an aid to comprehension. *Studies in Second Language Acquisition, 7,* 81–90.

Kihlstrom, J. F. (1987). The cognitive unconscious. *Science, 238,* 1445–1452.

Kleifgen, J. (1985). Skilled variation in a kindergarten teacher's use of foreigner talk. In S. Gass & C. Madden (Eds.), *Input in second language acquisition* (pp. 59–68). Rowley, MA: Newbury House.

Klein, W., & Dittmar, N. (1979). *Developing grammars.* Berlin: Springer-Verlag.

Knox, L. (1992, April). *Cooperative fellow speakers and the enrichment of input: An application of relevance theory.* Paper presented at the 12th Second Language Research Forum, Michigan State University.

Krashen, S. (1977). Some issues relating to the Monitor Model. In H. Brown, C. Yorio, & R. Crymes (Eds.), *On TESOL '77* (pp. 144–158). Washington, DC: TESOL.

Krashen, S. (1980). The input hypothesis. In J. Alatis (Ed.), *Current issues in bilingual education* (pp. 168–180). Washington, DC: Georgetown University Press.

Krashen, S. (1982). *Principles and practice in second language acquisition.* London: Pergamon.

Krashen, S. (1985). *The input hypothesis: Issues and implications.* New York: Longman.

Krashen, S. (1989). We acquire vocabulary and spelling by reading: Additional evidence for the input hypothesis. *Modern Language Journal, 73,* 440–464.

Krashen, S., & Terrell, T. (1983). *The natural approach.* Oxford: Pergamon.

Kumaravadivelu, B. (1994). Intake factors and intake processes in adult language learning. *Applied Language Learning, 5,* 33–71.

Larsen-Freeman, D. (1983). Second language learning: Getting the whole picture. In K. Bailey, M. Long, & S. Peck (Eds.), *Second language acquisition studies* (pp. 3–22). Rowley, MA: Newbury House.

Larsen-Freeman, D. (1995). On the teaching and learning of grammar: Challenging the myths. In F. Eckman, D. Highland, P. Lee, J. Mileham, & R. Weber (Eds.), *Second language acquisition theory and pedagogy* (pp. 131–150). Mahwah, NJ: Lawrence Erlbaum Associates.

Larsen-Freeman, D., & Long, M. H. (1991). *An introduction to second language acquisition research.* New York: Longman.

Lasnik, H. (1989). On certain substitutes for negative evidence. In R. J. Matthews & W. Demopoulos (Eds.), *Learnability and linguistic theory* (pp. 89–105). Dordrecht: Kluwer.

Levinson, K. (1987). *The right to talk: A sociolinguistic investigation of conversational dominance and social prestige in non-native speaker interactions.* Unpublished manuscript, Teachers College, Columbia University.

Lieven, E. (1994). Crosslinguistic and crosscultural aspects of language addressed to children. In C. Gallaway & B. Richards (Eds.), *Input and interaction in language acquisition* (pp. 56–73). Cambridge, England: Cambridge University Press.

Lieven, E., Pine, J., & Barnes, H. (1992). Individual differences in early vocabulary development: Redefining the referential–expressive distinction. *Journal of Child Language, 19,* 287–310.

Lightbown, P. (1985). Great expectations: Second language acquisition research and classroom teaching. *Applied Linguistics, 6,* 173–189.

Lightbown, P. (1992). Can they do it themselves? A comprehension-based ESL course for young children. In R. Courchêne, J. Glidden, J. St. John, & C. Thérien (Eds.), *Comprehension-based second language teaching* (pp. 353–370). Ottawa: University of Ottawa Press.

Liu, G. (1991). *Interaction and second language acquisition: A case study of a Chinese child's acquisition of English as a second language.* Unpublished doctoral dissertation, La Trobe University, Melbourne, Australia.

Loew, R. (1993). To simply or not to simplify: A look at intake. *Studies in Second Language Acquisition, 15,* 333–355.

Long, M. (1980). *Input, interaction, and second language acquisition.* Unpublished doctoral dissertation, University of California, Los Angeles.

Long, M. (1981). Input, interaction, and second language acquisition. In H. Winitz (Ed.), *Native language and foreign language acquisition: Annals of the New York Academy of Sciences, 379,* 259–278.

Long, M. (1983a). Linguistic and conversational adjustments to non-native speakers. *Studies in Second Language Acquisition, 5,* 177–193.

Long, M. (1983b). Native speaker/non-native speaker conversation and the negotiation of comprehensible input. *Applied Linguistics, 4,* 126–141.

Long, M. (1985). A role for instruction in second language acquisition: Task-based language training. In K. Hyltenstam &. M. Pienemann (Eds.), *Modelling and assessing second language acquisition* (pp. 77–99). Clevedon, Avon, England: Multilingual Matters.

Long, M. (in press). *Task-based language teaching.* Oxford, England: Blackwell.

Long, M., & Crookes, G. (1992). Three approaches to task based syllabus design. *TESOL Quarterly, 26,* 27–56.

Long, M., Gambhiar, S., Gambhiar, V., & Nishimura, M. (1982). *Regularization in foreigner talk and interlanguage.* Paper presented at the 17th annual TESOL convention, Toronto, Canada.

Long, M., & Porter, P. (1985). Group work, interlangauge talk, and second language acquisition. *TESOL Quarterly, 19,* 207–228.

Loschky, L. (1994). Comprehensible input and second language acquisition: What is the relationship? *Studies in Second Language Acquisition, 16,* 303–324.

Loschky, L., & Bley-Vroman, R. (1993). Grammar and task–based methodology. In G. Crookes & S. Gass (Eds.), *Tasks and language learning: Integrating theory and practice* (pp. 122–167). Clevedon: Multilingual Matters.

Mackey, A. (1995). *Stepping up the pace: Input, interaction and interlanguage development, an empirical study of questions in ESL.* Unpublished doctoral dissertation, University of Sydney.

MacWhinney, B. (1987). The competition model. In B. MacWhinney (Ed.), *Mechanisms of language acquisition* (pp. 249–308). Hillsdale, NJ: Lawrence Erlbaum Associates.

MacWhinney, B. (1989a). Competition and categorization. In. R. Corrigan, F. Eckman, & M. Noonan (Eds.), *Linguistic categorization* (pp. 195–241). Amsterdam: John Benjamins.

MacWhinney, B. (1989b). Competition and teachability. In M. Rice & R. Schiefelbusch (Eds.), *The teachability of language* (pp. 63–104). Baltimore, MD: Brooks-Cole.

Marcel, A. J. (1983a). Conscious and unconscious perception: An approach to the relations between phenomenal experience and perceptual processes. *Cognitive Psychology, 15,* 238–300.

Marcel, A. J. (1983b). Conscious and unconscious perception: Experiments on visual masking and word recognition. *Cognitive Psychology, 15,* 197–237.

Marcel, A., & Bisiach, B. (Eds.). (1988). *Consciousness in contemporary science*. Oxford, England: Clarendon.

McLaughlin, B. (1987). *Theories of second language learning*. London: Edward Arnold.

McLaughlin, B. (1990a). "Conscious" vs. "unconscious" learning. *TESOL Quarterly, 24*, 617–634.

McLaughlin, B. (1990b). Restructuring. *Applied Linguistics, 11*, 113–128.

McLaughlin, B., Rossman, T., & McLeod, B. (1983). Second language learning: An information-processing perspective. *Language Learning, 33*, 135–158.

McNeill, D. (1966). Developmental psycholinguistics. In F. Smith & G. Miller (Eds.), *The genesis of language: A psycholinguistic approach* (pp. 15–84). Cambridge, MA: MIT Press.

Meisel, J. (1977). Linguistic simplification: A study of immigrant workers' speech and foreigner talk. In S. P. Corder & E. Roulet (Eds.), *The notions of simplification, interlanguages and pidgins and their relation to second language pedagogy* (pp. 88–113). Geneva: Droz.

Meisel, J. (1980). Linguistic simplification. In S. Felix (Ed.), *Second language development* (pp. 9–40). Tübingen: Gunter Narr.

Merikle, P. M., & Cheesman, J. (1986). Consciousness is a "subjective" state. *The Behavioral and Brain Sciences, 9*, 42.

Miller, G. A. (1987). *Psychology: The science of mental life*. New York: Penguin.

Milroy, L. (1984). Comprehension and context: Successful communication and communicative breakdown. In P. Trudgill (Ed.), *Applied sociolinguistics* (pp. 7–31). London: Academic Press.

Nelson, K. (1977). Facilitating children's syntax acquisition. *Developmental Psychology, 13*, 101–107.

Nelson, K., Bonvillian, J., Denninger, M., Kaplan, B., & Baker, N. (1984). Maternal input adjustments and non-adjustments as related to children's linguistic advances and to language acquisition theories. In A. Pelligrini & T. Yawkey (Eds.), *The development of oral and written language in social contexts* (pp. 31–56). Norwood, NJ: Ablex.

Newport, E., Gleitman, H., & Gleitman, L. (1977). Mother, I'd rather do it myself: Some effects and non-effects of maternal speech style. In C. Snow & C. Ferguson (Eds.), *Talking to children: Language input and acquisition* (pp. 109–149). New York: Cambridge University Press.

Nissen, M. J., & Bullemer, P. (1987). Attentional requirements of learning: Evidence from performance measures. *Cognitive Psychology, 19*, 1–32.

Nissen, M. J., Knopman, D. S., & Schacter, D. L. (1987). Neurochemical dissociation of memory systems. *Neurology, 37*, 789–794.

Nobuyoshi, J., & Ellis, R. (1993). Focused communication tasks and second language acquisition. *English Language Teaching, 47*, 203–210.

Novak, W., & Waldoks, M. (1981). *The big book of Jewish humor*. New York: Harper & Row.

Nunan, D. (1989). *Designing tasks for the communicative classroom*. Cambridge, England: Cambridge University Press.

Nwokah, E. (1987). Maidese vs. motherese: Is the language input of child and adult caregivers similar? *Language and Speech, 30*, 213–237.

Ochs, E. (1985). Variation and error: A sociolinguistic approach to language acquisition in Samoa. In D. Slobin (Ed.), *The crosslinguistic study of language acquisition* (pp. 783–838). Hillsdale, NJ: Lawrence Erlbaum Associates.

Oliver, R. (1995). Negative feedback in child NS–NNS conversation. *Studies in Second Language Acquisition, 17*, 459–481.

Olshtain, E., & Blum-Kulka, S. (1985). Degree of approximation: Nonnative reactions to native speech act behavior. In S. Gass & C. Madden (Eds.), *Input in second language acquisition* (pp. 303–325). Rowley, MA: Newbury House.

Olshtain, E., & Cohen, A. (1989). Speech act behavior across languages. In H. Dechert & M. Raupach (Eds.), *Transfer in language production* (pp. 53–67). Norwood, NJ: Ablex.

Onaha, H. (1987). Foreigner talk in Japanese: A comparison of ellipsis of particles and noun phrases between foreigner talk and speech to native speakers. *JACET Journal, 18,* 89–107.

Parker, K., & Chaudron, C. (1987). The effects of linguistic simplifications and elaborative modifications on L2 comprehension. *University of Hawaii Working Papers in ESL, 6,* 107–133.

Peck, S. (1980). Language play in child second language acquisition. In D. Larsen-Freeman (Ed.), *Discourse analysis in second language research* (pp. 154–164). Rowley, MA: Newbury House.

Perruchet, P., & Amorim, M. (1992). Conscious knowledge and changes in performance in sequence learning: Evidence against dissociation. *Journal of Experimental Psychology: Learning, Memory, and Cognition, 18,* 785–800.

Peters, A. (1977). Language learning strategies: Does the whole equal the sum of the parts? *Language, 53,* 560–573.

Pica, T. (1987). Second language acquisition, social interaction, and the classroom. *Applied Linguistics, 8,* 3–21.

Pica, T. (1988). Interlanguage adjustments as an outcome of NS–NNS negotiated interaction. *Language Learning, 38,* 45–73.

Pica, T. (1991). Classroom interaction, participation, and comprehension: Redefining relations. *System, 19,* 437–452.

Pica, T. (1992). The textual outcomes of native speaker-non-native speaker negotiation: What do they reveal abut second language learning? In C. Kramsch & S. McConnell Ginet (Eds.), *Text and context: Cross-disciplinary perspectives on language study* (pp. 198–237). Lexington, MA: Heath.

Pica, T. (1994). Research on negotiation: What does it reveal about second–language learning conditions, processes, and outcomes? *Language Learning, 44,* 493–527.

Pica, T., & Doughty, C. (1985). Input and interaction in the communicative language classroom: A comparison of teacher-fronted and group activities. In S. Gass & C. Madden (Eds.), *Input in second language acquisition* (pp. 115–132). Rowley, MA: Newbury House.

Pica, T., Doughty, C., & Young, R. (1986). Making input comprehensible: Do interactional modifications help? *ITL Review of Applied Linguistics, 72,* 1–25.

Pica, T., Holliday, L., Lewis, N., Berducci, D., & Newman, J. (1991). Language learning through interaction: What role does gender play? *Studies in Second Language Acquisition, 13,* 343–376.

Pica, T., Holliday, L., Lewis, N., & Morgenthaler, L. (1989). Comprehensible output as an outcome of linguistic demands on the learner. *Studies in Second Language Acquisition, 11,* 63–90.

Pica, T., Young, R., & Doughty, C. (1987). The impact of interaction on comprehension. *TESOL Quarterly, 21,* 737–758.

Pienemann, M. (1992). Assessing second language through rapid profile. *Language acquisition research centre occasional papers, 1.*

Pienemann, M., & Johnston, M. (1987). Factors influencing the development of language proficiency. In D. Nunan (Ed.), *Applying second language acquisition research* (pp. 45–141). Adelaide: University of Sydney, Australia, National Curriculum Resource Centre, AMEP.

Pine, J. (1994). The language of primary caregivers. In C. Gallaway & B. Richards (Eds.), *Input and interaction in language acquisition* (pp. 15–37). Cambridge, England: Cambridge University Press.

Pinker, S. (1994). *The language instinct.* New York: Morrow.

Pinker, S., & Lebeaux, D. (1982). *A learnability–theoretic approach to children's language.* Unpublished manuscript, Stanford University, CA.

Plough, I. (1994). *A role for indirect negative evidence in second language acquisition.* Unpublished doctoral dissertation, Michigan State University.

Plough, I., & Gass, S. (1993). Interlocutor and task familiarity: Effects on interactional structure. In G. Crookes & S. Gass (Eds.), *Tasks and language learning: Integrating theory and practice* (pp. 35–56). Clevedon, Avon, England: Multilingual Matters.

Posner, M. (1994). Attention: The mechanisms of consciousness. *Proceedings of the National Academy of Sciences, 91*, 7398–6403.

Preston, D. (1989). *Sociolinguistics and second language acquisition.* Oxford, England: Blackwell.

Richards, J., Platt, J., & Weber, H. (1986). *Longman dictionary of applied linguistics.* New York: Longman.

Riggenbach, H., & Samuda, V. (1993). *Dimensions of grammar: Form, meaning and use, book two.* Boston: Heinle & Heinle.

Robinson, P. (1995). Review article: Attention, memory and the "noticing" hypothesis. *Language Learning, 45*, 283–331.

Robinson, P. (1996). Introduction: Connecting tasks, cognition and syllabus design. *University of Queensland working papers in language and linguistics, 1*, 1–14.

Rost, M. (1990). *Listening in language learning.* New York: Longman.

Rumelhart, D. E., Smolensky, P., McClelland, J. L., & Hinton, G. E. (1986). Schemata and sequential thought processes in PDP models. In J. L. McClelland, D. E. Rumelhart, & the PDP research group (Eds.), *Parallel distributed processing: Explorations in the microstructure of cognition* (Vol. 2, pp. 7–57). Cambridge, MA: MIT Press.

Rumelhart, D., & McClelland, J. L. (1986). PDP models and general issues in cognitive science. In D. E. Rumelhart & J. L. McClelland (Eds.), *Parallel distributed processing: Explorations in the microstructure of cognition* (Vol. 1, pp. 110–146). Cambridge, MA: MIT Press.

Rutherford, W., & Sharwood Smith, M. (1985). Consciousness-raising and universal grammar. *Applied Linguistics, 6*, 274–282.

Sachs, J., & Johnson, M. (1972). *Language development in a hearing child of deaf parents.* Paper presented at the International Symposium on First Language Acquisition, Florence, Italy.

Saleemi, A. (1990). Null subjects, markedness, and implicit negative evidence. In I. Roca (Ed.), *Logical issues in language acquisition* (pp. 235–258). Dordrecht: Foris.

Saleemi, A. (1992). *Universal grammar and language learnability.* Cambridge, England: Cambridge University Press.

Samuda, V. (1993, October). *Grammar tasks: Creating a need to mean.* Paper presented for the English Language Center Colloquium, Michigan State University.

Sato, C. (1986). Conversation and interlanguage development: Rethinking the connection. In R. Day (Ed.), *Talking to learn* (pp. 23–45). Rowley, MA: Newbury House.

Sato, C. (1990). *The syntax of conversation in interlanguage development.* Tübingen: Gunter Narr Verlag.

Scarcella, R. (1983). Discourse accent in second language performance. In S. Gass & L. Selinker (Eds.), *Language transfer in language learning* (pp. 306–326). Rowley, MA: Newbury House.

Scarcella, R. (1992). Interethnic conversation and second language acquisition: Discourse accent revisited. In S. Gass & L. Selinker (Eds.), *Language transfer in language learning* (pp. 109–137). Amsterdam: John Benjamins.

Scarcella, R., & Higa, C. (1981). Input, negotiation and age differences in second language acquisition. *Language Learning, 31*, 409–438.

Schachter, J. (1983). A new account of language transfer. In S. Gass & L. Selinker (Eds.), *Language transfer in language learning* (pp. 98–111). Rowley, MA: Newbury House.

Schachter, J. (1986). Three approaches to the study of input. *Language Learning, 36*, 211–226.

Schachter, J. (1988). Second language acquisition and its relationship to Universal Grammar. *Applied Linguistics, 9*, 219–235.

Schachter, J. (1990). On the issue of completeness. *Second Language Research, 6*, 93–124.

Schachter, J. (1992). A new account of language transfer. In S. Gass & L. Selinker (Eds.), *Language transfer in language learning* (pp. 32–46). Amsterdam: John Benjamins.

Schachter, J., Rounds, P., Wright, S., Smith, T., & Magoto, J. (1996). A dual mechanism model for adult syntax learning. Unpublished manuscript.

Schacter, D. L., McAndrews, M. P., & Moscovitch, M. (1988). Access to consciousness: Dissociations between implicit and explicit knowledge in neuropsychological syndromes. In L. Weiskrantz (Ed.), *Thought without language* (pp. 242–278). Oxford, England: Oxford University Press.

Schieffelin, B. (1985). The acquisition of Kaluli. In D. Slobin (Ed.), *The crosslinguistic study of language acquisition* (pp. 525–594). Hillsdale, NJ: Lawrence Erlbaum Associates.

Schmidt, R. (1990). The role of consciousness in second language learning. *Applied Linguistics, 11*, 129–158.

Schmidt, R. (1993a). Awareness and second language acquisition. *Annual Review of Applied Linguistics, 13*, 206–226.

Schmidt, R. (1993b). Consciousness, learning and interlanguage pragmatics. In G. Kasper & S. Blum-Kulka (Eds.), *Interlanguage pragmatics* (pp. 21–42). New York: Oxford University Press.

Schmidt, R. (1993c). *Consciousness in second language learning: Introduction.* Paper presented at AILA 10th World Congress of Applied Linguistics, Amsterdam.

Schmidt, R. (1994a). Deconstructing consciousness in search of useful definitions for applied linguistics. In J. Hulstijn & R. Schmidt (Eds.), *Consciousness and second language learning: Conceptual, methodological and practical issues in language learning and teaching* (pp. 11–26). *AILA Review- Revue de l'AILA, 11.*

Schmidt, R. (1994b). Implicit learning and the cognitive unconscious: Of artificial grammars and SLA. In N. Ellis (Ed.), *Implicit and explicit learning of languages* (pp. 165–209). London: Academic Press.

Schmidt, R. (1995). Consciousness and foreign language learning: A tutorial on the role of attention and awareness in learning. In R. Schmidt (Ed.), *Attention and awareness in learning.* Honolulu: University of Hawaii at Manoa.

Schumann, J. (1976). Social distance as a factor in second language acquisition. *Language Learning, 26*, 391–408.

Schumann, J. (1978). *The pidginization process: A model for second language acquisition.* Rowley, MA: Newbury House.

Schwartz, B. (1993). On explicit and negative data effecting and affecting competence and linguistic behavior. *Studies in Second Language Acquisition, 15*, 147–163.

Schwartz, B. (in press). On two hypotheses of "transfer" in L2A: Minimal trees and absolute influence. In S. Flynn, G. Martohardjono, & W. O'Neil (Eds.), *The generative study of second language acquisition.* Mahwah, NJ: Lawrence Erlbaum Associates.

Schwartz, B., & Gubala-Ryzak, M. (1992). Learnability and grammar reorganization in L2A: Against negative evidence causing the unlearning of verb movement. *Second Language Research, 8*, 1–38.

Schwartz, B., & Sprouse, R. (1994). Word order and nominative case in nonnative language acquisition: A longitudinal study of L1 Turkish German interlanguage. In T. Hoekstra & B. Schwartz (Eds.), *Language acquisition studies in generative grammar* (pp. 317–368). Amsterdam: John Benjamins.

Selinker, L., & Douglas, D. (1985). Wrestling with 'context' in interlanguage theory. *Applied Linguistics, 6*, 190–204.

Sharwood Smith, M. (1981). Consciousness-raising and the second language learner. *Applied Linguistics, 2*, 159–168.

Sharwood Smith, M. (1986). Comprehension vs. acquisition: Two ways of processing input. *Applied Linguistics, 7*, 239–256.

Sharwood Smith, M. (1991). Speaking to many minds: On the relevance of different types of language information for the L2 learner. *Second Language Research, 7*, 118–132.

Sharwood Smith, M. (1993). Input enhancement in instructed SLA: Theoretical bases. *Studies in Second Language Acquisition, 15*, 165–179.

Sharwood Smith, M. (1994). *Second language learning: Theoretical foundations.* New York: Longman.

Sheldon, A., & Strange, W. (1982). The acquisition of /r/ and /l/ by Japanese learners of English: Evidence that speech production can precede speech perception. *Applied Psycholinguistics, 3,* 243–261.

Skehan, P. (1996). A framework for the implementation of task-based instruction. *Applied Linguistics, 17,* 38–62.

Slobin, D. (1985). Crosslinguistic evidence for the language-making capacity. In D. Slobin (Ed.), *The crosslinguistic study of language acquisition* (pp. 1157–1256). Hillsdale, NJ: Lawrence Erlbaum Associates.

Smith, S., Scholnick, N., Crutcher, A., Simeone, M., & Smith, W. (1991). Foreigner talk revisited: Limits on accommodation to nonfluent speakers. In J. Blommaert & J. Verschueren (Eds.), *The pragmatics of intercultural and international communication* (pp. 175–185). Amsterdam: John Benjamins.

Snow, C. (1977). The development of conversations between mothers and babies. *Journal of Child Language, 4,* 1–22.

Snow, C., Arlman-Rupp, A., Hassing, Y., Jobse, J., Joosten, J., & Vorster, J. (1976). Mothers' speech in three social classes. *Journal of Psycholinguistic Research, 5,* 1–20.

Sorace, A. (1993a). Incomplete vs. divergent representations of unaccusativity in non-native grammars of Italian. *Second Language Research, 9,* 22–47.

Sorace, A. (1993b). Unaccusativity and auxiliary choice in non-native grammars of Italian and French: Asymmetries and predictable indeterminancy. *Journal of French Language Studies, 3,* 71–93.

Sorace, A. (1995). Acquiring linking rules and argument structures in a second language: The unaccusative/unergative distinction. In L. Eubank, L. Selinker, & M. Sharwood Smith (Eds.), *The current state of interlanguage: Studies in honor of William E. Rutherford* (pp. 153–175). Amsterdam: John Benjamins.

Swain, M. (1985). Communicative competence: Some roles of comprehensible input and comprehensible output in its development. In S. Gass & C. Madden (Eds.), *Input in second language acquisition* (pp. 235–253). Rowley, MA: Newbury House.

Swain, M. (1995). Three functions of output in second language learning. In G. Cook & B. Seidlhofer (Eds.), *Principle and practice in applied linguistics: Studies in honour of H. G. Widdowson* (pp. 125–144). Oxford, England: Oxford University Press.

Swain, M., & Lapkin, S. (1995). Problems in output and the cognitive processes they generate: A step towards second language learning. *Applied Linguistics, 16,* 371–391.

Swain, M., & Lapkin, S. (in press). Interaction and second language learning: Two adolescent French immersion students working together. *Modern Language Journal.*

Takashima, H. (1995). *A study of focused feedback, or output enhancement, in promoting accuracy in communicative activities.* Unpublished doctoral dissertation, Temple University.

Tannen, D. (1990). *You just don't understand.* New York: Ballantine.

Tarone, E. (1990). On variation in interlanguage: A response to Gregg. *Applied Linguistics, 11,* 392–399.

Tarone, E., & Liu, G. (1995). Situational context, variation, and second language acquisition theory. In G. Cook & B. Seidlhofer (Eds.), *Principle and practice in applied linguistics: Studies in honour of H. G. Widdowson* (pp. 107–124). Oxford, England: Oxford University Press.

Tomasello, M. (1988). The role of joint attentional processes in early language development. *Language Sciences, 10,* 69–88.

Tomasello, M., & Herron, C. (1988). Down the garden path: Inducing and correcting overgeneralization errors in the foreign language classroom. *Applied Psycholinguistics, 9,* 237–246.

Tomasello, M., & Herron, C. (1989). Feedback for language transfer errors: The garden path technique. *Studies in Second Language Acquisition, 11,* 385–395.

Tomasello, M., & Herron, C. (1991). Experiments in the real world: A reply to Beck and Eubank. *Studies in Second Language Acquisition, 13,* 513–517.

Tomlin, R. S., & Villa, V. (1994). Attention in cognitive science and second language acquisition. *Studies in Second Language Acquisition, 16,* 183–203.

Trahey, M., & White, L. (1993). Positive evidence and preemption in the second language classroom. *Studies in Second Language Acquisition, 15,* 181–204.

Tsimpli, I., & Roussou, A. (1991). Parameter resetting in L2? *UCL Working Papers in Lingusitics, 3,* 149–169.

Tulving, E. (1989). Memory: Performance, knowledge, and experience. *European Journal of Cognitive Psychology, 1,* 3–26.

Vainikka, A., & Young-Scholten, M. (1994). Direct access to X'-theory: Evidence from Korean and Turkish adults learning German. In T. Hoekstra & B. Schwartz (Eds.), *Language acquisition studies in generative grammar* (pp. 265–316). Amsterdam: John Benjamins.

Valian, V. (1990). Logical and psychological constraints on the acquisition of syntax. In L. Frazier & J. de Villiers (Eds.), *Language processing and language acquisition* (pp. 119–145). Dordrecht: Kluwer.

Van Riemsdijk, H. (1978). *A case study in syntactic markedness: The binding nature of prepositional phrases.* Lisse, The Netherlands: The Peter de Ridder Press.

VanPatten, B. (1993). Grammar teaching for the acquisition rich classroom. *Foreign Language Annals, 26,* 435–450.

VanPatten, B. (1995). Input processing and second language acquisition: On the relationship between form and meaning. In P. Hashemipour, R. Maldonado, & M. van Naerssen (Eds.), *Festschrift in honor of Tracy D. Terrell* (pp. 170–183). New York: McGraw-Hill.

VanPatten, B., & Cadierno, T. (1993). Explicit instruction and input processing. *Studies in Second Language Acquisition, 15,* 225–243.

VanPatten, B., & Sanz, C. (1995). From input to output: Processing instruction and communicative tasks. In F. Eckman, D. Highland, P. Lee, J. Mileham, & R. Weber (Eds.), *Second language acquisition theory and pedagogy* (pp. 169–186). Hillsdale, NJ: Lawrence Erlbaum Associates.

Varonis, E., & Gass, S. (1982). The comprehensibility of non-native speech. *Studies in Second Language Acquisition, 4,* 114–136.

Varonis, E., & Gass, S. (1985a). Miscommunication in native/non-native conversation. *Language in Society, 14,* 327–343.

Varonis, E., & Gass, S. (1985b). Non-native/non-native conversations: A model for negotiation of meaning. *Applied Linguistics, 6,* 71–90.

Velmans, M. (1991). Is human information processing conscious? *Behavioral and Brain Sciences, 14,* 651–726.

Wagner-Gough, J., & Hatch, E. (1975). The importance of input data in second language acquisition studies. *Language Learning, 25,* 297–307.

Watanabe, S. (1993). Cultural differences in framing: American and Japanese group discussions. In D. Tannen (Ed.), *Framing in discourse* (pp. 176–197). New York: Oxford University Press.

White, L. (1985). The "pro-drop" parameter in adult second language acquisition. *Language Learning, 35,* 47–62.

White, L. (1986). Implications of parametric variation for adult second language acquisition: An investigation of the 'pro-drop' parameter. In V. Cook (Ed.), *Experimental approaches to second language acquisition* (pp. 55–72). Oxford: Pergamon.

White, L. (1987). Against comprehensible input: the input hypothesis and the development of second language competence. *Applied Linguistics, 8,* 95–110.

White, L. (1989a). The principle of adjacency in second language acquisition: Do L2 learners observe the subset principle? In S. Gass & J. Schachter (Eds.), *Linguistic perspectives on second language acquisition* (pp. 134–158). Cambridge, England: Cambridge University Press.

White, L. (1989b). *Universal grammar and second language acquisition.* Amsterdam: John Benjamins.

White, L. (1991). Adverb placement in second language acquisition: some effects of positive and negative evidence in the classroom. *Second Language Research, 7,* 133–161.

White, L. (1992). On triggering data in L2 acquisition: A reply to Schwartz and Gubala-Ryzak. *Second Language Research, 8,* 120–137.

White, L. (1996a). Clitics in child L2 French. In H. Clahsen (Ed.), *Generative perspectives on language acquisition: Empirical findings, theoretical considerations, crosslinguistic comparisons.* Amsterdam: John Benjamins.

White, L. (1996b). The tale of the ugly duckling (or the coming of age of second language acquisition research). In A. Stringfellow, D. Cahana-Amitay, E. Hughes, & A. Zukowski (Eds.), *Proceedings of the Boston University Conference on Language Development* (pp. 1–17). Somerville, MA: Cascadilla Press.

Widdowson, H. (1991). The contexts of use and learning. In L. M. T. Kral, S. Tanewong, A. Wongsothorn, S. Tiancharoen, D. Chulasai, & P. Navarat (Eds.), *Explorations and innovations in ELT methodology* (pp. 1–17). Bangkok: Chulalongkorn University.

Willingham, D. B., Nissen, M. J., & Bullemer, P. (1989). On the development of procedural knowledge. *Journal of Experimental Psychology: Learning, Memory, and Cognition, 15,* 1047–1060.

Woken, M., & Swales, J. (1989). Expertise and authority in native-non-native conversations: The need for a variable account. In S. Gass, C. Madden, D. Preston, & L. Selinker (Eds.), *Variation in second language acquisition: Discourse and pragmatics* (pp. 211–227). Clevedon. Avon, England: Multilingual Matters.

Wolfe-Quintero, K. (1996). Nativism does not equal universal grammar. *Second Language Research, 12,* 335–373.

Yano, Y., Long, M., & Ross, S. (1994). The effects of simplified and elaborated texts on foreign language reading comprehension. *Language Learning, 44,* 189–219.

Zobl, H. (1982). A direction for contrastive analysis: The comparative study of developmental sequences. *TESOL Quarterly, 16,* 169–183.

Zobl, H. (1992). Prior linguistic knowledge and the conservation of the learning procedure: Grammaticality judgments of unilingual and multilingual learners. In S. Gass & L. Selinker (Eds.), *Language transfer in language learning* (pp. 176–196). Amsterdam: John Benjamins.

Zuengler, J. (1989a). Assessing an interaction-based paradigm: How accommodative should we be? In M. Eisenstein (Ed.), *The dynamic interlanguage* (pp. 49–67). New York: Plenum.

Zuengler, J. (1989b). Performance variation in NS–NNS interactions: Ethnolinguistic difference, or discourse domain? In S. Gass, C. Madden, D. Preston, & L. Selinker. *Variation in second language acquisition: Discourse and pragmatics* (pp. 228–244). Clevedon, Avon, England: Multilingual Matters.

Author Index

Subject Index